THE MANAGEMENT ANTHOLOGY SERIES

Edited by
Marlene G. Mayers, R.N., M.S., F.A.A.N

Theme I.

The Organization: People and Structures

Organizational Theories and Structures
Organizational Units and Groups
Individuals in Organizations
Intraorganizational Conflict
Organizational Change

Theme II.
Management Functions

Communicating Effectively

Planning
Organizing
Staffing
Controlling
Leadership in Nursing

Theme III.

Product and Service Cost Effectiveness

Philosophy, Goals, and Criteria
Quality Measurement Methods
Maintaining Cost Effectiveness
Management Goals

Theme IV.

Employee Growth and Satisfaction

Motivation
Job Enrichment
Development Through Education
Development of Nurse Managers
Personal Growth

Theme V.

Organizational Security and Longevity

Organization-Environment Relationships
Social Policy and Nursing Services
The Women's Movement and Nursing
New Human Services and Technologies
Labor Relations in Nursing
Legal Protection of Patients and Nurses
The Politics of Nursing

Several volumes were in preparation when Communicating Effectively was published.

Communicating
Effectively

Communicating Effectively

Edited by

Ann J. Huntsman, R.N., M.S.
Director, Education and Training
El Camino Hospital
Mountain View, California

and

Jane L. Binger, R.N., M.S.
Doctoral Candidate, Administration & Policy Analysis
School of Education, Stanford University
Stanford, California

The Management Anthology Series
Theme Two: Management Functions

Nursing Resources
An information activity of Concept Development, Inc.
12 Lakeside Park, 607 North Avenue
Wakefield, Massachusetts 01880

Contents

CONTRIBUTING AUTHORS

Jane L. Binger, R.N., M.S.
Doctoral Candidate
Administration & Policy
  Analysis
School of Education
Stanford University
Stanford, California

Doris Bloch, R.N., Dr.P.H.*
Chief, Research Grants Section
Nursing Research Branch
Division of Nursing
Bureau of Health Manpower
Health Resources Administra-
  tion, PHS
Department of Health, Educa-
  tion & Welfare
Hyattsville, Maryland

Joyce Brothers †

Nancy A. Brunner, R.N., M.S.
Director, Special Projects
Nursing Services Division
Mount Carmel Medical Center;
Doctoral Candidate, Adaptive
  Systems Research and Man-
  agement Science
The Ohio State University
Columbus, Ohio

Myron R. Chartier, Ph.D.*
Director, Doctoral Program
Associate Professor of Ministry
The Eastern Baptist Theological
  Seminary
Philadelphia, Pennsylvania

Signe S. Cooper, R.N., M.Ed. Professor & Chairman
Continuing Education in Nursing
University of Wisconsin—
    Extension;
Associate Dean
    Continuing Education
University of Wisconsin
Madison School of Nursing
Madison, Wisconsin

Paul R. Corts †

Jack R. Gibb †

Judy Grubbs* Bobrow/Thomas & Associates;
Former Lecturer
University of California
School of Nursing
Los Angeles, California

Ann J. Huntsman, R.N., M.S. Director, Education and
    Training
El Camino Hospital
Mountain View, California

Patricia M. Joy, R.N.* Head Nurse, Surgical Unit
Monterey Hospital
Monterey, California

Mark L. Knapp †

Karren E. Kowalski, R.N., M.S. Lecturer
School of Nursing
University of Colorado
Health Sciences Center
Denver, Colorado;
Sociology Doctoral Student
University of Colorado
Boulder, Colorado

Rose S. LeRoux, R.N., Ph.D.
Associate Professor
School of Nursing;
Assistant Professor
School of Medicine
University of Colorado
Denver, Colorado

Joanne Comi McCloskey,
R.N., M.S.
Assistant Professor
University of Illinois
College of Nursing;
Doctoral Candidate in Higher
  Education
University of Chicago
Chicago, Illinois

Naomi Domer Medearis,
M.B.A.*
Associate Professor
Division of Continuing
  Education
University of Colorado
School of Nursing
Denver, Colorado

Helen I. Okorafor, R.N.*
Doctoral Candidate, Health and
  Safety
Indiana University
Bloomington, Indiana

Pearl P. Rosendahl, R.N.,
Ed.D.*
Assistant Professor
Graduate Program
Boston University
School of Nursing
Boston, Massachusetts

Stephen J. Short*
Senior Associate
Bobrow/Thomas & Associates
Los Angeles, California

Sylvia H. Simmons†

Barbara J. Stevens, R.N., Ph.D. Director
Division of Helath Services,
  Science and Education
Teachers College
Columbia University
New York, New York

Marvin H. Swift* Associate Professor of
  Communication
General Motors Institute

C. William Welch, A.P.R.†

Lynne Brodie Welch, Assistant Professor of Nursing
  R.N., M.S.N.* Western Connecticut State
  College
Danbury, Connecticut;
Certified Doctoral Student
Teachers College
Columbia University
New York, New York

M.G. Williams†

Jack N. Wismer, Ph.D.* Employee Development
  Specialist
Bureau of Land Management
Denver, Colorado

---

*This information reflects the author's position when the selection included in this anthology was originally published.

†No biographical information available.

Foreword

During recent years all of us have been coping with the information explosion. Not only have the means of communication changed radically but the amount of information directed at everyone has increased at an incredible rate. If we were to devote our entire attention to all of the messages being directed at us we would soon lose our sanity! Thus, in self-defense, we develop various methods of selection based on a basic criterion: "What's in it for me?" As a nursing administrator, if you think about communication that way, you will have a clue to how to communicate effectively: communicate so that it is clear to the listener what's in it for him or her.

Of course that is much more easily said than done. Thus, there are many books on the subject of communication and many workshops and periodical selections devoted to teaching managers and administrators how to communicate more effectively. In organizations such as nursing services, a major objective of all communication is to assist various departments in achieving their objectives. Since nursing services' objectives are concerned with what happens not only in the organization but also in its community and with the clients it serves, the communication challenge is magnified. Communication, both internal and external to the organization, is like a lubricant which keeps the operation running smoothly and friction-free. And in the best of all worlds communication should flow through and out of the organization in such a way that it is always of the same consistency and quality.

Some wise person has said: "Blessed are those who understand, for they have listened wisely and well." We all know that an important part of communicating is understanding. It is amazing to consider how may hundreds, perhaps thousands, of courses are designed to teach speaking, and yet how very few are designed to teach listening. One of the keys to becoming a successful administrator or manager may be to listen more and talk less. We are all born with ears to hear; unfortunately we also have an inborn desire to hear the sound of our own voices! For the nursing administrator to listen carefully and empathically as well as speak and write clearly is crucial for the success of all the other elements of organization management.

No one can expect to communicate perfectly. A more reasonable objective is to learn ways to penetrate the static and distractions that get in the way. How can we get attention? How can we keep it? How can we enhance our spoken words? How can we use audiovisuals, the environment? How should we dress, gesture, sit, or stand to aid in clarifying our spoken words?

When we write, how can we organize our thoughts and translate them into brief, understandable, and interesting reports, memos, or publications? When should we use symbols or graphics as clarifiers of our written words?

How can we establish something in common between speaker and listener? What builds a sense of rapport and common purpose that lays the human relations groundwork for effective communication? How do we get useful feedback?

How can we efficiently read and gather data for planning programs, objectives, meetings, and special projects? Reading selectively and with understanding is another important element in the communications arena.

These questions and many more are answered in this book, whose purpose is to show how nursing managers and administrators can enhance their personal skills for communication and build organizational structures and channels that facilitate, rather than obstruct, the communications flow. This anthology has been designed by its editors to minimize talking about communicating and to maximize learning to communicate well. The selections and editors' commentaries represent the finest collection of articles on how to communicate that has yet been made available for nursing administrators.

As editor of the Management Anthology Series, I am proud to present this book to the world of nursing administration, a world that is constantly filled with communications interactions. These interactions, when enacted well, will not only result in more satisfied, motivated, and objectives-oriented staff but will also result in more excellent care for our patients.

Marlene G. Mayers, R.N., M.S., F.A.A.N.
Series Editor

Preface

How many hours a day do you spend communicating with other individuals in your immediate work environment? How often are poor or inadequate communication techniques the source of interdepartmental conflicts and problems in your own nursing department? What resources do you personally use to enhance your own communication skills or recommend to staff members interested in improving their verbal, written, or nonverbal skills?

Regardless of organizational structure, hospital size, or location, nursing administrators are constantly communicating—sharing and exchanging ideas, feelings, hopes, and dreams—with colleagues on staff in their hospital and health care community. Indeed, no process is more integral, or potentially problematic, in day-to-day leadership activities.

The purpose of this anthology is to provide nursing administrators, managers, and staff development educators with a comprehensive collection of timely, practical publications from the professional literature on relevant trends and practices in oral, written, and nonverbal communication. Special attention is given to "how to" publications on important, yet easily learned, leadership practices and skills.

For quick, easy reference, this volume has been divided into three units: Oral Communication, Written Communication, and Nonverbal Communication. After a short introduction, each unit begins with selections that discuss current trends and practices in communication and closes with "how to" contributions on essential skills and techniques. Unit I explores the complexities and potential impact of oral communication in human service organizations. Among the selections are readings on such time-consuming activities as interviewing, attending conferences, directing committees, preparing a speech, and listening. Unit II highlights the professional literature: reference sources relevant to the needs of busy nursing administrators, how one group of administrators (staff development educators) keeps up with the professional literature, and writing for publication. In the second chapter in this unit, readings offer practical instructions on organizing policies and procedures, developing standards and nursing audit tools, making visual aids for meetings and conferences, and drafting a memo. Unit III concludes the volume by addressing widely used, yet often unintentional, modes of nonverbal communication such as the physical design of a nursing unit, body language, clothes, and the environment created in an administrator's office.

A Communication Framework for the Nursing Administrator

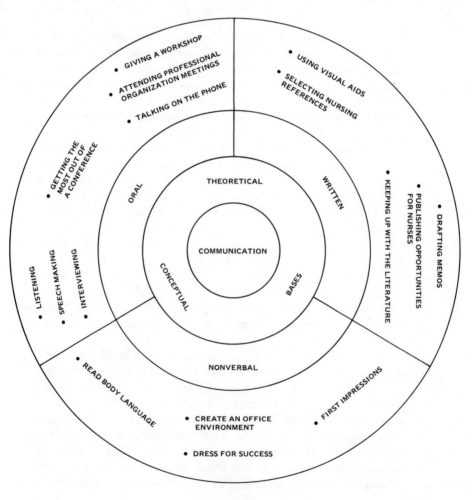

The volume's organizational scheme—from narrative and descriptions to "how to" makes this a multipurpose reference and source book. A nursing administrator may recommend the anthology to a supervisor about to give her first speech at a professional conference, to a group of visiting students who have a question about the systems approach in communication, or to a staff development educator or head nurse trying to prepare a manuscript for publication. Selections have been edited to stand alone as self-contained units of information rather than as parts of a volume to be read cover to cover. Thus, readers are encouraged to choose selections from the appropriate chapters as their communication needs and interests arise. Because of the multifaceted nature of communication, you may need to skim readings in all three units to cover a topic comprehensively.

"Suggested Readings" conclude each unit and offer additional information on the topics in the unit, discussed along with publications on a variety of related topics. These references have been organized alphabetically by topic for more efficient retrieval by the reader. Whenever possible in our editorial comments and unit introductions, we have cited specific readings that will assist nursing administrators with special needs (for instance, nursing administrators in small rural hospitals or those interested in preparing their first speech).

Cupertino, California   A.J.H.
Stanford, California   J.L.B.
January 1981

Acknowledgments

We are indebted to several individuals who have assisted us in preparing this volume. First, this project would have been impossible without the permission of numerous publishers to reproduce their work. We would also like to thank Marlene Mayers and Carol Wolfe for asking us to edit this enjoyable project and maintaining our enthusiasm through its development. In addition, scheduling flexibility approved by Greg Jackson and Lewis Mayhew in Administration & Policy Analysis at the School of Education at Stanford University and by Sharon Bird at Stanford University Hospital allowed the junior editor to complete her work on this volume while attending school full time and working. Bob Bernstein provided valuable editorial assistance and Jean Altman carefully typed our final manuscripts.

Finally, we wish to thank Laird, Chris, Sharon, and Robert for their continual support and love throughout our involvement with this project.

Introduction to the Management Anthology Series

As a nurse administrator or manager, have you often wished you could turn to your bookcase and select just the right book for the problem at hand? Or that you could talk with another nurse administrator who has faced a similar situation? Your time is limited, your problem is volatile, and the pressure merciless. Yet your bookcase contains no substantive reference source on current theories, thinking, or management methods.

Or if you are aspiring to become a nurse administrator or manager, do you wonder what you should read as part of your career development program? You may have scanned some management textbooks, only to find that, of necessity, they touch upon each subject briefly, leaving many questions unanswered and do not develop topics to any great depth.

If you are already a nursing manager or administrator or are planning to become a part of this challenging and important part of the nursing profession, you probably have discovered this problem; although there is a profusion of management applications available in the literature, they are scattered in a number of areas. And if you happen to stumble upon the application you need, it is not easy to relate it to a conceptual framework or to an overall philosophy of management. Thus you are left with a potpourri of articles and books that are as likely to be confusing as they are to be helpful.

The Management Anthology Series is designed to solve this problem by placing at your fingers a wealth of management information. Each book in the series focuses on one management topic; each is an anthology—a collection of the best selections from the literature—about a specific topic. The selections are chosen by talented people, usually nurses, who are experts in a particular field of management. These editors have generously added their own wisdom, opinions, and nursing examples to the management literature, producing not just a compendium of articles, but a logical conceptual flow of current thought by the most respected experts on that subject.

The selections in each book are chosen to provide a specific progression of concepts, and each book, in turn, contributes to the overall conceptual framework of the series. Each article in each book is an integral part of a set of beliefs, goals, and content.

PREMISE STATEMENT

This series of books on nursing management is based on several premises. The interrelated components of this belief system illustrate the dynamics of the world of nursing administration and can be seen as a conceptual framework that ties each theme and each book into an understandable whole. The five major components, or themes, are:

1. The organization, its people, and its structures
2. Management functions
3. Products, services, and cost effectiveness
4. Employee growth and satisfaction
5. Organizational security and longevity

Theme 1: The Organization, Its People, and Its Structure

The organization is the basic social matrix of the conceptual framework because it contains the concrete interpersonal and intergroup processes through which social action is accomplished. Formal organizations require conscious and purposeful cooperation among people. As individuals, we recognize that cooperation is crucial; through it we can accomplish purposes that alone we are biologically unable to do. Cooperation is essential to the survival of an organization, and because cooperation depends upon communication and interaction, organizational units are usually limited in size.

Maintaining the fabric and patterns of cooperative enterprise is the job of managers, who are responsible for organizational structures, lines of accountability and authority, and individual and group responses to change. Theme 1, the organization as the basic social matrix of our conceptual model, is shown in Exhibit 1.

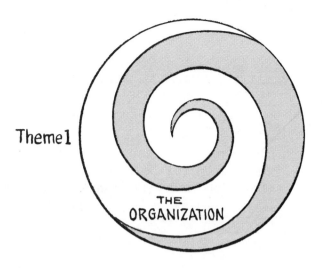

Theme1

THE
ORGANIZATION

Exhibit 1: **The Organization, Its People, and Its Structure. (Theme 1.)**

Theme 2: Management Functions

When Og, the prehistoric caveman, and his fellow tribespeople realized that they had to produce food to fill their hungry stomachs, they started communicating, planning, organizing, assigning jobs (staffing), and counting the cost (control and feedback). They also looked to someone to lead them. They didn't realize it, but they had to engage in management functions in order to achieve their goal—full stomachs!

Throughout the ages, this has been true of all collective human endeavor. Whether we realize it or not, we must fulfill management functions if we wish to achieve our goals. Seen in this way, management is not something forced upon people, it is a set of processes that we create for ourselves in order to ensure that we will be productive, satisfied, and secure.

The group initiates management tasks: communicating, planning, organizing, staffing, controlling, and leading. These management functions are universal processes based upon a body of knowledge. When a group is small, the processes simple, and the products uncomplicated, each person may incorporate many elements of management into his or her day-to-day activities, such as patient care. As the group enlarges, as processes become more complex and specialized, and as products become harder to evaluate and count, the group designates certain people to do the jobs of management on behalf of the entire group.

In contemporary society, with its large corporations comprising thousands of people, various management functions have been assigned to certain people. This has led to a belief by some people that management is an unnecessary, arbitrary, and capricious group of people at the top. It is true in some situations that management has deteriorated to the level of capriciousness, but in the most it is, and must be, a way of group thinking, planning, acting, communicating, and influencing that makes life better for both workers and consumers. Management functions arising from the needs of the organization and its people are illustrated as Theme 2 in the developing conceptual model shown in Exhibit 2.

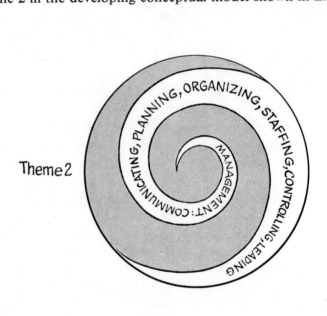

Theme 2

Exhibit 2.   Management Functions. (Theme 2.)

Theme 3: Product and Service Cost Effectiveness

People band together as an organization to produce something. Nurses come together to provide a service called nursing care, which is the profession's most obvious product.

An enterprise survives only so long as its "official," publicly offered products or services are marketable, or valued by society. Society expects an organization to produce products or services of quality at prices that are justifiable. To achieve this, nurse managers are responsible for defining values, formulating criteria, devising measurement methods, and setting forth, in understandable terms, the quality and cost of nursing care services. Theme 3, product and service cost effectiveness, is shown in Exhibit 3 as one of nursing's outputs.

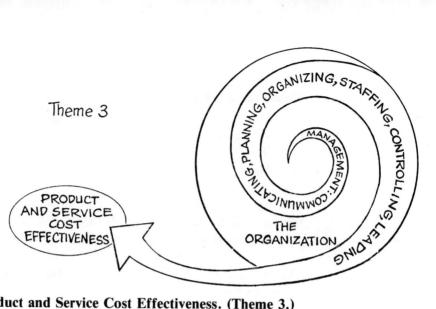

Theme 3

Exhibit 3.   Product and Service Cost Effectiveness. (Theme 3.)

Theme 4: Employee Growth and Satisfaction

People want to grow and develop, and work enterprise has the potential for being one of society's most powerful instruments for individual growth. People are always "wanting and growing"; when one need is satisfied, another appears. This process is unending, continuing throughout one's life. Therefore, nurse managers provide for: a motivating environment, job enrichment, and educational opportunities for the group's members. An important organizational output is personal and professional growth and the satisfaction of its members. This component of the developing conceptual model is shown in Exhibit 4 as Theme 4.

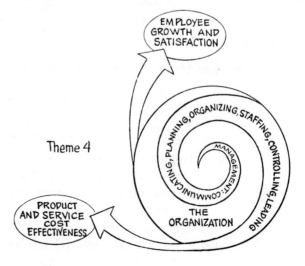

Theme 4

Exhibit 4.   Employee Growth and Satisfaction. (Theme 4.)

Theme 5: Organizational Security and Longevity

Finally, organizations must engage in transactions with both the internal and external environments simply to survive, and even more importantly, to grow. If they cannot cope with their environments, they die.

Managers, who foster the quality of the group's transactions, develop sense organs to detect environmental changes. They forecast, plan, and develop strategies for survival and growth, always looking as far into the future as possible. The security and longevity of the organization is itself an organizational output. This is illustrated as Theme 5 in the completed conceptual model shown in Exhibit 5.

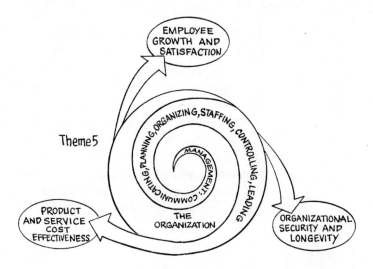

Exhibit 5.   Conceptual Model for the Management Anthology Series. (Theme 5.)

Summary

In summary, this conceptual framework incorporates the belief that a nursing organization must have three major outputs: cost-effective patient care; satisfaction and growth for its members; and organizational security and longevity. The absence or diminution of any one of these three can jeopardize the others.

The conceptual model illustrates the organization of the Management Anthology Series. The major principles of management practice are interrelated in a comprehensive conceptual framework, whose basic elements are derived from the theories more of the resource books. Some subtopics of each of the major themes are listed in the series outline at the front of this book.

Of course, any conceptual framework represents an arbitrary, yet defensible, division of content. The purpose of the division is to simplify a universe of knowledge so that one can grasp its essential nature. This accomplished, one can then deal with the myriad of details that logically (and sometimes arbitrarily) follow.

The conceptual framework of this series of books is designed specifically to provide nursing administrators and managers with current, comprehensive, and practical resources for dealing with management problems and issues. Each book relates to just one facet of management, and each selection covers theory as well as practical applications for nursing management situations, making it possible to review current thinking and practice quickly and efficiently.

Marlene G. Mayers, R.N., M.S., F.A.A.N.
Series Editor

THEME TWO: MANAGEMENT FUNCTIONS

There are certain activities that all managers perform. These functions are generic to management and neceesary for any kind of organization to meet its objectives. Whether a group of people is producing cars, dairy products, safety pins, soap, or nursing care, management functions are universal processes that are based on a recognized body of knowledge. All administrators or managers must *communicate, plan, organize, staff, control* and *lead.* The proportion of time and energy spent on each of these functions varies widely from day to day, situation to situation, and from one level of management to another, however. The hierarchy of management roles determines which functions are most crucial at each level. Investigators have identified at least three different management levels: the institution, general management, and department management[1].

At the institutional level, the top executives (board of directors, chief executive officer, and so on) set overall objectives, assess the organization's environment, gather and allocate resources, and are accountable to stockholders or the public at large. Theirs is a trustee function. Top level managers make long-run, life-or-death organizational decisions rather than perform the daily operations work of the organization. Their major management functions are planning, controlling, communicating, and leading.

Persons at the next level, general management, are responsible for specifying the overall objectives, implementing action plans, and utilizing allocated resources to the best advantage. The functions crucial to these managers are communicating, planning, organizing, staffing, controlling, and leading.

Departmental level managers (department heads, first-line supervisors, and so on) are primarily concerned with on-line production. They must utilize people, money, and technology to coordinate the work flow and ensure that their departments contribute to the effective accomplishment of the organization's goals.

Not all organizations are large enough to provide for three discrete levels of management. However, every management or administrative group must fill these three levels of functions, either by incorporating two or three levels in one or more persons' roles or by changing focus from time to time.

Each of the series of books in this theme, Management Functions, attends to one of the tasks of a manager. These management functions represent the technology of management—the intellectual, physical, and psychological tools that administrators and managers must have at their disposal in order to carry out their work effectively.

How to communicate effectively is the focus of the present book. The anthology's editors, Ann Huntsman and Jane Binger, in an upbeat and easy-to-read style, have brought together and commented on a selection of excellent and fascinating articles pertinent to the various elements of communication. They have made very perceptive observations on applications of the ideas presented in the articles to the world of nursing administration and its communication functions.

References

1. Holden, P., Fish, L., and Smith, H. *Top Management Organization and Control.* New York:McGraw-Hill, 1975.

UNIT I ORAL COMMUNICATION

It is not surprising in a television-oriented society that so much attention is given to the subject of communication. Political futures can be launched or devastated with a publicly expressed point of view.

Nurses are moving into the public arena of health legislation and planning. Now more than ever we need to deliver articulate messages containing the professional nursing perspective on health care issues.

We believe that nurses have tremendous amounts of information and innovative ideas about health care which frequently go unheard because of deficient verbal communication skills and consequent self-consciousness. We nurses have not perfected our verbal communication skills. We have not practiced presenting our ideas publicly or learned techniques to capture audience attention and argue our case. We have not received expert coaching by skilled senior practitioners on a daily basis for two or three years as have attorneys, politicians, schoolteachers and professionals in marketing and business. Perhaps we need to create in basic nursing education more opportunities for verbal exchange of views on health care issues.

In our employment settings, we can use the many structured and unstructured opportunities to improve our verbal communication skills. The principles of effective speaking apply whether you are in a thirty-bed hospital or a thousand-bed hospital. Articulate representation of the nursing department's problems, issues, and proposals is the responsibility of the nursing administrator. Equally important, that representation can also be an opportunity to positively influence the environment. Careful preparation for a meeting with the nursing management group can yield rewards in their support for your ideas. Confident and businesslike conduct of meetings with good verbal skills provides the much needed role modeling for nurses in your organization.

Are you satisfied with the communication network in your organization? Is there meaningful discussion, dialogue, and collegial

1

exchange among the professional nurses? Or does it seem that directives are dispatched from the top of the hierarchy, explained and defended to the caregiver levels of the nursing department? What we say and how we say it, both on an interpersonal level and an organizational level, have tremendous impact on employees' attitudes and self-esteem, on the patient care environment, and on the future progress of our health care programs.

Chapter 1 focuses on the importance of communication in nursing—to the profession, to our organizations, and to society. As you read these selections, ask yourself how the verbal communication in your setting advances professional, organizational, and societal objectives.

Chapter 2 concentrates the reader's attention on effective verbal communication skills of individuals, for instance, on clarity of expression and active listening. Also described are common blocks that hamper effective communication.

Chapter 3 concludes the unit with practical "how to" discussions on conducting an interview, attending conferences, preparing a speech, organizing and chairing a committee, intershift reporting, conducting a workshop, and giving a press interview.

1. The Importance of Communication

The first selection in this chapter, by Brunner, contains an overview of the fundamentals and goals of the communication process. It highlights technical and semantic problems of communications found in many nursing service departments.

It has long been our contention that nurses have more accurate information about health care clients than any other group and better ideas about how the health care system should respond. Yet we are frequently the least heard because (1) we erroneously assume that everyone else has the same information, awareness, and value system as we do and (2) we lack the skills to articulate our ideas in the appropriate arenas. In the second reading, Le Roux states that "the ability to influence social action is primarily a communication process" and makes a good case for nursing's responsibility to influence and change the health care system

and to teach its members the art and skill of public communication.

The senior editor's father-in-law, whose hobby for many years was teaching "Effective Presentation" tells this story: There was a popular country preacher whose church was always full of eager listeners. One Sunday a visiting preacher asked his host for the secret to such excellent sermons and attentive audiences. His reply, "Well it's like this: First I tell'em what I'm gonna tell 'em; then I tell 'em; then I tell 'em what I told 'em." The value of a simple, straightforward approach to the introduction, body, and conclusion of a speech cannot be overstated. The selection by Rosendahl contains excellent and concise guidelines for effective public speaking, from approaching the platform to organizing, outlining, and delivering the speech.*

---

*In adapting previously published literature, the editor has added original commentary. Throughout the rest of this book, the editor's contributions are italicized to distinguish them from reprinted material.

COMMUNICATIONS IN NURSING SERVICE ADMINISTRATION

By Nancy A. Brunner

Reprinted with permission from *The Journal of Nursing Administration,* Volume 7, Number 10, October 1977, pp. 29–32.

One of the most frequently cited problems occurring in nursing service administration is termed "communications." Medication and treatment errors, unusual incidents, and policy infractions are often labeled "communication problems." Usually there is no attempt to study the problem further, and communications problems continue to exist in the clinical setting. To begin to resolve communications problems we must understand the communications process and some basic elements of information theory. Our knowledge can then guide us in identifying, defining, and resolving specific communications problems when they occur.

Information and communications theorists have developed models describing how we communicate as well as the barriers to effective communication. The communications model presented in Exhibit 1-1 demonstrates the basic elements of the communications process[1]. Communications can be defined as the flow of a message from a sender to a receiver via a channel. Channels include the spoken or written word, pictures, physical gestures, etc.

Cherry sees communications as the process "which links any organization together," and views the flow of information among the parts of an organization as essential to its survi-val[2]. Messages about the assignment of personnel, the location of specialized equipment, and the performance of personnel are vital to the functioning of the nursing service department. Patient information is also of great importance, for it provides the basis for assignments, treatments, medications, etc. Each of us can readily cite examples of communications failures within our own organization.

Shannon and Weaver believe that organizations and individuals have three types of communications problems: technical, semantic, and influential[3]. These three types include the communications problems usually occurring in nursing services; for that reason, they will be used as a framework for discussion of communications in nursing service organizations.

TECHNICAL PROBLEMS

Technical problems address the question of accuracy of message transfer—is the sent message accurately received? Here we are assuming that an intelligible message was sent. Often, in nursing, there is no clear-cut, intelligible message. Many messages sent between nursing personnel are incomplete, jargon-laden, and based on erroneous

---

Exhibit 1-1.   Basic Communication Model [1]

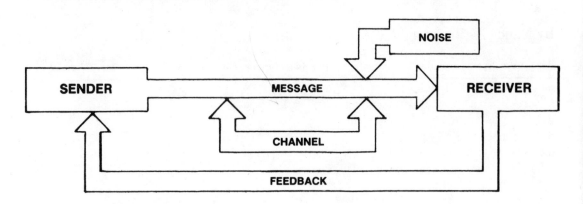

assumptions regarding the receiver's knowledge of the situation. Technical communications problems can create life-threatening situations—as when incomplete patient information is assumed to be complete. A receiver may demand clarification, repetition, or further information. However, our bureaucratic system discourages this; a receiver's position in the hierarchy may preclude a request for clarification or further information. The newly employed nurse or nurse's aide is not likely to ask her superordinate to give clearer directions.

In order to determine whether the message sent is the message received, the sender may request feedback. Requests for clarification of additional information (from the sender or receiver) can be utilized to test for message completeness or distortion. Requesting or obtaining feedback need not be a complicated or painful process. It may be done simply by asking the receiver to interpret a specific point or to summarize a prior discussion.

Positive and negative feedback are two terms which are used frequently, although not always correctly, in nursing. Feedback is positive when the sender gets information indicating that the message sent was received. Negative feedback indicates to the sender that the

message sent was not received or was misunderstood.

Both positive and negative feedback can provide information regarding system performance[4]. Positive feedback indicates that the system is functioning in the manner desired, while negative feedback indicates that something is wrong in the system. For example, when the supervisor asks the head nurse if a specific activity has been completed on the nursing unit, the supervisor is requesting feedback regarding the system's performance. If the head nurse indicates that the activity had been completed, the supervisor receives positive feedback.

The basic communications model demonstrates that there can be noise in the system while messages are being sent. According to Cherry, noise is a disturbance or interference in the communications process[5]. Since it can enter the communications channel in different places, noise may take several forms. The sender can be the source of the noise. If experiencing stress, the sender may produce garbled messages. If the sender attempts to send multiple messages simultaneously, noise may be the result. Contradictory messages are another form of noise.

Receivers should also be checked for noise.

It is possible that that their concerns are of sufficient magnitude to cause them to block out all information, including that which is positive or helpful.

Receivers may have noise in their own systems if they have ideas, emotions, or problems occupying their attention when a message is sent to them. An individual may not receive a message accurately while experiencing stress; we listen more closely to good news. A receiver tends to ignore neutral, nonthreatening messages; those that have little or no immediate significance get tuned out very easily. Information that increases stress tends to be rejected; this response is observed frequently among patients. We forget that the same phenomenon occurs among nursing and other personnel as well. To ensure that the message will be received, it is necessary to remove the noise prior to sending the message.

There are many possible sources and types of noise in most health care systems, whether in the nurse-patient setting, the nurse-nurse setting, or the nurse-physician setting. Removing the noise to permit effective communication can be a monumental task. For example, the distractions and interruptions occurring in a hospital nursing station often generate noise that can be avoided only by leaving the area.

Channel selection can also affect communication success. Senders should make certain that they are using the appropriate channel. For example, is face-to-face communication appropriate in all situations? Perhaps an indirect channel would be more advantageous. The right channel must be selected to avoid distortion or omission of the signal and to avoid unnecessary opportunities for noise to interfere with the message. Factors to be considered in selecting the appropriate channel include knowledge of the receiver as an individual, desired time of message receipt, and need for immediate feedback. Noise (in the form of receiver stress) resulting in message distortion may occur if face-to-face communications is attempted in the presence of the receiver's peer group.

In nursing, part of the communications problem is often due to a lack of clarity regarding what messages should be sent. Frequently, a staff nurse or supervisor learns too late that a certain incident should have been reported to the director, physician, or administrator. Nursing department policies should include a concise statement regarding what events should be reported to whom, by whom, and at what times.

SEMANTIC PROBLEMS

Semantic problems refer to the interpretation of a message by the receiver. Does the receiver clearly comprehend the message's information content? Information content can be distorted by noise, and something very different from that which was sent may be received. Some messages are distorted because "buzz words," slang, or jargon is used. Sometimes, the real message is buried under emotional overtones or is hidden in body language. The receiver can be confused when the sender uses subtle hints and innuendos as a means of communicating. This may be appropriate for private personal exchanges, but it is inappropriate in a work setting

One major semantic problem in hospitals is the use of abbreviations. Almost every disease, treatment, surgical procedure, and medication seems to have an abbreviation. The nurse tends to forget this when caring for patients and often assumes that the patient knows a given abbreviation. Later the nurse may wonder why the patient is upset. She may find it is because she used an abbreviation and failed to check whether the patient understood it. Likewise, the nurse must be careful in her use of medical or nursing jargon when communicating with patients. She must consider the vocabulary of her listener. It is the sender's responsibility to use language that is understandable to the receiver. Senders must rely on feedback to ascertain the receiver's comprehension of their messages. Similarly, the receivers have an obligation to give feedback to the sender regarding the clarity of the message.

INFLUENCE PROBLEMS

The influence problem refers to the message's effects on the behavior of the receiver. It is generally accepted that the only way we can influence the behavior of others is through communication[6]. However, it should not be assumed that the receiver of a message will act in the manner desired by the sender.

The sender's knowledge of the communications process alone may not be adequate to change behavior. The sender may need to appeal to the receiver's sense of motivation and desire for job satisfaction in order to bring about a desired behavior change. Knowledge of these concepts provides cues as to how information should be communicated. For example, behavioral change may be effected by nonverbal communication of the rewards that can be obtained by performing in the same manner as the unit clinical specialist.

To know whether the transmitted information has any impact on the individual, the sender must obtain feedback. For influence problems, observing the receiver's behavior may be the best means of obtaining feedback. When the desired behavior does not occur, senders should look for technical or semantic problems in the communications system before blaming the receiver for lack of cooperation.

INFORMATION OVERLOAD

People can absorb and process only a very limited amount of information at any one time. Information overload may develop when an esoteric or incomprehensible message is presented, or when listeners are given too much information. When an individual's limit has been reached, he or she will block out further information. Some people do this by inattentiveness in a conversation, sleeping during a meeting, or talking with another person during a lecture.

The treatment for information overload is quite simple: eliminate messages that are not relevant to the main topic. When the primary message is complex, the presentation should be very concise and to the point. If small amounts of information are given over an extended period of time, the probability of accurate reception is greater.

There are other techniques for treating and/or preventing information overload. When messages are repeated frequently, the sender and receiver may agree upon a chunking or coding procedure. "Chunking" or "coding" refers to the use of one special word term, number, or symbol to represent a larger amount of information. For example, by referring to pulmonary toilet, as spelled out in a procedure book, nurses can communicate more easily. For this approach to be effective, everyone involved must understand the code.

Another approach to information overload, particularly during a lecture, speech, or lengthy conversation, is for the speaker to provide some thinking time for the audience. Thinking time can be gained through a brief digression from the main topic, a question period, or a simple coffee break. The thinking time approach permits the audience to consider and process the information received before being subjected to additional messages.

COMMUNICATIONS AND ORGANIZATIONAL SURVIVAL

The technical, semantic, and influence problems associated with the flow of information can be found in many nursing service organizations. These problems must be identified and resolved for nursing service to function effectively. Whatever the source or cause of interference, ineffective communication can have deleterious consequences for any organization. Noise in the channel is the most frequent cause of a breakdown of effective communications. It is the most difficult communications problem to deal with.

At all levels in nursing service organization, decision making depends upon the availability of accurate, reliable, up-to-date information. Bedside patient decisions require accurate patient information. Decisions at the nursing unit level require that the head nurse have information regarding both patients and personnel. The director of nursing makes decisions on the basis of information about one or more patients and/or personnel and/or nursing units. Equitable decisions are arrived at only when information is received without noise or distortion.

Within the nursing organization, feedback regarding system performance and feedback regarding messages sent are of the utmost importance. Negative feedback regarding system performance indicates a need for corrective messages to refocus the system's performance. Positive feedback requires that reinforcements and rewards be provided to maintain performance at satisfactory levels.

In nursing service organizations, feedback on messages sent may be obtained in individual conversations between supervisory personnel and staff members or in meetings (such as head nurse–supervisor meetings or staff-nurse meetings). The nursing staff may be the senders of information and may require feedback from persons higher in the system. When messages are freely exchanged and information flows without noise or distortion in the channels, the organization has a much better chance of survival.

COMMUNICATION AND INFLUENCE IN NURSING

By Rose S. LeRoux

Reprinted from *Communication and Influence in Nursing*, by permission of Nursing Administration Quarterly, ©1978.

You can have expert knowledge; but if you cannot communicate your ideas to others clearly, forcefully, and fluently, you will have little influence.

You can have expert skill; but if you cannot demonstrate your skills to others and move them to action, you will have little power.

You can have an excellent department of nursing service; but if you cannot sell your products and services to others, the activities of your department members will be relatively underused and unappreciated.

Too often in nursing we are reactive rather than proactive. Too often the system controls us rather than our controlling the system. Often when we try to influence the system and do not meet with complete success, we think we have lost the total war rather than just one of many battles.

Some of this has to do with our expectations of how people should be. Sometimes we assume that what motivates us motivates others; what we value, others value; and because of our status and position we will be granted a priori trust and confidence. In a sense we are a bit out of step because we are fighting for autonomy in an age when society demands our interdependence. The energy crisis is a dramatic illustration.

We must know when to be autonomous and when to be interdependent. We must decide when to advance and when to hold our ground. This requires a sense of timing, political astuteness, knowledge of marketing skills, familiarity with diffusion of innovation theories, and an ability to communicate effectively.

In the past, we inadvertently set our nursing administrators up for a "one-down" position by preparing them for patient-focused clinical practice while many of their colleagues (health administrators) were prepared in two-year master's programs in administration. It is a testimonial to their considerable talent and personal fortitude that many survived the challenges of the job. This lack of preparation in the tools of management, however, may have made them reticent to communicate their ideas forcefully. The ability to influence social action is primarily a communication process. That we have not influenced the health care system in proportion to our potential strength may be due to our inability to attract an audience, to be granted credibility, or to express ourselves forcefully.

We are beginning to offer rigorous management graduate programs for nurses. Prospective administrators will learn much about what it takes to administer programs and departments and to manage people. We are also promoting doctoral preparation in nursing so that we will produce scholars and researchers who will develop and expand nursing knowledge and theory. Knowledge is an absolute necessity, but it is not sufficient to influence the health care system in a powerful way. Skill and knowledge must be demonstrated to be useful.

COMMUNICATION EFFECTIVENESS

Oral communication plays a fundamental part in human interaction. History reveals that public communication has exerted considerable influence in human affairs. The Greeks prepared people for political leadership by prescribing methods for rhetorical success. Their audiences were small and localized. Our modern media makes it possible for us to reach a potential worldwide audience. Whether the audience is small or large, localized or worldwide, nursing administrators will be expected to stand on their feet before a group of people and address them.

In nursing we are still not teaching people the rudiments of effective speaking: how to speak up and speak out; how to present logical, effective argumentation; how to modify attitudes and opinions through persuasive communication. Poorly chosen words and ineffectual delivery can weaken the impact of excellent ideas.

Many women lack confidence in their ability to speak publicly. This may be due to years of conditioning ("Silence is a woman's glory") and negative feedback ("It is better to remain silent and be thought a fool than to speak and remove all doubt") or a belief that what we have to say is not important for others to hear. There are few females fluent in oral discourse who can serve as models. Women are also affected by prevalent beliefs and social restrictions about their speech. There is a belief that the things women talk about are trivial; social restrictions reinforce this assumption. Women are expected to use more:

- "Polite" construction: "Would it be all right if we . . .?"
- Tag questions: "Won't you . . .?"
- Wh-imperatives: "Why don't you . . .?" [7]

Women are more likely to say, "Goodness, the health care system is a mess, isn't it?" or "Would you mind answering that light?" Men are more likely to use declarative sentences and outright commands.

Lakoff believes that even when women use declarative sentences to state their opinions, they frequently use an intonation pattern which makes them *sound* like questions. All of which make women appear less self-confident, more deferential, and approval-seeking[8]. These social expectations about women's speech maintain their stereotyped social roles; and nursing administrators, as a predominantly female group, are affected by them.

Whenever we speak we reveal something about ourselves and risk the possibility of rejection. But the consequences of not speaking out forcefully can be dire for the administrator, the nursing staff, and the patients under their care. To have power and not use it in behalf of one's constituency is an abdication of responsibility.

Our communication effectiveness depends on our ability to manipulate linguistic symbols orally or in writing, privately or publicly. Spoken discourse differs from written, however, in that receivers tend to respond more holistically and subjectively[9]. There is little time to critically analyze, to review the message, to dissect it. The speaker's voice, manner, and personality may enhance or distract from what is being said. Substance and style are both important for maintaining the listener's attention and interest.

VARIABLES OF COMMUNICATION

Although ultimately meaning lies in the mind

of the receiver, there is much we can do to prepare our messages and improve our delivery. Every act of public communication involves the following variables:

- The communicator
- The context
- The audience
- The message
- Style and delivery

The Communicator

Some speakers project more vitality than others. Some are dynamic and adept in oral communication. The speaker's image is as important a factor in speaking today as it was when Aristotle defined it as "ethos" or "credibility" centuries ago.

The status, position, and reputation of the speakers operate to establish speaker credibility. This "prestige" factor often accounts for favorable response to a message. The speakers' image often benefits or suffers because of the image of the group, institution, or interest they represent[10]. This image is subject to change, depending on such image-changing factors as accuracy and importance of what the speakers say, the method of delivery, how it is said, the perceived similarities between the communicators and the listeners, whether or not the speakers can argue against their own best interest, and if they initially express some views that are also held by the audience[11].

These elements operate to establish the speakers' sincerity, trustworthiness, and expertise, and leave the audience with a residual image as well as a residual message. In addition, people tend to expose themselves to speakers they respect and to messages with which they agree. If receivers feel they do not possess sufficient knowledge or the subject is too complex, reaction to the speech may be largely in terms of the credibility of the message source. Credibility is a variable, not a constant; it varies with topic, receivers, and time[12]. The nurse administrator will do well to remember this. We are improving our collective image as professional nurses and we as individuals will benefit from this. It is up to us to communicate in the public domain. Our many publics will not know who we are unless we inform them; they will not know what we do unless we demonstrate our skills.

The Context

Every act of public communication operates in a climate of public opinion and is screened by the traditions, rituals, and myths of the particular culture of the listeners[13]. Many politicians, movie producers, and advertisers pretest their products by performing some type of public opinion sampling. They realize that a public message is part of a larger public dialogue[14]. An entire matrix of prior events will influence how the message is received and whether or not it is acted upon[15].

The situational context and physical surroundings also prescribe the type of oral discourse permitted. The physical characteristics of the immediate situation may convey messages in their own right[16]. For example, presenting a budget request at the capitol building will restrict the range of viable options. A speaker must improvise within the framework of situational constraints, but "there remains considerable room for rhetorical invention in most cases"[17].

The prior social situation, the context of the communication, the climate of public opinion all influence the reception and interpretation of the message.

The nursing administrator must ask and answer some critical questions about prevailing public opinion prior to delivering a message to achieve a particular goal. The following are but a few:

- What are the current negative and positive social forces?
- Where does nursing fit into the total health care delivery system?
- What is the prevailing public opinion toward nursing and the services it offers?
- What are the benefits of conducting a public opinion survey prior to making some major changes in nursing care delivery?

The Audience

There are many publics. It is important for nurse administrators to find out about the values, beliefs, and opinions of their listeners. They must identify with them in order to present material in the most favorable light. Often we may be speaking to the battle weary, and we should choose our words accordingly. The more diversified the audience, the wider the appeal of the message must be.

Some publics are more attentive than others and therefore receive more messages. Some are more informed and rational than others; some are more actively concerned with certain issues than others[18]. Borden, Gregg, and Grove identify the mass public, the attentive public, and the opinion-making public. A very small percentage of the potential audience may be involved in active formulation of public policy[19]. This is a critical group to address.

King reminds us that our aim should be to influence as many people as possible in behalf of the goals espoused[20]. The speaker must speak to maintain the allegiance of the committed, win the support of the uncommitted, and modify or soften the attitudes of the opposition[21]. This requires all of a person's persuasive skills and means that we cannot continue to speak to only our partisan, nurse audiences. We must speak to different audiences, sometimes bypassing the active

opposition to discover groups which will provide a support base.

The group affiliation of the audience, conformity to the norms of that group, and individual personality factors affect message attendance, reception, and acceptance. The speaker must consider in what ways listeners may be affected by proposals made. Such questions as the following should be asked:

1. How much personal investment do the listeners have in maintaining the status quo?
2. Is there a possibility of listeners giving up some autonomy in order to advance a higher goal?
3. What is the latitude of acceptance-rejection among individuals?

The more personally involved and committed individuals are on an issue, the greater is their latitude of rejection and the smaller their latitude of acceptance. Message distortion occurs frequently if the message runs contrary to a person's established beliefs[22].

Attitude change toward the direction advocated by a speaker occurs when the following conditions are obtained:

1. The message is relatively unstructured and permits for a variety of interpretations and responses.
2. Listeners are not highly involved in the topic, or it is unfamiliar to them.
3. There is not a maximum discrepancy between the listener's initial attitude and the proposal.
4. The communicator is acceptable in terms of the listener's reference group affiliation [23].

The health care system will benefit from our addressing various consumer groups, interested politicians, and supportive physicians, as well as other nurses. In order to have influence we must be able to attract listeners, maintain their attention, alienate the fewest possible, and accomplish our purpose. Careful audience analysis will enable us to communicate effectively with these various groups.

The Message

The message links the source with the receiver and should be carefully prepared and organized to influence others. Although much communication is nonverbal, humans are basically a speaking species. For maximum effect words and actions should be congruent.

Although there is no foolproof way to gain support for one's goals, it is helpful to begin with the point of most agreement and to convey information about one's own attitude or belief on the topic in a nonopinionated way. A simple "I believe that . . ." is preferable to an opinionated rejection statement, "Only an idiot would suggest that," or an opinionated acceptance statement, "Any intelligent person knows . . ."[24].

It is important to address the issues, the questions which are inherent in the proposal. King states that the speaker must come to grips with those matters that are the basis of opposition and doubt, take a stand, meet logical objections without belittling the audience, and gain support on the basis of the audience's aspirations and attitudes[25]. If you think a program is needed, you will probably be asked why you should be supported, who will bear the financial support, and how it will benefit others. You must use evidence to support your contentions. The evidence should be factual and strong.

We should be able to argue on both sides of an issue so that we can anticipate the objections of our listeners and be able to refute legitimate concerns with careful, well-thought-out, persuasive answers[26]. A problem-solution approach will be successful in modifying attitudes and gaining support if the solution proposed will actually solve the problem. Insulting an audience or imputing negative characteristics to them will only succeed in erecting further barriers to communication.

Style and Delivery

If you have something worthwhile to say, and if you have thoroughly researched your topic, your style and delivery can help maintain your audience's attention. A clear, direct, conversational tone, words which are familiar and create images in the minds of your receivers help to drive home your message. Distracting mannerisms (for example, clearing the throat, adjusting your dress, disfluencies such as "you know, er, ah," apologizing for not being prepared) should be avoided. If you really believe what you are saying, you can communicate your own sense of involvement, personal conviction, and commitment. Unless you transmit this to others you cannot expect to influence them toward accepting your ideas[27].

Public communication can not only illuminate issues; it can create them. We should not expect immediate results, but as advertisers and politicians know, many messages delivered over an extended period of time will inevitably produce a subtle awareness of the issues, arouse public opinion, reinforce attitudes, and cause attitude change[28].

We, as nurses, have important things to say about improving the health of our nation. We also have vital, critical services to offer. We must enter the public arena to become visible and to communicate with our various publics. Knowledge of the variable involved in every act of public communication is helpful. As with every skill, however, practice is essential. Let us teach nurses how to influence the system through effective speaking.

It is time to begin.

THE VERBAL SIDE OF EFFECTIVE COMMUNICATION

By Pearl P. Rosendahl

Reprinted with permission from *The Journal of Nursing Administration*, Volume 4, Number 5, September–October 1974, pp. 41–44.

The time for "silent service" is past. Today, nursing needs articulate leaders to define professional goals and communicate them to both the recipients of services and the principals who authorize those services. If society still asks, "What does the nurse do?," nurses themselves must answer by initiating continuous dialogue to clarify their philosophies and responsibilities.

Heide states that medicine fails to understand attempts by nurses to strive for autonomy[29]. Fundamental to our success in achieving autonomy are leadership efforts, which can be greatly strengthened by effective oral communication. Specifically, nurses must speak in the public forum about professional matters in order to convince more people of their expanding competencies and open up new frontiers of responsibility. They must develop the speaking expertise that "turns on" their listeners.

Public speaking is a practitioner's art; the term itself implies interaction with people. Most of the principles that apply to oratory and other formal presentations also apply to all purposeful conversation. One major nursing goal is to develop such purposeful conversation in the nurse-patient relationship. To do so, every nurse needs to acquire the techniques of effective public speaking, which also provide excellent opportunities for self-expression and the development of a sense of identity.

The ability to communicate effectively has impressive advantages. The insight of Charles W. Schwab, when he was president of U.S. Steel, continues to influence industry, business, and government. He said he would pay more for a man's ability to speak and express himself than for any other quality he might possess. Schwab believed that to speak clearly, cogently, and persuasively broadens social acceptance, increases personal satisfaction, and lays a foundation for personal leadership[30].

My initiation into public speaking was via a Toastmasters Club, where my progress has been slow, but measurable. Toastmasters International, which has local clubs throughout the world, is seriously concerned with improving its members' communication and leadership skills through reciprocal self-help techniques. Our local chapter assembles weekly around a dinner table. Everyone speaks at each meeting and is evaluated.

If our listeners do not comprehend our message, it matters little how well we know our subject, how well we have done our research, or how well we have organized our thoughts—we have not achieved our objective. The effective speaker cultivates the listener and stirs him to action. He should be fluent and congruous, utilizing the following guidelines for the best effect.

PLATFORM MANNER

Project a Feeling of Natural Poise.

Approach the platform and pause before speaking. Look at your audience and smile. Do not speak until you are ready. Stand with your shoulders back and your head up; good posture makes you appear alert. Let your legs, not the speaker's stand, support your weight. The stand should be used only to hold your reference resources.

Use Appropriate Gestures.

The hands, body, and feet are essential visual aids for adding variety to your exposition. Learn to control and capitalize on their usage.

Gestures serve to illustrate, emphasize, and interpret your speech. The more involved in your subject you become, the more you will need to use them. However, too many gestures are as bad as none, and awkward movements detract from your presentation.

Start with illustrative gestures, using your hands to indicate size, distance, and numbers. Point to objects to focus attention on them. Emphatic gestures, such as striking your palm or extending both hands, help to accentuate key words, a specific message, or a definitive goal and add emphasis as you repeat words. You may also use your hands to portray your thought process. For instance, try to pantomime your explanation of such topics as cardiopulmonary resuscitation.

Make Direct Eye Contact.

Eyes are one of the most effective nonverbal means of communication. Direct eye contact serves as a stimulus to each person in the audience and is an excellent technique for gaining and holding his attention. You should make the listener feel that you are talking to him alone.

Keep your eyes moving from person to person, pausing momentarily for individual eye contact. Address yourself first to one listener, then concentrate on others in turn until you have reached them all. Continue talking to specific individuals throughout your speech. If the audience is very large, concentrate initially on a small group in one area and then divert your attention to other groups.

Should You Use Notes?

No, they get between you and your listeners. Your role as a speaker is to communicate thoughts and ideas to each member of your audience. A "reading" is not a speech, and listening evaporates when a speech is read. If you need assurance, put your outline on bibliography cards. Visual aids may also serve to expand your listeners' comprehension and to shore up your own confidence.

Be Enthusiastic.

Enthusiasm is the priceless ingredient that brings your words to life. You must believe in your message! Authentic enthusiasm is the outward reflection of true emotions originating within you. The secret of a full life or a great speech is enthusiasm of the kind that recognizes no obstacles.

The prescription is, "Take your natural intelligence, add profound motivation, which drives off apathy and cynicism, stir in the excitement of doing—the result is enthusiasm and accomplishment"[31].

VOICE

Your voice is a reflection of your personality

and a sensitive barometer of your feelings. A good speaking voice, one that can be clearly and easily understood, is essential to success in public speaking. Be yourself. Keep your voice natural. Consider the four criteria of (1) pitch, (2) loudness, (3) timing and (4) quality.

Pitch.

The range from alto to soprano or bass to tenor is the quality of voice defined as pitch. A high pitch suggests excitement, uncertainty, or possibly anger, whereas a low pitch projects an air of confidence, relaxation, and assurance.

Use your natural pitch when speaking, with modulation to express doubt, enthusiasm, conviction, and other attitudes or emotions. Whenever the pitch level remains unchanged, your voice becomes monotonous.

If your natural speaking voice is high, try a slight drop in pitch to maintain interest; conversely, if your voice is naturally low, raise the pitch. Vocal variety creates a melodious speech and avoids dullness and monotony.

Loudness.

Loudness is regulated by the amount of breath you force through your vocal cords and amplify in the air-filled cavities in and around your mouth. A good speaker controls this amount of air and its amplification to suit his subject matter. Speak clearly. Do not force your voice; project it. Talk to the person in the back row: Look at that person and project your voice to him. Remember that middle and higher pitched voices usually have better carrying power. Vary the loudness of your voice to provide emphasis and variety.

Timing.

In general the optimum rate for achieving understanding is from 125 to 150 spoken words per minute. The speaker can vary the grouping of words and phrases, pausing to provide emphasis and intelligibility. A pause can also be an attention-getter; your listener will sense a change in tempo and this will stimulate his curiosity.

Quality.

Vocal quality may be described as husky, hoarse, nasal, melodious, or flat. It may be influenced by the emotional and physical state of the speaker. Fatigue and sickness can often be clearly detected in the quality of a speaker's voice. Try to be relaxed, friendly, eager to communicate. Practice reading aloud to help you enunciate every syllable and improve your tonal quality.

THE SPEECH

Here are some pointers for preparing well-constructed speeches that really communicate:

Subject.

Choose stimulating subjects you understand and in which you are strongly interested (your listeners will seldom care more about something than you do). Learn as much as you can about the people who will constitute your audience. If you know something about their personalities, attitudes, and beliefs, you will know how to select your subject matter and structure your thoughts and ideas effectively, thereby stimulating the attention of your audience.

Organize Your Speech.

First, make an outline which presents your message step by step and develops it coherently. Every talk should have an introduction, a body, and a conclusion. The introduction must get immediate attention, warm up your audience, and prepare them for your subject matter.

You should make your point in the body of

your talk. It contains the vitals of your speech. You can develop your idea by progressing from the general to the specific, then back to the general and to the specific. Whatever your message, it must be worthy of your listeners. It must provoke them to think objectively, motivate them to make subjective explorations, or prompt them to act spontaneously.

Toastmasters recommends a reading program to enrich your own background before preparing to speak on your chosen subject. Select an area that interests you and do serious reading about it. Information derived from your reading will give added impact to your speech.

Keep your speech on a constructive note, with a positive message. To hold an audience, never scold. When you pose a problem, your listeners should feel that it is their problem you are helping to solve. The conclusion should inspire your audience to take that action your speech was designed to achieve. For a dynamic closing, you can use an informational summary, an appropriate quotation, or a rhetorical question. Strive to create a lasting impression. Your closing should be unforgettable.

Choice of Words.

Constantly strive to increase your vocabulary. Words are your tools. The right ones can generate desired actions. Learn to use words to accomplish your goals. Make them work for you. Your choice of words will affect the way you think and the degree to which you influence others. Make lively, exciting, enthusiastic, imaginative words become your natural way of speaking. The use of such words

quickly gets the attention of your listeners and makes verbal pictures much clearer.

Use Specific Instances.

Give names, places, dates, and events. Present your ideas like a newsreel, creating successive pictures. The good speaker brings all elements of speaking into harmony. Performance and content are not in competition; rather, they reinforce each other and thereby enhance the clarity of the speech.

Practice speaking in public as often as you can. Make every conversation an exercise in good speech making. Always speak as well as you can, whether it be to one person or a thousand.

Tape record your speeches to provide a basis for analysis and evaluation to promote future improvement. Listen to, evaluate, and emulate successful speakers. Apply their principles to your own style.

The form I have devised to evaluate speakers (Exhibit 1–2) may help you to evaluate your own performance. Toastmasters believe that growth in speaking effectively is facilitated through evaluation by self and others. This form suggests ways in which you may look at yourself as a public speaker. How do you score yourself?

Speech making is now a major part of the public relations effort of progressive organizations. The growing awareness of the importance of public speaking is manifested by the increase of company speaker activities, speaker's bureaus, and efforts to train good speakers. The ability to communicate effectively is the means whereby nurses may become leaders in the rapidly changing area of health care.

Exhibit 1-2. Evaluation of Speaker Performance

Speaker _____

Date _____

Subject _____

Key: 4—Superior
3—Above average
2—Average
1—Needs improvement
0—Unsatisfactory

Behavior	4	3	2	1	0	Comments
Platform Manner:						
Uses natural poise						
Uses appropriate gestures						
Exhibits enthusiasm						
Makes direct eye contact						
Voice:						
Varies the pitch of the voice						
Maintains a moderate level of loudness						
Controls talking speed to hold maximum interest						
The Speech						
Opens speech with material that arouses the listener's interest						
Organizes material for logical movement from point to point						
Prepares a conclusion that restates the message, summarizing its main points						
Accomplishment:						
Presents information that is clearly understood						
Adapts the message to the listener's capacities						
Attempts to satisfy the listener's needs						

2.   Effective Verbal Skills

In the first selection of this chapter, Chartier puts forth seven principles for increasing the accuracy and clarity of messages. If each of us could always keep these principles in mind, we would greatly reduce the time, energy, and frustration common to so much interpersonal and organizational miscommunication. The reader who wishes to achieve greater clarity in his or her interpersonal communication will find the guidelines on the last page helpful.

In "Defensive Communication," Gibb encourages understanding of communications by viewing it as a "people process" rather than as a language process. This selection is concerned with reducing the degree of defensiveness in interpersonal relationships. The author describes categories of behavior characteristic of both supportive and defensive climates in small groups. It contains the best description of blocks to communication that we have read.

If we had to select the single most important skill in oral communication it would be active listening. Chapter 2 concludes with a selection by Wismer, who states that "in active listening, the listener is involved with the sender's need to communicate." What a fine way to characterize intelligent listening! Wismer presents excellent examples of communicating acceptance of the other person, which is so vital to personal and work relationships.

CLARITY OF EXPRESSION
IN INTERPERSONAL COMMUNICATION

By Myron R. Chartier

Reprinted from J.W. Pfeiffer and J.E. Jones (Eds.), *The 1978 Annual Handbook for Group Facilitators*. San Diego, CA: University Associates, 1978. Used with permission.

"Why can't people get things straight?" is a question often asked when communication breaks down. Since many factors contribute to a lack of clarity in communication, no easy answers are available.

FAULTY ASSUMPTIONS

Misunderstandings between persons can occur because of faulty assumptions people make about communication. Two such faulty assumptions are (1) *"you"* always know what *"I"* mean and (2) *"I"* should always know what *"you"* mean. The premise seems to be that since people live or work together, they are or should be able to read each other's minds. Some people believe that since they are transparent to themselves, they are transparent to others as well. "Since I exist, you should understand me," they seem to be saying. Persons who make this assumption often presume that they communicate clearly if they simply say what they please. In fact, they often leave the persons listening to them confused and guessing about the message being communicated. Misunderstanding is common because clarity of communication does not happen.

A third assumption often made is that communication happens naturally, like walking across a room. The communication process, however, is complex, and achieving a correspondence between messages sent and messages received is difficult. Some people ascribe to a "conveyor belt" theory of communication—meaning moves from one head to another with 100-percent accuracy. The shortcoming of a "conveyor belt" theory of communication, however, is that it suggests that meanings are inherent in the words used or messages sent. However, the meaning one person has is never identical to that which another person has because meanings are in people's minds, not in the words they use. Total accuracy in communication would require that two persons have an identical history of shared experiences. Only then could they perceive exactly the same meaning for a given message. Given the reality of different life experiences, this is impossible.

A DEFINITION OF CLARITY

"Getting things straight" is a difficult communication task; yet people must communicate clearly with each other in order to receive information to accomplish the mundane tasks of life and to experience the depths of dialogue with another person.

Fortunately, absolute clarity is unnecessary; *effective communication is accomplished when the amount of clarity or accuracy achieved is sufficient for handling each situation adequately.* According to information theorists, the purpose of communication is to reduce uncertainty. Total accuracy in communication would lead to an absence of uncertainty. However, uncertainty can never be totally eliminated. Accurate or clear communication, then, is designed to reduce uncertainty in a given situation to a point where necessary understanding can occur.

Certain practical principles and guidelines for reducing uncertainty and increasing the accuracy and clarity in interpersonal communication can be suggested. To achieve greater clarity in speaking, the individual should have the desire to do so and want to understand the communication process more completely. The communicator can try to analyze and shape his message according to the following factors; sending and receiving, the communication context, encoding a message, and communication channels. Of course, the degree of clarity achieved in a given situation is likely to result from the combined effects of several of these factors. Since communication is a process, the factors being considered are interrelated, making it difficult to differentiate one from another.

SENDING AND RECEIVING

Several principles and guidelines are observable in any attempt to send a clear message from one person to another. These guidelines can be seen in terms of pictures, attitudes, skills, and the frame of reference.

Pictures

A person needs to have a clear picture of what he hopes to communicate to another individual. The preacher needs a proposition to help him know what he is trying to accomplish with a sermon. The teacher needs instructional objectives to help him know what he wants his pupils to learn. The administrator needs both short- and long-range objectives to help him plan organizational goals and interpret them to his colleagues. Well-stated goals or objectives aid the effective communicator in developing a clear picture of what he wants to say.

This first guideline is particularly valid when dealing with complex, ambiguous, or vague topics. If a topic or idea is unclear to the person sending the message, its lack of clarity is likely to be magnified by the person trying to understand it. Although there are times when a person may find interpersonal communication helpful in clarifying the pictures in his own head, it is imperative that the communicator first be clear about his ideas before he attempts to convince or influence others, give data, or share feelings.

Attitudes

Accuracy in communication varies with the attitudes of the communicators toward their topic. If a person's attitudes are very positive or very negative, the resulting communication tends to be less accurate. Indeed, persons often organize data according to their biases.

Communication clarity is also influenced by the attitudes of the communicators toward each other. It seems reasonable that communication between people who respect or love each other would be more accurate. However, research indicates that accuracy is inversely correlated with either positive or negative attitudes that the communicators hold toward each other. Thus, an analysis of the extent of one's positive or negative attitudes toward the topic and toward the listener is important for clarity and accuracy of communication.

Communication Skills

Clarity of communication is also influenced by the extent to which those listening and those sending are aware of their communication skills. It is possible to evaluate the assumptions one holds about his ability to communicate messages. Persons with careless speech communication habits are often convinced that they are successful communicators because they are able to open their mouths and utter a stream of words. Actual skills in interpersonal communication, however, are quite different. An accurate assessment of one's own communication weaknesses and strengths is important. Often, strengths can be maximized and weaknesses improved. One person may have a sparkling personality that aids him in communication. Another may have a way with words. Yet another may be able to communicate in such a way that others feel he understands them.

The communicator should also try to assess the listening skills of the person receiving the message. Good "hearing" is not necessarily good "listening." As listening is an active rather than a passive process, people's poor listening habits often take the form of daydreaming, defensiveness, inattention, etc.

Psychological Frame of Reference

Because communication is a function of shared or common meanings, meaning does not occur simply because words are spoken. Words have no meaning in and of themselves. Meaning is what people attribute to words; meanings lie within the experiences and feelings of persons. Thus meanings are within people.

Each person is unique. What he is has been determined by his individual experiences and choices in or with his family, friends, school, church, and culture. Each person has his own set of perceptions, thoughts, feelings, and behaviors. This uniqueness has a profound impact upon the success or failure of communication.

It is impossible to know what another person is sensing or feeling. Because a listener can only guess about the communicator's meaning, it is essential that the person speaking avoid basing his communication on unexamined assumptions about that person.

To assess what he is communicating, the sending person needs to know the psychological frame of reference of the person receiving the message. How does the listener see, feel, and act with respect to others and the world? The psychological frame of reference of a child is quite different from that of an adult. Persons from Maine see life differently than do people from California. Some people prefer to quench their thirst with Pepsi-Cola rather than 7-UP; others choose Dr. Pepper.

People respond quite differently to the words they hear. One person may react warmly to the words "Jesus saves," while another person may become angry and hostile, and yet another may be indifferent and display no strong sentiment. Indeed, what is clear and rational to one person may seem vague or ridiculous to someone else.

A person can increase the clarity of his communication by constantly trying to place himself inside the psychological framework of the other person. He must try to see the communicative situation from the listener's point of view. If the person communicating understands the other person, he can make his communication more relevant to this person's self-understanding and needs.

COMMUNICATION CONTEXT

A second set of factors affecting the clarity of communication is the context in which communication occurs. Is the setting an office, someone's home, or the golf course? Communicating with a professor in his office is altogether different from communicating with a friend at the bowling alley. The rules in the two situations are distinctly different.

The context of communication is important in determining the amount of accuracy needed or possible between persons in a given situation. How much clarity can be achieved is somewhat determined by the persons' communication skills, the number of communication channels available to the person sending, how much repetition he can incorporate into his message, and the nature of the relationship between the persons communicating. Attempting to communicate with a person in another room presents more difficulties for the clarification process than does speaking face-to-face. In short, the speaker needs to develop a realistic expectation for the degree of clarity obtainable in a given context.

ENCODING A MESSAGE

In order to make ideas clear, an individual must encode his message in order to reduce the amount of uncertainty the other person experiences in hearing that communication. Encoding is the process of translating ideas into a message appropriate for delivery. Once ideas are encoded into messages, they become the potential information that can reduce ambiguity in the other person's mind and produce a clearer picture. There are seven principles for increasing the accuracy and clarity of the messages persons use to communicate.

1. Principle of Relevance

Make the message relevant in the terms of the listening party. The most difficult task related to encoding a message is to assemble it in such a way that the words used accurately reflect the picture one intends and, at the same time, fall within the other person's psychological frame of reference. If a listener is to comprehend the sender's message, he must be able to relate the information he is receiving to what he already knows. Therefore, it is important that the message be presented in a context that says to the listener, "This is important and significant for you." This can be done by using the words of the listening person rather than one's own to encode a message. Such a strategy in communication requires adaptability and flexibility in communication behavior, so that, whether speaking to a child, a teenager, an adult, or persons from different cultural and subcultural backgrounds, the communicator employs appropriate behaviors for sending a clear message.

Just as the encoding of a message should be relevant to the person to whom one is speaking, so should it be appropriate to the situation or the context. The content of a conversation in the privacy of a home is not necessarily appropriate for a discussion at a church committee meeting. Even if the topic were the same in both situations, the message would very likely be encoded quite differently.

2. Principle of Simplicity

Reduce ideas to the simplest possible terms. The communicator should employ as few words as possible to communicate his ideas to a listener. Simplicity of language and economy of words are helpful in facilitating clarity of communication. Generally, the simpler the words, the more likely they are to be understood. However, simplicity really relates to the experience of the person receiving the message. What is simple to one person is complex to another. Theological material that is easily understood by the student of theology may seem quite complicated when presented to the layman in a Sunday morning sermon. The effective communicator calculates the extent to which material must be simplified if it is to be understood by those listening, and he uses the principle of simplicity to make sending messages more successful.

3. Principle of Definition

Define before developing, explain before amplifying. Even simple terms can be unclear. Where would a person go, for example, if someone said, "I'll meet you at the side of the building"? Terms more complicated than "side" increase the need for definition and explanation. The use of jargon also creates problems of clarity for those not acquainted with the words. Unfamiliarity with jargon may cause a person to become confused and frustrated in his efforts to understand. He may even stop trying. Unfamiliar or exceptional terms or concepts need to be defined and explained before they are used, to make the communicator's message as clear as possible.

4. Principle of Structure

Organize a message into a series of successive stages. Texts on public speaking emphasize the importance of making apparent the order or structure of a message. A well-organized speech, it is said, will increase the audience's understanding. However, there is little research evidence to support such a contention, especially in regard to face-to-face dialogue. Indeed, most people will structure the message in accordance with their own patterns of thinking even as they listen, regardless of how well a message is organized.

What is important is the clarity of thought and the expression of individual parts. In interpersonal communication it is probably best to develop one idea at a time. A message can be "packaged" into a series of stages, with one stage completed before the next is introduced.

Furthermore, the communicator can help the person listening by not overloading him with information. When people are asked to comprehend too much, they tend to forget or become confused. By developing one idea at a time and taking one step at a time, the person

speaking can facilitate accuracy in communication.

5. Principle of Repetition

Repeat the key concepts of the message. The principle of repetition is important. Very important. The words "very important" were repetitive. They repeated the idea of the second sentence in a slightly different manner in order to make the concept clearer. Repetition is particularly important in oral communication, where words are spoken only once. Obviously a communicator should not repeat everything he says since it would bore the listener. However, the person speaking needs to use enough repetition to ensure clear reception of his ideas. Some possible strategies: (a) repeating key ideas, (b) restating difficult ideas, (c) recycling ideas wherever feedback indicates they are weak or misunderstood, and (d) using examples, synonyms, analogies, or periodic summaries. In short, a person should use intentional repetition in his attempts to achieve clarity.

6. Principle of Comparison and Contrast

Relate new ideas to old ideas; associate the unknown with the known. The principle of comparison and contrast is essential to the achievement of clear communication, as understanding comes most often through association—the perception of similarities and differences among objects, events, and people. A person can understand a new, unknown idea more clearly if he is able to relate it to an old, known one.

Discriminating between those elements that rightfully belong to an idea and those that do not will help a listener understand a concept. Comparison helps individuals to identify the similarities in two or more ideas. Contrast helps to point out the differences in two or more ideas. When accurate discriminations occur, clarity in communication emerges: the sharper the discrimination, the greater the clarity.

Helpful devices for presenting comparisons and contrasts include the use of models, metaphors, analogies, and explanations.

7. Principle of Emphasis

Focus on the essential and vital aspects of the communication. Since the transitory nature of interpersonal communication makes it highly susceptible to loss of information, attention should be given to the essential and vital aspects of a message. Communication goals and key points should be sharply focused so as not to submerge the message in details and make it vague, ambiguous, and blurred. The impact of the significant points of a communication can be heightened by speaking louder, using a different tone of voice, pausing or using various other techniques to captivate the listener. *Reinforcing and underscoring ideas help in developing such impact.* For example: *this last principle is an important one—remember it and use it.*

Communication strategies based on these principles for developing or sending a message will result in a more accurate correspondence of ideas between persons.

COMMUNICATION CHANNELS

Once a message is constructed for sending to another person, it must be sent through a communication channel. Several factors related to communication channels affect clarification in the speaking-listening process. Four of these are discussed here.

Channels Available

An important aspect of communication that affects accuracy and clarity is the number of channels available for sending a message. For example, in a letter only one channel—the written word—is in use. Face-to-face interaction, however, utilizes several channels, e.g., body tension, facial expressions, eye contact, hand and body movements, relative positions of each person, vocal sounds accompanying a verbal message, etc.

To communicate clearly, a person should be aware of the various channels available to him and utilize as many of them as possible. When messages are sent through more than one channel, repetition is increased. As repetition increases, uncertainty is reduced, and the chances for clarity are increased. It is important, however, that whenever multichannel communication occurs, the messages be consistent across all channels or the results will be confusing for the listener.

Feedback

An awareness and use of feedback is important to the communicator. Feedback, which is a term from cybernetic theory, is an essential element in any control process. This phenomenon can be observed in the operation of a self-adjusting camera in which a built-in light meter measures the amount of illumination in the environment and automatically adjusts the camera accordingly. In a comparable manner, feedback can be used to correct and adjust meanings and thus increase communication clarity. A person sending a message should elicit feedback following his communication attempts in order to determine whether the picture received was the one transmitted. On the basis of this feedback, the next step in the communication process can be taken. The following conversation between Joe and Sally is an example of feedback as purposive correction:

Joe: "Feedback is a process of correcting inaccuracy in communication."

Sally: "Do you mean that feedback is simply a process of correcting errors?"

Joe: "Not exactly, although that is a part of what I mean. Feedback is a way of being sure that what I say to you is adequately perceived by you."

Sally: "Now you're really getting complicated. What does 'adequately perceived' mean?"

Joe: "Well, I think 'adequately perceived' means that you understand the idea as I would like for you to understand it."

Sally: "Oh, then you mean that feedback is a device for checking whether or not I got the idea you wanted me to get."

Joe: "Exactly."

Sally: "Do you think I used feedback effectively?"

Joe: "Well, how do you feel about it?"

In the same way that communication clarity can be increased by using a variety of available channels, a number of feedback channels can also be an aid to accuracy.

Noise

Communication accuracy is affected by "noise," a term frequently used to refer to any disturbance that interferes with the sending of a message. Although noise may occur in almost any aspect of the communication process, such interference appears often as an obstruction in the channel between two interacting persons. The interfering noise may be other people talking, the whir of a vacuum cleaner, or the sound of a lawn mower coming through an open window. The greater the noise, the more difficult it becomes to communicate clearly. For this reason it is important for the communicator to find ways of eliminating or reducing sources of distracting noise.

Speed and Pacing

Clarity of communication is related to how much information a channel can carry and a listener can receive at one time. Because the oral channel requires those listening to depend heavily on their memories for comprehension, it is less effective than other channels for handling large amounts of verbal information. Effective lecturers know that it is the rare audience that can absorb more than one or two new ideas. In contrast, the written channel can carry much more verbal information, as it allows individuals to reconsider the material. Therefore, the speed of oral communication must be determined by the listening persons' rate of comprehension. The communicator should pace his message according to the information-processing capacities of the channel and the hearers.

A SUMMARY OF GUIDELINES FOR CLEAR INTERPERSONAL COMMUNICATION

A person wishing to achieve greater clarity in his interpersonal communication should find the following guidelines helpful.

The communicator seeking to improve his communication clarity should:

1. Have a clear picture of what he wants the other person to understand

2. Analyze the nature and magnitude of his attitudes toward both the topic and the person with whom he is communicating

3. Assess his own communication skills and those of the person listening

4. Seek to identify himself with the psychological frame of reference of the person receiving his ideas

5. Develop a realistic expectation for the degree of clarity obtainable in a given context

6. Make the message relevant to the person listening by using that person's language and terms

7. State ideas in the simplest possible terms

8. Define before developing and explain before amplifying

9. Develop one idea at a time; take one step at a time

10. Use appropriate repetition

11. Compare and contrast ideas by associating the unknown with the known

12. Determine which ideas need special emphasis

13. Use as many channels as necessary for clarity

14. Watch for and elicit corrective feedback in a variety of channels

15. Eliminate or reduce noise if it is interfering

16. Pace his communication according to the information-processing capacities of the channel and the person listening

DEFENSIVE COMMUNICATION

By Jack R. Gibb

Reprinted with permission from *The Journal of Communication,* Volume 11, Number 3, 1961, pp. 141–148. Published by The International Communication Association.

One way to understand communication is to view it as a people process rather than as a language process. If one is to make a fundamental improvement in communication, he must make changes in interpersonal relationships. One possible type of alteration—and the one with which this paper is concerned—is that of reducing the degree of defensiveness.

DEFINITION AND SIGNIFICANCE

"Defensive behavior" is behavior which occurs when an individual perceives threat or anticipates threat in the group. The person who behaves defensively, even though he also gives some attention to the common task, devotes an appreciable portion of his energy to defending himself. Besides talking about the topic, he thinks about how he appears to others, how he may be seen more favorably, how he may win, dominate, impress, or escape punishment, and/or how he may avoid or mitigate a perceived or an anticipated attack.

Such inner feelings and outward acts tend to create similarly defensive postures in others; and, if unchecked, the ensuing circular response becomes increasingly destructive.

Defensive behavior, in short, engenders defensive listening, and this in turn produces postural, facial, and verbal cues which raise the defense level of the original communicator.

Defensive arousal prevents the listener from concentrating upon the message. Not only do defensive communicators send off multiple value, motive, and affect cues, but also defensive recipients distort what they receive. As a person becomes more and more defensive, he becomes less and less able to perceive accurately the motives, the values, and the emotions of the sender. The writer's analyses of tape recorded discussions revealed that increases in defensive behavior were correlated positively with losses in efficiency in communication[32]. Specifically, distortions became greater when defensive states existed in the groups.

The converse also is true. The more "supportive" or defense reductive the climate, the less the receiver reads into the communication distorted loadings which arise from projections of his own anxieties, motives, and concerns. As defenses are reduced, the receivers become better able to concentrate upon the structure, the content, and the cognitive meanings of the message.

Exhibit 2–1.   Categories of Behavior Characteristic of Supportive and Defensive Climates in Small Groups

Supportive Climates	Defensive Climates
1. Description	1. Evaluation
2. Problem orientation	2. Control
3. Spontaneity	3. Strategy
4. Empathy	4. Neutrality
5. Equality	5. Superiority
6. Provisionalism	6. Certainty

CATEGORIES OF DEFENSIVE AND SUPPORTIVE COMMUNICATION

In working over an eight-year period with recordings of discussions occurring in varied settings, the writer developed the six pairs of defensive and supportive categories presented in Exhibit 2–1. Behavior that a listener perceives as possessing any of the characteristics listed in the left-hand column arouses defensiveness, whereas that which he interprets as having any of the qualities designated as supportive reduces defensive feelings. The degree to which these reactions occur depends upon the personal level of defensivenss and upon the general climate in the group at the time[33].

Evaluation and Description

Speech or other behavior that appears evaluative increases defensiveness. If by expression, manner of speech, tone of voice, or verbal content the sender seems to be evaluating or judging the listener, then the receiver goes on guard. Of course, other factors may inhibit the reaction. If the listener thinks that the speaker regards him as an equal and is being open and spontaneous, for example, the evaluativeness in a message will be neutralized and perhaps not even perceived. This same principle applies equally to the other five categories of potentially defense-producing climates. The six sets are interactive.

Because our attitudes toward other persons are frequently, and often necessarily, evaluative, expressions that the defensive person will regard as nonjudgmental are hard to frame. Even the simplest question usually conveys the answer that the sender wishes or implies the response that would fit into his value system. A mother, for example, immediately following an earth tremor that shook the house, sought for her small son with the question: "Bobby, where are you?" The timid and plaintive "Mommy, I didn't do it" indicated how Bobby's chronic mild defensiveness predisposed him to react with a projection of his own guilt and in the context of his chronic assumption that questions are full of accusation.

Anyone who has attempted to train professionals to use information-seeking speech with neutral affect appreciates how difficult it is to teach a person to say even the simple "Who did that?" without being seen as accusing. Speech is so frequently judgmental that there is a reality base for the defensive interpretations that are so common.

When insecure, group members are particularly likely to place blame, to see others as fitting into categories of good or bad, to make moral judgments of their colleagues, and to question the value, motive, and affect loadings of the speech which they hear. Since value loadings imply a judgment of others, a belief that the standards of the speaker differ from his own causes the listener to become defensive.

Descriptive speech, in contrast to that which is evaluative, tends to arouse a minimum of uneasiness. Speech acts that the listener perceives as genuine requests for information or as material with neutral loadings are descriptive. Specifically, presentations of feelings, events, perceptions, or processes that do not ask or imply that the receiver change behavior or attitude are minimally defense-producing. The difficulty in avoiding overtone is illustrated by the problems of news reporters in writing stories about unions, Communists, blacks, and religious activities without tipping off the "party" line of the newspaper. One can often tell from the opening words in a news article which side the newspaper's editorial policy favors.

Control and Problem Orientation

Speech which is used to control the listener evokes resistance. In most of our social intercourse someone is trying to do something to someone else—to change an attitude, to influence behavior, or to restrict the field of activity. The degree to which attempts to control produce defensiveness depends upon the openness of the effort, for a suspicion that hidden motives exist heightens resistance. For this reason attempts of nondirective therapists and progressive educators to refrain from imposing a set of values, a point of view, or a problem solution upon the receivers meet with many barriers. Since the norm is control, noncontrollers must earn the perceptions that their efforts have no hidden motives. A bombardment of persuasive "messages" in the fields of politics, education, special causes, advertising, religion, medicine, industrial relations, and guidance has bred cynical and paranoid responses in listeners.

Implicit in all attempts to alter another person is the assumption by the change agent that the person to be altered is inadequate. That the speaker secretly views the listener as ignorant, unable to make his own decisions, uninformed, immature, unwise, or possessing wrong or inadequate attitudes is a subconscious perception that gives the latter a valid base for defensive reactions.

Methods of control are many and varied. Legalistic insistence on detail, restrictive regulations and policies, conformity norms, and all laws are among the methods. Gestures, facial expressions, other forms of nonverbal communication, and even such simple acts as holding a door open in a particular manner are means of imposing one's will upon another and hence are potential sources of resistance.

Problem orientation, on the other hand, is the antithesis of persuasion. When the sender communicates a desire to collaborate in defining a mutual problem and in seeking its solution, he tends to create the same problem orientation in the listener; and, of greater importance, he implies that he has no predetermined solution, attitude, or method to impose. Such behavior is permissive in that it allows the receiver to set his own goals, make his own decisions, and evaluate his own progress—or to share with the sender in doing so. The exact methods of attaining permissiveness are not known, but they must involve a constellation of cues, and they certainly go beyond mere verbal assurances that the communicator has no hidden desires to exercise control.

Strategy and Spontaneity

When the sender is perceived as engaged in a stratagem involving ambiguous and multiple motivations, the receiver becomes defensive. No one wishes to be a guinea pig, a role player, or an impressed actor, and no one likes to be the victim of some hidden motivation. That which is concealed, also, may appear larger than it really is, with the degree of defensiveness of the listener determining the perceived size of the suppressed element. The intense reaction of the reading audience to the material in the *Hidden Persuaders* indicates the prevalence of defensive reactions to multiple motivations behind strategy. Group members who are seen as "taking a role," as feigning emotion, as toying with their colleagues, as withholding information, or as having special sources of data are especially resented. One participant once complained that another was "using a listening technique" on him!

A large part of the adverse reaction to much of the so-called human relations training is a feeling against what are perceived as gimmicks and tricks to fool or to "involve" people, to make a person think he is making his own decision, or to make the listener feel that the sender is genuinely interested in him as a person. Particularly violent reactions occur when it appears that someone is trying to make a strategem appear spontaneous. One person has reported a boss who incurred resentment by habitually using the gimmick of "spontaneously" looking at his watch and saying, "My gosh, look at the time—I must run to an appointment." The belief was that the boss would create less irritation by honestly asking to be excused.

Similarly, the deliberate assumption of guilelessness and natural simplicity is especially resented. Monitoring the tapes of feedback and evaluation sessions in training groups indicates the surprising extent to which members perceive the strategies of their colleagues. This perceptual clarity may be quite shocking to the strategist, who usually feels that he has cleverly hidden the motivational aura around the "gimmick."

This aversion to deceit may account for one's resistance to politicians who are suspected of behind-the-scenes planning to get one's vote; to psychologists whose listening apparently is motivated by more than the manifest or content-level interest in one's behavior; or to the sophisticated, smooth, or clever person whose "oneupmanship" is marked with guile. In training groups the role-flexible person frequently is resented because his changes in behavior are perceived as strategic maneuvers.

Conversely, behavior that appears to be spontaneous and free of deception is defense-reductive. If the communicator is seen as having a clean id, as having uncomplicated motivation, as being straightforward and honest, and as behaving spontaneously in response to the situation, he is likely to arouse minimal defense.

Neutrality and Empathy

When neutrality in speech appears to the listener to indicate a lack of concern for his welfare, he becomes defensive. Group members usually desire to be perceived as valued persons, as individuals of special worth, and as objects of concern and affection. The clinical, detached, person-is-an-object-of-study attitude on the part of many psychologist–trainers is resented by group members. Speech with low affect that communicates little warmth or caring is in such contrast with the affect-laden speech in social situations that it sometimes communicates rejection.

Communication that conveys empathy for the feelings and respect for the worth of the listener, however, is particularly supportive and defense-reductive. Reassurance results when a message indicates that the speaker identifies himself with the listener's problems, shares his feelings, and accepts his emotional reactions at face value. Abortive efforts to deny the legitimacy of the receiver's emotions by assuring the receiver that he need not feel bad, that he should not feel rejected, or that he is overly anxious, though often intended as support-giving, may impress the listener as lack of acceptance. The combination of understanding and empathizing with the other person's emotions with no accompanying effort to change him apparently is supportive at a high level.

The importance of gestural behavioral cues in communicating empathy should be mentioned. Apparently spontaneous facial and bodily evidences of concern are often interpreted as especially valid evidence of deep-level acceptance.

Superiority and Equality

When a person communicates to another that he feels superior in position, power, wealth, intellectual ability, physical characteristics, or other ways, he arouses defensiveness. Here, as with the other sources of disturbance, whatever arouses feelings of inadequacy causes the listener to center upon the affect loading of the statement rather than upon the cognitive elements. The receiver then reacts by not hearing the message, by forgetting it, by competing with the sender, or by becoming jealous of him.

The person who is perceived as feeling superior communicates that he is not willing to enter into a shared problem-solving relationship, that he probably does not desire feedback, that he does not require help, and/or that he will be likely to try to reduce the power, the status, or the worth of the receiver.

Many ways exist for creating the atmosphere that the sender feels himself equal to the listener. Defenses are reduced when one perceives the sender as being willing to enter into participative planning with mutual trust and respect. Differences in talent, ability, worth, appearance, status, and power often exist, but the low-defense communicator seems to attach little importance to these distinctions.

Certainty and Provisionalism

The effects of dogmatism in producing defensiveness are well known. Those who seem to know the answers, to require no additional data, and to regard themselves as teachers rather than as coworkers tend to put others on guard. Moreover, in the writer's experiment, listeners often perceived manifest expressions of certainty as connoting inward feelings of inferiority. They saw the dogmatic individual as needing to be right, as wanting to win an argument rather than solve a problem, and as seeing his ideas as truths to be defended. This kind of behavior often was associated with acts which others regarded as attempts to exercise control. People who were right seemed to have low tolerance for members who were "wrong"—i.e., who did not agree with the sender.

One reduces the defensiveness of the listener when he communicates that he is willing to experiment with his own behavior, attitudes, and ideas. The person who appears to be taking provisional attitudes, to be investigating issues rather than debating, and to be willing to experiment and explore tends to communicate that the listener may have some control over the shared quest or investigation of the ideas. If a person is genuinely searching for information and data, he does not resent help or company along the way.

CONCLUSION

The implications of the foregoing material for the parent, the teacher, the manager, the administrator, or the therapist are fairly obvious. Arousing defensiveness interferes with communication and thus makes it difficult—and sometimes impossible—for anyone to convey ideas clearly and to move effectively toward the solution of therapeutic, educational, or managerial problems.

COMMUNICATION EFFECTIVENESS: ACTIVE LISTENING AND SENDING FEELING MESSAGES

By Jack N. Wismer

Reprinted from J.W. Pfeiffer and J.E. Jones (Eds.), *The 1978 Annual Handbook for Group Facilitators.* San Diego, CA: University Associates, 1978. Used with permission.

I know you believe that you understand what you think I said, but I am not sure you realize that what you heard is not what I meant.

When a person communicates a message to another person, the message usually contains two elements: content and feeling. Both elements are important because both give the message meaning. However, we often do not understand other people's messages or are misunderstood by others because we forget that meanings are in people, not in words.

The Risk of Communicating Nonacceptance

The communication of mutual acceptance is vital to developing and maintaining work and personal relationships. However, various ways of responding to situations run the risk of communicating nonacceptance. To understand a person's point of view effectively, it is necessary not to communicate nonacceptance. According to Gordon, author of several books on active listening, most people, in a listening situation, commonly respond in one or more of the following twelve ways[34]:

1. Ordering, directing: "You have to . . ."
2. Warning, threatening: "You'd better not . . ."
3. Preaching, moralizing: "You ought to . . ."
4. Advising, giving solutions: "Why don't you . . ."
5. Lecturing, informing: "Here are the facts . . ."
6. Evaluating, blaming: "You're wrong . . ."
7. Praising, agreeing: "You're right . . ."
8. Name-calling, shaming: "You're stupid . . ."
9. Interpreting, analyzing: "What you need . . ."
10. Sympathizing, supporting: "You'll be okay . . ."
11. Questioning, probing: "Why did you . . ."
12. Withdrawing, avoiding: "Let's forget it . . ."

These modes of response may communicate to the sender that it is not acceptable to feel the way he or she feels. If the sender perceives one of these messages as indicating nonacceptance, there is a risk that he will become defensive about new ideas, will be resistive to changing behavior, will tend to justify certain feelings, or will turn silent because the listener is perceived as only passively interested in the sender.

ACTIVE LISTENING

A more effective way of responding to a listening situation is called "active listening." Gordon[35] defines active listening as a communication skill to help people solve their own problems. In active listening, the listener is involved with the sender's need to communicate. To be effective, the listener must take an "active" responsibility to understand the content and feeling of what is being said. The listener can respond with a statement, in his own words, of what he feels the sender's message means. For example:

Sender: "The deadline for this report is not realistic!"

Listener: "You feel you're pressured to get the report done."

If the listener is to understand the sender's meaning, he will need to "put himself in the other person's place." Feeding back perceptions of intended meaning allows the listener to check the accuracy of his listening and understanding.

Benefits of Active Listening

An open communication climate for understanding is created through active listening. The listener can learn to see what a person means and how the person feels about situations and problems. Active listening is a skill that can communicate acceptance and increase interpersonal trust among people. It can also facilitate problem solving. Therefore, the appropriate use of active listening increases the communication effectiveness of people.

Pitfalls in Active Listening

Active listening is not intended to manipulate people to behave or think the way others think they should. The listener also should not "parrot" someone's message by repeating the exact words used. Empathy is a necessary ingredient—the listener should communicate warmth toward and feeling about the sender's message by putting himself in the sender's place. Timing is another pitfall; active listening is not appropriate when there is no time to deal with the situation or when someone is asking only for factual information. Also, it is important that the listener be sensitive to nonverbal messages about the right time to stop giving feedback. Avoiding these common pitfalls will make active listening a more effective communication skill.

Principle of Problem Ownership

Since active listening is most appropriate when a person expresses feelings about a problem, it is necessary to ask who owns the problem. The principle of problem ownership can be demonstrated in the following situations.

1. Person A's needs are not being satisfied by his or her own behavior, and A's behavior does not directly interfere with Person B's satisfaction of his or her own needs. Therefore, A owns the problem.

2. Person A's needs are being satisfied, but his or her behavior interferes in some way with Person B's satisfaction of his or her own needs and thus creates a problem for B. B then owns the problem.

3. Person A is satisfying his or her own needs, and his or her behavior does not directly interfere with Person B's needs. In this case, there is no problem.

Active listening is very useful, but it is not appropriate to use if another person's behavior is creating the problem.

COMMUNICATING ONE'S NEEDS

Ineffective Approaches

It is necessary for the person who owns the problem to know how to confront it and communicate his or her needs so that other people will listen. However, people frequently confront problems in a way that tends to stimulate defensiveness and resistance. The two most common approaches:

1. *Evaluating*—which communicates judgment, blame, ridicule, or shame ("Don't you know how to use that machine?"; "You're late again!"). This method has several risks: (a) it makes people defensive and resistant to further communication; (b) it implies power over the other person; and (c) it threatens and reduces the other person's self-esteem.

2. *Sending solutions*—which communicates what the other person should do rather than what the speaker is feeling ("If you don't come in on time, I'll have to report you"; "Why don't you do it this way?"). Sending solutions carries risks: (a) people become resistive if they are told what to do, even if they agree with the solution; (b) this approach indicates that the sender's needs are more important than the receiver's; (c) it communicates a lack of trust in other people's capacities to solve their own problems; and (d) it reduces the responsibility to define the problem clearly and explore feasible alternatives to a problem.

A More Effective Approach

Problems can be confronted and one's needs can be made known without making other people feel defensive. An effective communication message involves three components: (1) owning feelings, (2) sending feelings, and (3) describing behavior.

Ownership of feelings focuses on "who owns the problem." The sender of a message needs to accept responsibility for his or her own feelings. Messages that own the sender's feelings usually begin with or contain "I."

Sometimes, communicating feelings is viewed as a weakness, but the value of sending feelings is communicating honesty and openness by focusing on the problem and not evaluating the person.

Describing behavior concentrates on what one person sees and hears and feels about another person's behavior as it affects the observer's feelings and behavior. The focus is on specific situations that relate to specific times and places.

It is useful to distinguish between descriptions and evaluations of behavior. The boldface parts of the next statements illustrate **evaluations** of behavior:

"I can't finish this report **if you are so inconsiderate as to interrupt me.**"

"**You're a loudmouth.**"

The boldface parts of the following statements are **descriptions** of behavior:

"**I can't finish this report if you constantly interrupt me.**"

"I feel that **you talked considerably during the meetings.**"

A design for sending feeling messages can be portrayed as follows:

Ownership + Feeling Word + Description of Behavior = Feeling Message

Example:

"I (ownership) am concerned (feeling word) about finishing this report on time" (description of behavior).

The effectiveness of feeling messages can be attributed to several factors:

- "I" messages are more effective because they place responsibility with the sender of the message.
- "I" messages reduce the other person's defensiveness and resistance to further communication.

- Behavioral descriptions provide feedback about the other person's behavior but do not evaluate it.

- Although "I" messages require some courage, they honestly express the speaker's feelings.

- Feeling messages promote open communication in work and personal relationships.

SUMMARY

Sending feeling messages and listening actively are skills that can be applied to work, family, and personal relationships.

No one is wrong. At most someone is uninformed. If I think a man is wrong, either I am unaware of something, or he is. So unless I want to play a superiority game I had best find out what he is looking at.

"You're wrong" means "I don't understand you"—I'm not seeing what you're seeing. But there is nothing wrong with you, you are simply not me and that's not wrong.[36]

3.   Daily Uses

Chapter 3 focuses on several everyday experiences in verbal communications that can
return much benefit when done well.

Interviewing prospective nursing employees
can be a time-consuming and exhausting process. The article by Kowalski describes the basics of interviewing selectively so that you end
up with the right people in the right jobs,
where they will be happiest and contribute the
most to the mission of the unit.

Another expensive process is sending a
nurse to a conference. What kind of preplanning and follow-up of outside educational
events takes place in your organization? In
"You Can Help It Happen!," Medearis points
out that attending outside learning experiences can provide a rich resource for making
changes in your nursing organization.

Most of us have a strong desire to make our
beliefs known to others, to influence and
modify our environment, to make things better for those following after us. An important
opportunity to do this is in the medium of
public speaking. In this arena, we can convey
important messages, stir others to action, and
help shape the future. The excerpt from Simmons' New Speakers Handbook: How to Be
the Life of the Podium covers the fundamen-

tals of speech preparation in ten practical
steps from the time you are invited until you
approach the dais. It shows you how to optim-
ize such real-world problems as procrastina-
tion and conflicting demands on your time in
the weeks before your speaking event. The
suggestions can also benefit the nursing
administrator in preparing "little" talks for
meetings, committees, or one-to-one communications with the hospital administrator.

The readings by Cooper and Joy focus on
those frequent and common group communications in nursing—committees and change-
of-shift report.

Whether you are coordinating and hosting
a workshop or are the workshop speaker or
leader, you will find Stevens' thorough list of
"do's" and "don'ts" helpful.

Finally, "Making Press Interviews Work
for You" offers nursing administrators
success-proven suggestions in preparing for
and following up on an interview with the
press. Readers interested in promoting newly
developed patient education programs or in
sharing their views and constraints in an
upcoming strike with the public will find this
selection especially valuable for interacting
effectively with newspaper reporters.

JOB INTERVIEWING: AN EFFECTIVE TOOL FOR HIRING STAFF NURSES

By Karren E. Kowalski

Reprinted with permission from *The Journal of Nursing Administration,* Volume 5, Number 1, January 1975, pp. 28–32.

Oftentimes a nursing service has been so desperate for general duty staff nurses that they have hired anyone who walked through the door and possessed a current license to practice. Traditionally, these nurses have been placed where they were "needed" regardless of their previous experience, area of expertise, or desires. If a nurse needed a job, she took whatever she could get.

With the current emphasis on the quality of patient care, however, it is inappropriate to place nurses on hospital units or in agencies regardless of experience, expertise, or desire. The modes utilized for improving the quality of patient care must include employing nurses in the area of their choice and specialization.

One of the managerial functions of the head nurse is to assume the responsibility for hiring and firing the personnel who are accountable to her. A fundamental aspect of this responsibility must be to hire the best people for the job. These people cannot be found or hired without an effective job interview. Most head nurses have not been involved either as interviewees or interviewers in positive, constructive, and informative job interviews.

Recent research indicates that, in the business world, trained interviewers have a success rate for hiring appropriate job applicants which is double that of untrained interviewers. In addition, on-the-job performance can be predicted by utilizing the information trained interviewers elicit from applicants[37]. I propose that the same result can be achieved in employing nurses.

The author's interest in the interviewing process was stimulated after several nurses were hired to participate in a new obstetrical independent practice role[38]. It was soon discovered that some of these nurses had interests which were not what they had seemed to be during their job interviews. This indicated that some serious mistakes must have been made in the interviewing process. In fact, the four most common basic errors of interviewing had all been committed in each instance:

1. The interviewer talked too much (more than half of the time) and did not listen enough.

2. The interviewer jumped to conclusions on the basis of inadequate data which was never validated.

3. The interviewer consistently lead the applicant into giving the desired responses to questions. For example, "Do you think you can function independently?"

4. The interviewer failed to apply the facts she did obtain from the interview to on-the-job performance probability. For example, an applicant who never mentioned patients or patient care, though she was given numerous opportunities to do so, gave a strong indication that she was not a "patient-oriented nurse."

BASIC INTERVIEWING PRINCIPLES

It is important to examine the basic principles of job interviewing as they apply to nursing. A job interview is both a directed interview, which is planned and led by the interviewer, and a nondirected interview, during which the interviewer asks many open-ended questions and concentrates on being a responsive listener[39].

Most authors agree that there is some basic preparation which should be done before an interview. First, the application form should be reviewed to brief the interviewer on the background of the applicant. Second, a plan or an outline for the interview should be devised, setting forth all the essential items to be covered in the interview. These may not follow a proposed order, but may be covered in the natural course of the conversation.

The setting for the interview is also very important. There should be privacy and comfort (including such social amenities as serving coffee). A relaxed atmosphere will help to keep the applicant's anxiety and nervousness to a minimum[40].

An informal, low-key opening is desirable, but irrelevant; "small talk" should be avoided as it usually increases the anxiety level of the applicant. It is more helpful for the interviewer to move right into the subject matter with a preliminary remark, such as, "I was very interested in several areas of your application form. Let's make the most of the time we have together and move immediately into the interview." The interviewer must establish and maintain an atmosphere of confidentiality and inspire a feeling of trust in order to obtain reliable information concerning what might be construed as unfavorable factors in the applicant's character or background. Once under way, one of the most important considerations is to avoid interruptions: answering telephone calls or having people walk into the office during the interview not only distracts the interviewer, but also gives the applicant time to reflect excessively on specific aspects of the interview.

The attitude of the interviewer and the way she handles herself are also very important. She should be straightforward throughout the interview[41], thereby contributing to the desired atmosphere of trust. Attempts to be shrewd and clever are usually transmitted to the applicant, who can sense the effort to trick her into revealing something unfavorable about herself. If, however, the applicant feels she is doing well and making a favorable impression, she is more likely to be open and candid about her shortcomings[42].

The interviewer should play down unfavorable information. For example, if an applicant has admitted an inability to get along with a former supervisor, the interviewer might say, "Almost everyone has had a supervisor with whom she has had difficulty. Could you tell me a little more about the situation?"

The interviewer should avoid disagreeing openly with the applicant as this will certainly stop the flow of information. This does not mean that principles should be sacrificed but that the interviewer should remain neutral. For example, if an applicant says, "I don't believe fathers should be allowed in the delivery room," the interviewer may respond, "That's an interesting concept. Please elaborate a little more about your feelings."

One technique to help the applicant develop confidence in herself is to give sincere praise, such as, "Nursing school is so demanding, it is very admirable that you worked your way through school and maintained above-average grades."

THE DRAKE METHOD

A method for interviewing devised by John Drake is particularly useful and applicable to nursing. This method includes four areas in which the interviewer must have adequate information by the time the interview is concluded (Exhibit 3–1).

1. Intellectual skills and aptitudes—How does she organize her thoughts? How effectively does she communicate? Is she reflective or impulsive? Is her thinking penetrating or shallow? Is she concise or does she go off on tangents? What is her nursing philosophy?

2. Motivational characteristics:
   a. Interests—How does she feel about the activities in which she engages and why?
   b. Aspirations—What are her long- and short-range goals and objectives? Why has she chosen them?
   c. Energy level—Have the applicant describe a typical working day. A high energy level implies the ability to function for long hours and yet show considerable zest and vitality.

3. Personality strengths and limitations—Interpersonal relationships are assessed. Is she shy, confident, aggressive, withdrawn, forceful, persuasive, arrogant, open, outgoing, passive?

4. Knowledge and experience—Is her training and job experience appropriate and helpful to the task? (It is not necessary that they be specific to the present position.)

Drake also stresses the importance of having a plan to follow throughout the interview. In addition to the plan, he suggests that the interviewer use her experience to formulate a valid list of test questions to ask in almost every interview. The categories for discussion and test questions used by the author are shown in Exhibit 3–2.

The interviewer introduces each topic by asking a broad general question, such as, "Tell me some things you would like me to know about your nursing school days." This forces the applicant to take the initiative and choose what she will tell the interviewer, which is often revealing. For instance, in response to the question on nursing school, an applicant might say, "Well, I had a B average. I guess I studied an average amount. The group I ran around with had a lot of fun. We went to parties and played bridge. I got to be a pretty good bridge player. I'm not sure what you want to know . . . ." This also relieves the interviewer of the need to direct the proceedings for a short time, so that she can concentrate on the responses and assess such items as the applicant's ability to organize her thoughts and her degree of skill in verbal communications.

From a broad general question, the interviewer can move into a self-appraisal question:

Interviewer: "What qualities do you have which you believe have contributed to your success as a labor and delivery nurse?"

Applicant: "Well, I think I am very efficient and function well in a crisis. The doctors had a lot of respect for my ability and they liked me as a person. I got along pretty well with other members of the staff. We only had a few run-ins."

Interviewer: "It certainly is a good feeling to know that you are liked and respected. We all have occasional problems with coworkers. If you had to describe one problem area that you and the other staff

**Exhibit 3–1.   The Drake Method: Areas in which the interviewer must have informa-
tion by the end of the interview. Adapted by permission of the publisher from *Interviewing for Managers* by John Drake ©1972 by the American Management Association, Inc.**

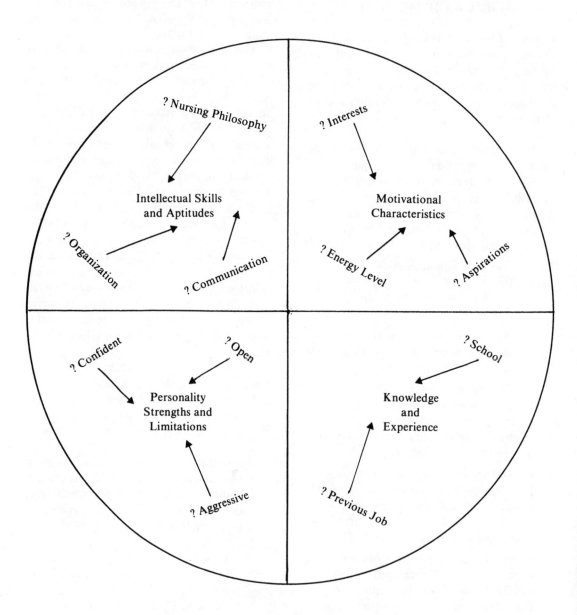

Exhibit 3-2. Sample Interview Plan

I. Introductions (The applicant has already gone through an initial screening and knows in which area(s) of nursing the interviewer(s) work.)

II. Categories and questions

    A. Early life—Tell me a little bit about your family or anything you would like me to know about your life when you were growing up.

    B. Education

        1. High school—What are some things you particularly remember about high school?

        2. College and other studies—What would you like me to know about your nursing school days?

    C. Military experience—What kinds of experiences did you have? What did you think about them?

    D. Summer and full-time work experience—Tell me about your last job. What did you like and dislike about it? How would you assess the nursing care given? Why? Describe your philosophy of nursing. Why? Tell me why you left that job.

    E. General attitudes toward job and agency—What is it about this kind of position that might appeal to you? What would you like to do with this job if you get it? What attracts you to this institution? What do you see in this position that wasn't in your previous job? Are there any things about this hospital that would make it a desirable place to work? What do you feel you would need to know more about before you could do this job?

    F. Aspirations and goals—Where would you like to be five years from now? Why? How will you accomplish this? What might be some goals and objectives for this job?

    G. Self-assessment of candidate's strengths and limitations—What would you say accounts for the success you attained in your previous position? What would you say there is about yourself that could be improved or strengthened? On a continuum of dependence to independence, where would you place yourself and why? How would you describe your peer relationships? How would you describe your leadership style and why?

    H. Leisure-time activities—What are they? What makes you good at them? What satisfactions do you get from them?

III. Describe job—Complete any data the applicant may need about the job and ask for questions.

IV. Conclusion—Is there anything else you would like to tell me? Is there something you would like to know?—Give a time limit within which you will get in touch with the applicant.

Exhibit 3–3.   Suggested Method for Taking Notes

Applicant Responses	Interviewer Hypotheses

Self-appraisal Attributes
  Functions well in crisis
  Efficient
  Respected by M.D.s
  Liked by M.D.s
  Worked fairly well
    with coworkers
	Competent techniques
	Reward system from M.D.s
	Didn't mention patients
	  or patient care

members had, what would it be?"

After a few self-appraisal questions, most applicants will become uncomfortable about continuing to praise themselves and will begin to give some clues as to possible problem areas (e.g., a few run-ins with staff members). Two more important follow-up questions are (1) how she arrived at a certain point or decision and (2) why she has a specific goal, problem, or success. These questions produce data concerning the applicant's thinking processes and provide the basis for an analysis of her assessment processes. Another helpful tool is to give the applicant a hypothetical situation and ask her what she would do, step by step, and why.

Frequently, the very strong applicants will be essentially interviewing the interviewer during their time together. It is very positive for an applicant to ask many questions of the interviewer concerning the job, the institution, and the supervision she will receive.

In order to evaluate the information received, the interviewer must take notes on almost all comments made by the applicant, not just the negative ones, without letting the applicant see what she is writing. One effective method is to divide a lined page of paper in half; use one side for the applicant's responses and the other for the interviewer's hypotheses, such as friendly, confident, vague,

personable, shows limited energy and drive, originator of reward system, appears organized (Exhibit 3–3). The latter derive directly from specific comments made by the applicant and from observed behavior. Hypotheses which appear repeatedly are considered confirmed.

By completing questions in all of the major categories suggested in Exhibit 3–2 and by beginning each category with a broad general questions followed by self-appraisal questions, the interviewer will acquire information in all of the four major areas designated in Exhibit 3–1. After the session, the interviewer can classify the confirmed hypotheses from her notes. All applicants will have some limitations; the deciding factor will be whether the limitations will affect the job for which an applicant is being considered.

USE OF THE GROUP INTERVIEW

A group interview, an alternative to a one-to-one session, gives the applicant an opportunity to meet and interact with members of the staff other than the head nurse. This allows the several interviewers to compare their data and share their assessments of the applicant. It also provides a learning opportunity for the staff to develop interviewing skills. In addition, it gives increased input to use as a basis for the continued evaluation and revision of future interview settings.

There are some basic guidelines which should be followed in planning a group interview. The staff must decide prior to the interview who will conduct specific portions of the questioning. The interview must be non-threatening. The anxiety level of the applicant can be increased by having more than one other person in the room. It is important to have only one person at a time ask the questions. When two or more interviewers are talking simultaneously, the applicant becomes frustrated and defensive. Appropriately conducted, group interviews can be beneficial for the interviewers and a pleasant experience for the applicant.

SUMMARY

Effective interviewing skill can be very advantageous as a tool to aid in selecting the nurse whose strengths and limitations are best suited to a particular job. It is recommended that the hospital or agency staff development services offer workshops to head nurses in order to improve their job interviewing skills.

The days when a nurse was assigned to a unit because that was where she was needed, regardless of her preparation, experience, or desires, are disappearing. Administrators have discovered that the proper placement of nurses not only increases their job satisfaction, but also decreases personnel turnover; and nurses who are happy and effective in their jobs give better-quality patient care than those who are not.

Readers interested in a step-by-step system of interviewing—from reviewing the application to evaluating your interviewing methods—will want to read P. Kaiser's article listed in suggested readings for this unit, which also includes tips for job applicants.

Many nurse administrators are concerned about what they can or cannot ask during a pre-employment interview in terms of federal Equal Employment Opportunity laws. Most interview questions pose no problem if the individual being interviewed is subsequently hired. But questions must be asked in such a way that, should the individual not be hired, they cannot be construed as discriminatory. An example: "Can you work every other weekend?" is a question of concern to many nurse managers when interviewing prospective staff nurses. If the applicant answers "No," and happens not to be hired, that question could be construed as discriminatory against those whose religious practices would prevent them from working weekends. A better way to cover the same issue in an interview would be as follows: "Our staffing policy states that staff nurses and assistant head nurses work every other weekend and have the alternate weekend off. Could you comply with this policy?" Sounds like hairsplitting? Maybe, but it is difficult to challenge an interview question when the policy necessitating it is stated first. A good rule of thumb is to ask interview questions that specify expectations of the job.

Nurse managers new to the function of interviewing and selection of personnel should have the benefit of thorough orientation by the personnel department or through a management development program.

YOU CAN HELP IT HAPPEN!

By Naomi Domer Medearis

Reprinted with permission from *The Journal of Nursing Administration*, Volume 3, Number 1, January-February 1973, pp. 12–13.

As an adult educator in Continuing Education Services at the University of Colorado, I conduct many workshops for health professionals and I am dismayed by the number of participants who seem to have no idea of why they were sent to the event. In discussing the reasons why they came, their responses frequently go something like this:

"I really don't know why I'm here. My director (or supervisor) asked me if I would go, and here I am."

"This workshop interested me, so I asked to come, and they said 'Okay.' That was all."

"It was my turn to attend a conference, and I've always wanted to see Denver."

And when I ask, "What will you be expected to do when you go back to your work?" the replies follow a similar theme:

"I don't know. Nobody said."

"We have a policy that we must write a report."

"I'm supposed to present some kind of inservice."

Such responses communicate several implicit messages. One, that administration supports attendance but does not expect much in return. Another, that becoming a resource person to the nursing staff is not considered part of the RN's job. Still another, that the learning experience is for self-development and has no direct bearing on staff or organizational changes in nursing practice. And finally, that the experience is really not important, since there is no evidence that it ever happened. From my experience these messages are probably valid.

Nurses involved in educational programs who have developed a real sense of who they are personally and professionally, and who have a realistic idea of how to utilize newly acquired knowledge, skills, and values, offer a potential resource to facilitate change in nursing practice. As a director or supervisor of nursing, your support as a nurse colleague for such nurses is critical to freeing these resources.

Have you ever matched pennies with anyone? The outcome is always a win-lose situation, and the outcome is controlled strictly by chance. It seems to me that matching pennies is somewhat like the situation in which a nursing director and a member of her staff find themselves when the opportunity to attend a conference, workshop, or educational event occurs. Either the conference will prove beneficial or it will have been a waste of time. As in the game of matching pennies, the outcome may be the result of chance, but if the nurse administrator thoughtfully plans for the event, the element of chance can be eliminated and the likelihood of favorable results greatly enhanced. If the planning process includes dialogue between the director and the nurse participant, the likelihood of a favorable result is even further enhanced.

As an administrator in nursing, you are accountable for the costs of your staff development program. You should be giving the highest priority to ensuring that the conference or workshop attended by a member of your staff will ultimately benefit both the nursing service and the nurse attending the workshop. The energy required to support a decision to send someone from your staff to a workshop is considerable. Both you and the nurse participant spend much time and effort in the process.

In providing for staff development opportunities outside your agency, the energy you expend in preparing for such a learning experience requires financial support. The person attending the event usually receives his or her salary plus expenses while away from home. Frequently this includes fees, tuition, transportation, lodging, and food. Furthermore the absence of a nurse from her unit may necessitate arrangements for a staff replacement. Thus, when the nurse receives official approval to attend the conference, cold hard cash underwrites her participation.

In addition, there are adjustments that the nurse must make personally when she attends a conference. Her daily routine, and possibly that of her family, requires considerable adjustment, and often an outlay of money for child care as well. She must plan adequately for responsibilities at work, even at the risk of interpersonal conflict with other members of the staff. Such conflict may arise from the additional work load for persons in her unit or the orientation of a "float" nurse to assume her duties. And later, during the training program, she may risk the possibility of coming face to face with needed changes—in her own work or in her unit. This possibility poses a threat to her and may well influence her decision on how much time and effort she is willing to invest in the conference.

To feel comfortable in venturing into a new learning experience, the nurse participant needs and deserves genuine support in order to make more than a token investment in the learning experience. This requires more than administrative support. It requires support from an administrator who is willing to recognize that she is a member of the nursing profession and that the assistance offered is provided as a *professional* colleague as well as an administrator. In other words, the nurse administrator *must* acknowledge that she is a nurse—a nurse with special administrative functions, but still a nurse!

What about professional support? Professional support is more difficult to give than administrative assistance. It presupposes support from a *nurse colleague.* It is more than merely giving your permission to attend a conference. It includes the thoughtful and realistic integration of your goals, her goals, and the health agency's goals. Both your expectations and hers need to be discussed openly and your thoughts shared prior to making the decision for her participation in the education event. Such support includes creating a climate that will facilitate changes that may ultimately evolve from the learning experience.

How is nurse colleague support developed? Before making the decision to send a nurse to an education event, take time to do some thoughtful advance planning. To assess the potential value of such an experience to the nurse involved and to nursing service, reflect on questions like these:

What do you anticipate the education event will be like?

What philosophy and methodology lie behind the content of the program?

What are the potential changes that one might expect from such a learning experience?

What expectations do you have of this nurse colleague when she returns?

What back-up will she need if she comes back full of challenging ideas?

What will she expect from you? What can you give her?

Ask the nurse to reflect on her motivation for going. What does she expect the conference to be like? What is likely to "turn her on"? How does she anticipate using the experience? How will she feel about sharing the experience after the conference? How does the request to attend the education event relate to her personal and professional needs?

It is important to come to some kind of understanding or working agreement that clearly defines your expectations of each other when the conference is over. You should agree that there is more to come—attending a conference is part of a "whole" educational approach to the growth and effectiveness of the nursing service. You should clarify such basic things as how soon you will meet to talk about the conference on her return; how the experience will relate to your preplanning and discussions before the conference; how the learning can be used for the nurse's growth as well as for nursing service's benefit. In addition, consider what recommendations you both might make about similar future pro-

grams; what data and/or recommendations you could share with the sponsor or coordinator of the conference (either to encourage her to continue with similar conferences, to modify her offerings, to discontinue the program, or to identify new needs that could be met by future conferences or workshops).

The risk you run—and there is a risk—comes when you take off your administrative hat and don that of the nurse colleague. Wearing the hat of nurse colleague facilitates the supportive dynamic; it alters the relationship between administrator and subordinate. It balances power among professional nurse colleagues. This is a challenge as well as a risk. The potential payoff for you stems from reaffirming your professional identity as a nurse, and you will probably find your role in the nursing profession expanded and enriched as a result.

And finally, weight your choices. Will the "flip of the coin of opportunity" result in a merely temporary stimulation for the nurse participant? Will the learning, because of lack of follow-up, become irrelevant or impractical? Will the nurse's attendance finally provide no more than "face validity" or "window dressing" for the staff development program of nursing service?

I submit that some concrete planning toward a "resource bank" of new, creative inputs from nurses attending educational events will result in a new level of professionalism in your nursing staff. As nurse colleagues, you can plan to share your expectations with each other; you can mutually agree on the intent and potential outcome of the learning experience, and you can create a win-win situation for both yourself and the nurse participant, for the nursing profession, and for your agency. The next time one of your staff requests permission to attend an education conference or training program you can help it begin to happen.

YOUR SPEECH WILL ALMOST WRITE ITSELF IF YOU FOLLOW THESE EASY STEPS

By Sylvia H. Simmons

Reprinted from *New Speakers Handbook*. New York: Dial Press, 1972. Used with permission.

In most instances, you will probably have accepted your invitation to speak many weeks before the actual date of the speaking engagement. But if you are like most people, you are doubtlessly going to wait until you are up against the deadline before you actually sit down and commit your planned comments to paper.

With the exception of a handful of politicians and business tycoons who have their own ghostwriters on staff, the actual writing of a talk—even for a professional writer—looms as a ghastly task. Many a speaker faces his blank sheet of paper wondering what (besides the flattery inherent in the invitation) ever induced him to accept a place on the program.

Take heart! Over the years, having experienced my own share of the syndrome known as "writer's block" and having watched many a speech-writing colleague agonize over a cold typewriter, I have developed a foolproof system for organizing my thoughts and getting them down on paper in script form. I have introduced dozens of people to my system—not only speakers, but writers of articles and books, and even high schools and college students faced with term papers, book reports, and graduate theses. This system has yet to fail—provided the speaker, or writer, has anything at all to say.

For want of a better name, we'll call it the Simmons System. (For all I know, many other people may have independently come up with the same system; for it's a device born of need, perfected through usage, and heaven-made for anyone faced with an irrevocable deadline. There is no reason why The System should have evolved for me alone.)

The Simmons System is based upon a conviction that one's unconscious can be hard at work on a problem or an assignment even when one's conscious mind is not thinking about it. Take a typical situation: You agree to appear on a program some six weeks hence. You figure six weeks gives you time enough in which to write a brilliant and applause-winning talk. But you are busy. Other matters have greater priority or closer deadlines. So you procrastinate about getting started on the speech.

Actually, you may not be procrastinating at all. During the days and weeks when the project is set off on a back burner, thoughts relevant to your talk keep popping into your mind. An idea occurs to you. Sometimes it is only a phrase. Or you read something somewhere and think, "Maybe I ought to quote that." Pertinent facts come to you when you are in the shower, in a meeting, at dinner, often during a sleepless moment at night.

The basic trick, which might be called Step

No. 1 of the Simmons System, is to *write down every single one of these thoughts or items* as soon as possible after they come to you. And, for reasons that will become clear later on, each should be written or typed on the same size paper or card, one item per card or sheet. I prefer to use 5" x 8" index cards because each card gives me enough room for several paragraphs of copy, should I have that much to record or to add on at another time. A cheaper but equally effective method is to tear in half a pad of 8½" x 11" paper. This provides you with a stack of sheets, each approximately 5½" x 8½" in size—very close to the size of my favorite index cards.

Now, once you get these items down in writing, some of them may not look as good, or as wise, or as well phrased as when they were in your mind. Save them anyway. Later on, you may find these bits and pieces work well in conjunction with other thoughts you will be jotting down. There will be plenty of time to discard excess or inferior material when you get to writing your first draft.

Step No. 2 in the Simmons System begins when you eventually get to the point where you really have to devote some time to thinking about your talk on a conscious level. Armed with your stack of index cards, you are ready to concentrate on your topic. Perhaps the best way to start is to do some reading on the subject—articles, speeches, research, even books if you have the time—written by other people about, or close to, the subject. Hopefully, you have someone on your staff—an assistant, a researcher, a good secretary—or a smart wife or husband, who can save you many hours by going to the library for you (after thorough briefing) and finding source material for you to read or scan.

As you go through this material, you will unquestionably find things others have said that you agree with or take exception to. Transcribe such passages onto your cards (one item only per card) making certain to jot

down the source and putting quotation marks around anything you've excerpted verbatim so that you can properly credit the author, should you choose to quote him directly.

Another stimulus to your thinking will often be found in conversations with authorities on your speech subject, with smart friends whose opinions you respect, and occasionally, with people who hold the opposing point of view to your own. As you explore your topic with such persons, you are likely to unearth new information, facts, and figures, plus thoughtful or emotional viewpoints that had not previously occurred to you. Take notes. And remember to add them to your growing file of material.

If you cannot get to see or talk to all the people whose knowledge and opinions are of interest to you, write to them and request that they send you letters describing their attitudes or telling you what they know on the subject. You will be amazed at how many people reply to your inquiries with stimulating material! Bear in mind that most people like to be asked their opinions, particularly if they are to be quoted by name. One caution: if you are writing for information or an opinion, be certain to mention the deadline for receiving a usable reply.

The longer the lead time between agreeing to make a speech and the actual date of your talk, the fatter will be your file of accumulated ideas, arguments, phrases, quotations, examples, etc. You are now approaching the moment of truth—the day when you really have to clean your desk, unclutter your mind, unencumber your date book, *and begin to write.*

This brings you to Step No. 3 in the Simmons System. Go through your stack of index cards. In the upper right-hand corner of each card write, in pencil (because it's erasable, and therefore changeable), a key word or two that tells you what the card is about. Let me give you an example.

Say you are going to give a talk on "The Pros and Cons of Legalizing Marijuana." In the corner of one card, you might want to jot down "PRO: Non-addictive." On another, "CON: Unknown Factors." Then, "CON: Prevents Problem Solving." And, "CON: Appeal to Pre-Teens." Plus, "PRO: Millions Using It." And, "PRO: Comparison with Alcohol." One card might be marked "Better Laws Needed," another, "Accommodation to Reality." Several cards might bear the corner label "Experience—Other Countries."

You might come across several cards that appear to contain good things to say right at the outset of your speech. On each of these, write "INTRO" in the upper right-hand corner. Others might seem like things that should be held until the end. On those, write the word "CONCLUSION." Several cards may contain items pertinent to very young people. Perhaps they'll get the key corner word "YOUTH." Still others might contain quotations or opinions from the medical profession. These could be tabbed "MEDICAL OPINION." Here and there you will find a card that does not fall into any category you can designate. In the upper right-hand corner of those cards, put a question mark. (As your script starts to take shape, you'll find appropriate places where these items seem to fit.)

In Step No. 4 of the Simmons System, you are going to shuffle the cards, arranging them so that all cards with the same key word are together. Thus, all the CONS will be in one group, all the PROS will be in another, all the INTRO items together, etc. Clip together, or place a rubber band around each group

Now, Step No. 5. Lay out the card groupings on a clear area of your desk or table moving groups around until you have a subject sequence that appears sensible to you.

You have now created *a natural outline for your talk.* And it is totally unnecesary for you to "write an outline before your begin to write your speech"—which is what every textbook

on writing will advise you to do. You have similar material together, thus preventing the possibility of a disjointed address where the speaker's ideas ramble all over the place, giving the impression of inadequate preparation or, worse still, of a person who has not quite thought through his subject matter.

In Step No. 6, you are going to beef up your material, flavor it, make it come alive. Attack the first group of cards marked INTRO. Do you find in this batch anything that will provide you with your opening comment—any provocative quotation, interesting story, wisely paraphrased show-stopper? Do you have here anything that will make your audience want to listen? Provoke their undivided attention? Arouse their emotions? Make them laugh? Relieve the tension? If not, read through the chapter called "Openers" (Sylvia A. Simmons, *New Speakers Handbook.* New York: Dial Press, 1972), and see what you find that will make a suitable item with which to launch this platform appearance. If you find several possibilities, copy each one onto a separate card and add to the INTRO group. At this point you need not decide exactly which of the items you will eventually use—you're merely considering some possibilities.

Here is how it works. Sticking with the theoretical subject of our talk, "The Pros and Cons of Legalizing Marijuana," you might copy out this item on a card: "I have considerable respect for your tolerance in inviting me to address you—and for my courage in accepting." On the same card, immediately after this excerpt, you could add a sentence of your own, such as: "For the whole subject of drugs, is today, one about which most people feel very emotional and heated."

On another card, perhaps you will copy out this story: "As I stand before you, I can't help thinking about the man who was killed in the floods in Florence, Italy just a few short years ago. He made his way to heaven and at the Pearly Gates he was asked to give his case history—to tell the story of how he died and came to heaven. This he obligingly did. St. Peter thought the story so interesting that he asked the new arrival if he would agree to give a talk to the other angels in heaven, telling them all about the flood and his demise. The newly arrived resident of heaven was very flattered, and he immediately accepted the invitation. As he flew away, a kind young angel tugged at the sleeves of his robe and said, 'Sir, I think I ought to tell you that *Noah* will be in the audience.'

"My point is that I'm somewhat humbled at being up here and talking on the subject of *drugs*—when so many of you in the audience are experts in the field."

On still another card, you could jot down this comment: "I'm going to read my talk to you today, rather than deliver if off the cuff. That's because I believe it's a good idea to carefully think through my thoughts before I say something. The trouble is that it never sounds any better than if I had just blurted it out in the first place."

(Eventually, when you actually write your speech script, you might determine that you do not need all of the INTRO material you have now accumulated, and you might make the decision to discard one of these three items. Right now, however, it is better to have too much material than too little.)

In the same manner that you use this book, (Sylvia Simmons, *New Speakers Handbook.* New York: Dial Press, 1972) to enliven and strengthen your group of ideas for the introductory section of your talk, Step No. 6 of the Simmons System calls for you to go through each group of cards in your collection and, wherever you feel you could use more or better material, skim the appropriate chapters for additional content. *And be sure to use the Subject Index at the back of the book.* When you have finished with this step, you should have quite a bit more material than when you first put your file card items in sequential

groups.

In Step No. 7 you are going to draw upon your opinions and convictions to supplement the considerable copy you must now have in your index file. Check each group of cards again. Under each subject category, ask yourself if you have noted every thought, every belief, every argument, every example you wish to convey to your audience. If you did Step No. 1 over a period of many weeks, and if you are talking on a subject where you have strong convictions and have jotted them down whenever they occurred to you, do not be surprised if Step No. 7 finds you with little to add. On the other hand, additional thoughts might well come to mind as you concentrate on the various subheadings that you have written on the corners of the cards.

When you have exhausted your ideas, when the core of every thought you wish to convey has been noted, you are ready to write the first draft of your script.

Getting the first draft on paper is Step No. 8. But instead of it looming as a monumental and dreadful chore, you will find to your amazement that your talk is all but written! By using the Simmons System up to this point, your speech has almost written itself.

With your cards arranged in a sequence that makes sense to you, pick and choose the best material in each group and start writing. Much of it you will be able to copy off the cards. Some of it will require amplification, cutting, or improved phraseology. Do this as you go along, adding, subtracting, rewording, inserting bridges from idea to idea.

When you have gone through all your cards—discarding those which do not seem to fit in, perhaps moving a few into other groups where they fit better, utilizing the best of your material, and working in the previously uncategorized cards (the ones with the question marks in the corner)—you will have your rough draft. And no matter how many changes you may choose to make in the last two steps, the worst is behind you. You have committed to paper all the things you want to tell your audience, and you have done it in an organized, logical sequence.

The last two steps are the easiest. And they should be the most fun, because you will be doing them in the knowledge that the basics are already down on paper—and it wasn't as tough as you thought it would be. However, the last two steps, though easy, make the difference between an *ordinary* speech and a *great* one. It is this extra bit of work that separates the stars from the mediocrities.

In Step No. 9, you are going to study your rough draft very critically and objectively, searching for weak transitions, dreary stretches, passages that lack forcefulness, and sections where witticisms, anecdotes, or philosophical punch lines might be added. Use one-liners, proverbs, anecdotes, quotations—any and all material that can serve to perk up a sagging section or paragraph. Let me give you some examples of how Step No. 9 works.

Staying with our theoretical talk on "Legalizing Marijuana," you might well decide to use this item: "Theodore Roosevelt once told us that it is difficult to make our material condition better by the *best* laws. 'But,' he said, 'it is easy enough to ruin it by *bad* laws.'" Whichever side of the marijuana issue you take, you could use that quotation to make a point for the right sort of laws concerning the drug under discussion. Another anecdote might be, "It's like the man who emerged from a meeting and announced, 'There is a feeling of togetherness in there. Everyone is reasonably unhappy.'" This bit would work very well towards the conclusion of the talk on marijuana, if the speech writer were to use it and add a comment such as this: "The same might be said of us. Whichever side of the drug problem we may be on, I'm sure all of us are reasonably unhappy about the current situation. Well, polarized as we may be, at least that gives us a feeling of togetherness!"

And now for Step No. 10—the final editing of your speech. After incorporating into your rough draft the new material you added in the last step, read through your talk again—*but this time, read it aloud.* Stop at awkward phrases. Edit them as you go along, until you are comfortable saying every word. If something seems unclear, clarify it. If anything seems repetitious, eliminate it. If all your sentences seem to be the same length, cut some of them and add to others. The variety in sentence length will help you avoid a monotonous delivery. If some of the words you used in writing the talk looked good on paper but sound phony or artificial when spoken, substitute synonyms. Keep in mind that your talk is meant to be *heard,* not read. It makes a difference.

When you have edited the talk for *sound,* read it aloud once more. And *time* it. If you have written a speech that takes more time to read than the time allotted to you on the program, read it once again—and this time, cut out any sentence or paragraph that does not *strengthen your thesis* or *enliven the script.* It is very important to recognize that you cannot time a talk if you read it silently. *You must read it aloud.*

While you may continue to make word changes here and there each time you rehearse your talk (even professional actors rehearse; it's suicide for an amateur to deliver a speech without plenty of rehearsal time behind him), your script is now finished—in ten simple steps, some of which took only a few minutes. And, as the material was transferred from card file to manuscript paper, the first draft all but wrote itself!

Stone and Bactiner's Speaking Up *is an excellent reference for the novice speaker or the veteran who wants to refine her public speaking skills. It contains many helpful suggestions for dealing with the unforeseen and inevitable hassles that plague public speakers.*

Disparaging remarks about committees are not uncommon. They usually stem from negative experiences while working in groups where too few individuals, including the leader, understand the purpose of the group and have the basic skills to move the work assignment to successful completion. Staff nurses moving into management positions are generally accustomed to doing everything themselves. They may be frustrated by the slow process of doing things through others as in committee work. One should not equate educational preparation or status position with skill in conducting meetings or committee work. Whether you are in staff nursing, staff development, or nursing administration,

important skills to develop are learning how to conduct a meeting and how to participate in committees. A meeting participant skilled in conducting meetings can be very helpful to a chairperson who may lack these skills.

Committees present an excellent opportunity for professional nurse colleagues to advance the work of the profession or their employing organizations. Knowing the kinds of committees possible and how best to use them, a nurse leader can approach this important area with the best use of everyone's time and resources. Cooper describes the purpose of committees and the roles of various participants, and includes a helpful tool for recording.

COMMITTEES THAT WORK

By Signe S. Cooper

Reprinted with permission from *The Journal of Nursing Administration,* Volume 3, Number 1, January-February 1973, pp. 30–35, p. 59.

Search all your parks in all your cities . . .
You'll find no statues to committees.
This Week, 1961

Although it is true that statues do not commemorate committees, it is also true that much of the world's work is done through committees. While many of us may agree that "a camel is a horse put together by a committee," the sentiment is probably a reflection on how committees work rather than a denial of the need for committees to carry out certain tasks.

The typical American way to solve problems has been to appoint a committee, and many nurses are members of different kinds of committees, in both their personal and professional lives. Some of these committees are effective, others completely ineffective; too often considerable time and effort is wasted in accomplishing the designated goals. Since nursing administrators spend so much time in committee work, it is important to consider ways to use that time wisely.

Committee work is a good learning experience for all those involved, but there are no shortcuts to learning how to be an effective committee member. Committees are especially valuable in assuring that divergent ideas and points of view are considered, and working together, a group can take advantage of the special skills possessed by some of its members. Individual members often volunteer to do the tasks they do best in order to achieve the goals of the group.

The underlying philosophy of all committee work is that problems are solved more satisfactorily and certain tasks are done more effectively by pooling the abilities, resources, interests, and experiences of several persons. When the various abilities and contributions of each member are used, not only will the end product be better than that which any of the individuals alone could produce, but each member is committed to the result, such as trying the new product (e.g., nursing care plans) or supporting a new approach (e.g., hospital policies).

Time is money, and because considerable amounts of time are often spent in committee sessions, it is appropriate to consider if this time is spent wisely. "Is this committee really necessary?" is a moot question. It is not unusual for a committee to outlive its original purpose, so this question should be asked frequently. The question should also be asked before any committee is established.

PURPOSE OF A COMMITTEE

Committees are established for specific purposes. Most committees are problem solving or task oriented. The work of some of these committees may be stated in the by-laws or rules of the organization; examples include the committee on legislation of a state nurses' association or an executive committee of a school of nursing. The sections of the by-laws or rules relating to committees should be reviewed from time to time and amended in keeping with the needs of the organization.

Other committees are advisory, and the advice is sought by a specific group. Schools of nursing may have an advisory committee to advise the faculty on certain aspects of the curriculum or management of the school. Directors of hospital inservice education programs usually find an advisory committee helpful.

Members of advisory committees are selected on the basis of their qualifications; each member should understand the nature of his involvement as advisory. Final decisions are made by the group that appointed the committee. Once appointed, advisory committees should be used; it is disappointing to accept membership on such a committee and then find out that it is a committee in name only.

The purpose of a committee may often be inferred from its title: for example, the Procedure Revision Committee of a hospital nursing staff. If purposes have not been defined by the rules or by-laws of the parent organization, it often helps to expedite matters if the committee members define their own purposes. When purposes are stated broadly rather than specifically, it may be useful for committee members to delineate specific objectives, such as those attainable in a given period of time (usually the length of the appointment of the members).

An ad hoc committee is established for one specific purpose; by definition, *ad hoc* means "for this case alone." When its work is completed, the committee is disbanded. An ad hoc committee may be appointed to review a hospital's policies regarding visiting hours; when the task is completed, the committee goes out of existence.

Although not titled a committee, the Task Force on Continuing Education of the American Nurses' Association was appointed to function as an ad hoc committee. Its specific task was to examine the question of mandatory continuing education for relicensure and make recommendations to the ANA board of directors. With the completion of its ad hoc assignment, the task force was dissolved.

Task force is defined as "a temporary grouping . . . under one leader for the purpose of accomplishing a definite objective." The term is now often used to replace the word *committee* and may suggest the enormity or seriousness of the task to be done or the problem to be solved. Essentially this is a semantic distinction, since most task forces function as ad hoc committees, working on specific assignments or tasks. However the group is labeled, the same principles apply for effective functioning.

Committees often fail because their goals were not clearly identified or because members were not aware of the goals or did not believe in them. It is not unusual to have a committee meeting open with the words, "I wonder what we are supposed to do." When this happens, it is apparent that the purposes of the committee have not been clearly outlined.

Since committees are not appropriate for all types of tasks, before any committee is established, careful consideration should be given to the appropriateness of the task for committee activity.

COMMITTEE SIZE AND SELECTION

Cynics say that the ideal size of any committee is three, with two of its members out of town. (Again, this suggests that there are some activities better done by individuals than by committees, and this possibility should always be carefully considered.)

The size of a committee depends upon its function. In general, it should be large enough to do the job, but small enough to facilitate free discussion. The work of large committees (more than 25 members) is often accomplished through subcommittees, each of which has its own task or assignment.

Size may also relate to other factors. For instance, in some types of organizations, such as the American Nurses' Association or the National League for Nursing, geographic representation may be an important consideration. The mobility of nurses makes maintaining geographic representation difficult after committee members have been selected, but such representation is usually desirable for major committees. In other instances, it may be appropriate to have another type of representation, such as various fields of nursing, or, in the example of a hospital committee, representation from various nursing units. The size of the committee may also relate to the specific job to be done and the kind of competence required to do it.

Increasingly, nurses are involved with interdisciplinary groups. Some nurses are impatient in working with members of such groups, particularly those that also include public members, since certain kinds of interpretations take time. Such interactions are significant, however, and all nurses should welcome these opportunities to interpret nursing and to work with others in attempting to solve health problems. Nursing administrators may be asked for suggestions for members of interdisciplinary groups, and careful selection of nurses who will be contributing members is important.

The selection of the chairman may contribute substantially to the effectiveness of the committee. Members of the committee may wish to select their own chairman, but if

members are unknown to each other at the time the committee is established, it may be preferable to have the chairman selected by the person responsible for appointing the committee. This may be the director of nursing in an institution, the president of an organization, the inservice education coordinator, and so on.

It may be desirable to involve the chairman in the selection of committee members, since he must work with these persons. This may seem to be an undemocratic procedure, and should be done only for justifiable reasons. Often committee members have suggestions for additional members, so on occasion only a small number are selected by the appointing body, with the proviso that additional members be appointed by the committee.

ROLE OF THE CHAIRMAN

An effective chairman facilitates the work of the committee in a specific role, which varies somewhat, depending upon the purposes of the committee[40]. In an advisory committee, the chairman encourages all members to contribute to the discussions in order to elicit as many views and ideas as possible. With a task-oriented or problem-solving committee, the chairman often directs activities and coordinates the efforts of the group.

The role of the presiding officer of a large body such as the House of Delegates of the American Nurses' Association is to facilitate the deliberations of the organization. Thus, he must maintain his neutrality and objectivity. As the presiding officer, the president does not usually express his point of view unless specifically requested to do so. In contrast, a chairman is expected to contribute to the deliberations of a committee. Indeed, he may have been appointed chairman because of his expert knowledge in a given area. This knowledge may assist the committee in its work. An effective chairman does not misuse the knowledge he possesses, nor does he use his role as chairman to achieve his own purposes.

A good committee chairman generates interest, coordinates group efforts, and stimulates the group to action. This requires confidence in the members of the committee, as well as enthusiasm and persuasion. Obviously, the chairman must understand the purpose of the committee and be able to convey it to the members.

In order to move committees to action, the charman must be willing to spend time in preparation for meetings. It may involve locating resources and resource persons as well as necessary study materials to give members the facts and information they need to take appropriate action.

Although this seems a questionable practice for continuity, a chairman who has not previously served on the committee may be appointed. I recall attending a committee meeting where this was the case. The new chairman had obviously not read the minutes of previous meetings but came with a long list of suggested projects for the committee. Had she read the previous minutes, she would have learned that most of her suggested projects had been ruled out for one reason or another. Instead, valuable time was wasted in interpreting the previous actions and decisions to the new chairman.

The effective chairman seeks contributions from all members in establishing and reordering priorities and in determining the direction of the work of the committee. This can be a time-consuming process, and an effective chairman must be able to help the group advance toward its goals. Otherwise, valuable time may be wasted deciding what to do first—a not uncommon way of postponing action.

Developing a written agenda for meetings is a major responsibility of the chairman; this agenda is based on the decisions by the committee members for their priorities. Mailed to members several days in advance of the meeting, a prepared agenda gives members an opportunity for advance thinking on topics to be discussed and, for certain types of committee meetings, an opportunity to poll colleagues and others on the points to be considered. Such an opinion poll may be particularly useful for an inservice education planning committee.

The agenda should not be so long that the committee cannot discuss all the items without feeling hurried. If items are not listed in order of priority, the important items may not be considered until the end of a long meeting, often accounting for hasty and unwise decision making. Members need enough time to discuss all items without feeling pressed. However, the most effective meetings begin and end promptly.

A chairman has a responsibility for moving a meeting along, for keeping digressions at a minimum, for directing necessary action to achieve the goals of the committee. The chairman has a serious responsibility to expedite the business of the committee, yet encourage every member to contribute to the work of that committee. There is no "royal road" to effective committee action, but one significant factor is the selection of a chairman with leadership skills.

Being an effective chairman is not a skill with which persons are born. The nurse in a supervisory or administrative position can encourage and assist nurses to develop this particular skill. Opportunities abound for nurses to serve as committee chairmen, but individuals may be reluctant to accept this type of assignment, particularly if they are unsure of the encouragement and support they will receive when they agree to serve in this capacity.

Support and assistance to a new committee chairman is available from a variety of sources: the president of the organization (who often serves as an ex officio member of committees), the director of nursing or inservice coordinator, or a previous committee chairman. Under some circumstances, having any of these persons attending may *not* be helpful; the mentor must know when to offer help but, more importantly, when *not* to interfere. Leadership styles vary, and the neophyte needs freedom to try out his ideas and use his own approaches.

The new chairman who is anxious to learn will seek help from a variety of sources. He may wish to discuss the conduct of the meeting with someone who attended, or he may ask for suggestions and useful references. If meetings are recorded on tape, the chairman may find it most useful to listen to the playback of the session.

THE RECORDER

Among the witty remarks about committees is the one which suggests that "perhaps the reason committees keep minutes is on account of the hours they waste." If the meeting is important enough to be held, then it probably is important enough to be recorded.

Minutes are useful in recording decisions and noting progress. Members should be encouraged to review the minutes prior to subsequent meetings to help them take steps toward progress without going over ground already covered. Recall how many meetings you have attended in which valuable time was spent in orienting an absent member from the previous meeting! Minutes mailed in advance can help to save time—if members review them prior to the meeting.

It is rarely necessary to keep detailed records of meetings, but a good recorder summarizes the discussion and takes careful note of any actions or decisions. Some organizations follow a regular format (Exhibit 3–4); with others, the report of the secretary or recorder is less structured. If detailed records are essential, tapes of the sessions are more effective than written minutes by a member of the committee, but may be difficult to transcribe.

An annual report or other type of reporting may be expected of the committee. It may be the recorder's responsibility to prepare the report or to draft a report for the chairman to submit. Well-written records of the meetings facilitate the compilation of such reports.

The duties of the recorder should not preclude his participation in the deliberations of the committee. He, too, may have been selected because of his expert knowledge. He may also have a special contribution to make by his careful analysis of previous discussion and actions of the committee. Special skills needed by the recorder are the ability to distinguish between relevant and irrelevant discussions, and skill in developing records that portray an accurate picture of the work of the committee.

In addition to keeping records, the recorder is usually responsible for notifying members about meetings. Establishing a regular meeting time usually facilitates the work of the committee and assures attendance by the majority of members. If meetings are held at irregular intervals, the decision about the meeting time is usually made by the recorder and the chairman. Often a response by members is requested to make certain that a sufficient number will be attending the meeting. Notices of meetings should be sent several days (or sometimes weeks) in advance of the meeting.

RESPONSIBILITIES OF COMMITTEE MEMBERS

Each member of the committee can contribute to the productivity of the group. Effective meetings often result from members coming to meetings well informed and accepting a

Exhibit 3–4.   Suggested Format for Recording of Minutes. The specific information recorded depends upon the nature of the committee. (Courtesy Wisconsin Nurses' Association. Used with permission.)

_____
(Committee Title)

A meeting of the _____

(Committee)

was held at _____ on _____

(Place)   (Date)

at _____.

(Time)

ROLL CALL

   Presiding:
   Members Present:
   Also Present:
   Absent & Excused:
   Absent:

MINUTES OF PREVIOUS MEETINGS

CORRESPONDENCE

BUSINESS

SUMMARY OF RECOMMENDATIONS

NEXT MEETING

ADJOURNMENT (TIME)

_____   Date Approved _____
   SECRETARY

personal responsibility for attending to the business of the meeting. Unnecessary delays frequently result from members not having read committee materials in advance; this may cause resentment by those members who came to the meeting prepared. Each committee member has a responsibility for keeping the discussion on the topic and resisting the impulse to discuss irrelevant items until after the meeting has ended.

Committee members must be genuinely interested in the work of the committee and be patient with the time-consuming elements of group work. Those who are unable to fulfill their committee obligations should not accept the appointment to the committee or they should resign if changing circumstances prevent their participation in the work of the committee. Evidence of lack of interest may be detected by continued tardiness or absence from meetings, failure to prepare for the meeting, or inability or unwillingness to contribute to the work of the committee.

Many meetings are conducted informally, particularly when the committee is small. In larger committees, the business is expedited by observance of parliamentary procedure. In this instance, every member needs a familiarity with the rules of parliamentary procedure. Educational institutions and other agencies offer short courses in parliamentary procedure. Since the principles apply to many different meetings and organizations in which nurses participate, enrolling in such a course is often a worthwhile investment of time[37].

SUMMARY

The amount of time spent in committee activities is extensive. It is important, then, to consider ways of assuring that this time is spent productively. Attention and effort directed to improving the work of committees can lead to more effective committees and assure members of personal satisfaction of a job well done.

Committees are established on a belief in the soundness of group thought and decision; this is democracy in action, a basic concept for nurse administrators.

MAINTAINING CONTINUITY OF CARE DURING SHIFT CHANGE

By Patricia M. Joy

Reprinted with permission from *The Journal of Nursing Administration,* Volume 5, Number 6, November-December 1975, pp. 28–29.

Nurses' behavior at change-of-shift report is frequently related to tools used in that setting, such as Kardex, doctors' order sheets, ward work sheets, and tape recorders. Change-of-shift behavior can also reflect the internal communication system (or lack of same) of that nursing service.

What kind of communication occurs in your nursing service, as the responsibility for patient care is passed from one group of nurses to another three times each day? What purpose does or should this communication serve?

We believe that in addition to conveying important information about the patient and his reactions to illness and treatment, change-of-shift report offers another unique opportunity. During this frequent, scheduled exchange, nurses can give one another significant positive feedback regarding nursing interventions and the human caring offered to patients. It is a time for nurses to give support to other nurses tired after a hectic day, in short, for nurturing their professional colleagues.

How much serious thought is given to rituals in the nursing profession? The phrase "But we've always done it that way" is heard time and time again. One aspect of the profession of nursing that has become rigidly ritualistic is the change-of-shift report. With a few little twists here and there it remains the same—a nurse telling an oncoming group of nurses and ancillary personnel what she feels is important for them to know.

The disadvantages are numerous. The oncoming nursing team sits and absorbs information, relying on the nurse giving the report to tell them everything they need to know. They do not observe the patient, his chart, or the other "tools" necessary for his care. The oncoming charge nurse then makes assignments without seeing the patients.

Meanwhile, at the time this report is being taped or presented, few staff members are available on the patient care unit. Patients and physicians often complain of the scarcity of nursing personnel while "report" is taking place.

Those are a few of the reasons why a serious examination of the change-of-shift report took place at Boswell Memorial Hospital in Sun City, Arizona. Three East, a 26-bed medical-surgical unit, which practiced team nursing and where I was head nurse, was chosen as the site for a trial period of a new change-of-shift activity.

Preparation began approximately one month in advance. The nursing staff on Three

East was provided with background information on different change-of-shift activities instituted elsewhere and they were encouraged to seek out the advantages and disadvantages of the various methods.

Following many discussions with the nursing staff and resource people in nursing service administration, the idea of patient rounds came about. Nurses would observe patients while planning and evaluating their care.

This method was then discussed with the evening and night shift patient care coordinators in order to ensure continuity in implementing it on all shifts.

WHAT IT ACHIEVES

The objectives toward which our new change-of-shift activity was directed included:

Patient Objectives

1. To provide a means for the patient to communicate to the staff his care needs by expressing his likes, dislikes, and suggestions for change
2. To enable the patient to express his perception of how he is progressing and allow him to relate happenings that occurred in the course of his prior hospital day
3. To acquaint the patient with the person who will be responsible for the delivery of his care on a specific shift

Nurse Objectives

1. To provide the oncoming nurse with an opportunity to quickly determine the patient's cognizance of his care
2. To enable the nurse to initiate or reinforce patient teaching regarding scheduled procedures and tests
3. To allow the nurse to assess (at the beginning of her work day) the current physical and emotional status of the patient

4. To provide the nurse with an opportunity to inform the patient of what his care that day will consist
5. To assist the nurse in enhancing her observational skills and interviewing techniques

Team Objectives

1. To provide the ancillary team members with the opportunity to begin the delivery of their care immediately (with the aid of a temporary assignment)
2. To enable them to communicate and cooperate with the out-going team members so that together they can deliver quality patient care

HOW IT WORKS

Another staff nurse and I then demonstrated the new change-of-shift activity for the nursing staff.

After consulting with the team leader going off duty about work not completed, the oncoming team leader made out a temporary assignment for staff members not involved in patient rounds. For example an RN or LPN was assigned to count narcotics with the medication nurse who was finishing her shift. An LPN or nursing assistant was directed to complete A.M. or P.M. care that was unfinished, prepare patients for x-ray, make surgical beds, and check nursing supplies. The unit secretary ordered nourishments. After the staff received their temporary assignments, the oncoming staff nurses (including their team leader) began patient rounds (on the day and evening shifts there would usually be two to three staff nurses). The head nurse would also participate in these rounds during the morning and afternoon change of shift. The outgoing staff nurses (including their team leader) did not accompany these nurses. They utilized that time to complete any unfinished duties. All oncoming staff nurses were included in patient rounds and were responsible for assisting in the completion of the formal assignment following these rounds. They also were to be used by other staff members as resource persons in order to avoid interrupting the team leader. The oncoming medication nurse (usually an LPN) often was included on patient rounds and the focus of these rounds might center around the patient's medication regimen. When staffing patterns changed due to illness, etc., an LPN not assigned to medications might also accompany the staff nurses in order to be of greater assistance in the planning of patient care.

Different tools were utilized in the gathering of information on these rounds. These included the nursing care plan book, the nursing assessment, the patient's chart, medications records, and IV records.

The focus of the rounds would differ from patient to patient. Above all the patient was never talked *to* or *about*. His care was discussed *with* him. It was an opportune time to assess skin conditions, check dressings, catheters, IVs, traction, body alignment, and the patient's emotional status.

After rounds were completed, any questions or problems that had arisen could be discussed with the staff members preparing to leave. The team leader finishing her shift might also wish to further clarify certain things.

After having a chance to see the patient on rounds, the team leader would then complete the formal assignment with the assistance of the staff nurses who accompanied her. The formal assignment delegates responsibility for certain aspects of the patient's care: obtaining vital signs, assisting in admissions, providing patient teaching, checking and replenishing IV and examination trays, checking the crash cart, passing medications, and caring for IVs.

The assignment also showed the time of the patient care conference and the persons delegated to attend inservice programs that shift. Nursing orders were written as a part of the assignment, as much of this information had been obtained from patient rounds and the nursing care plan book. The assignment and the results of the rounds made were then discussed with the individual team members.

HOW LONG DOES IT TAKE?

The actual time spent making rounds and clarifying questions before the outgoing shift left was 30 minutes on the 26-bed unit. The entire process, including completing the assignment and discussing it with team members, consumed approximately one hour. This may seem excessively long until you stop and look at what occurred during that period. With the aid of the temporary assignment the work of the unit began immediately. Sufficient personnel were constantly available to meet patient needs and the formal assignment was more concise and accurate since the team leader completed it after she saw the patients. The new system also enabled the team leader to discuss her expectations with team members at the shift's start.

Patient rounds must be modified somewhat for the night shift as most patients are asleep. The concept remains the same, but following rounds there is a more involved verbal exchange between the nurses leaving and coming on duty.

The patient care coordinators were accustomed to holding their change-of-shift report away from the patient units. It would consist of a verbal exchange regarding patient and staff problems and requests that needed follow-up. However, during the beginning phase of initiating the "patient rounds" the coordinators agreed to begin their shift 15 minutes earlier. This enabled them still to receive a verbal report of general occurrences throughout the hospital and then proceed to Three East to join the nurses there for patient rounds. After the new change-of-shift activity had been instituted on other patient units, the patient care coordinators elected to continue in this manner, and their choice of units would vary from day to day.

Since "patient rounds" were implemented, at no time has lack of information jeopardized patient safety. This change-of-shift activity was implemented on a unit that practiced team nursing, but the basic concept of "patient rounds" could be extended and modified to accommodate other care concepts. It could also be adjusted to variations in the size of the unit and staff.

"Patient rounds" are now used almost everywhere in our hospital at shift change. The success of this activity has been indicated by: (1) positive verbal responses elicited from patients, staff nurses, ancillary personnel, and patient care coordinators when interviewed by the head nurse either individually or collectively and (2) the realization that the objec-tives formulated had been met and were definite advantages.

We were able to make the change-of-shift activity an integral part of the nursing process—for planning and evaluating patient care was one of our overall objectives. Written nursing care plans became a tool to be read, utilized, and updated daily since they were a necessary part of the rounds. It was also noted that time allotted for the care of the patient was now utilized more efficiently, and job productivity, which had been hampered by lack of organization at the beginning of the work shift, was increased. The resulting smooth and orderly change of shift made the concept of continuity of care a reality.

Readers interested in specific tools to facilitate change-of-shift report will want to see Mezzanotte's checklist and Lavoie and Foley's recording tools cited in the Wiley's guidelines for change-of-shift report, also cited, clarify what is important for content and process in this frequent exchange between nurses.

THE SUCCESSFUL WORKSHOP: HOW TO BRING IT OFF

By Barbara J. Stevens

Reprinted with permission from *Nurse Educator*, Volume 2, Number 1, January-February 1977, pp. 16–20.

The workshop is an educational form with its own unique characteristics, problems, and potentialities. It may be the most difficult educational form for teachers to master. In this article "workshop" refers to a concentrated group educational experience focusing on a single subject, usually lasting from one to five days, and typically attended by from 20 to 150 persons from diverse work settings.

This article is directed toward two audiences: (1) those who serve as workshop speakers and leaders and (2) those who sponsor and organize workshops. Obviously, in some circumstances one person may fill both roles. I will address the extreme case (which also happens to be a typical case) in which an outside "expert" is called in to design and run a workshop singlehandedly, except for the support services of the sponsoring institution's staff. Clearly, this extreme case has a greater chance of failure because it relies so heavily on the abilities of a single person. The principles that will be discussed in relation to this most difficult case also apply, though less critically, to simpler workshops where several speaker-leaders are employed or where speaker-leaders are familiar with the participant audience.

The need for this article emerged when a fellow faculty member, preparing to run her first workshop, asked for advice. Although she queried me and a fellow educator who was also familiar with the workshop circuit separately, we produced remarkably similar lists of "do's and don'ts." Those lists are addressed and expanded in this article.

The reader should be warned that what follows is not an erudite discussion of correct teaching methodologies or content organization for workshops. The separate lists of suggestions and subsequent joint discussion made it clear to us that the success or failure of a workshop really hangs on mundane and "non-educational" factors. The reader should also know that both lists were produced from the perspective of the outside "expert" rather than from the perspective of the host and sponsor; that bias will be evident as the items are discussed.

DEFENSIVE MANEUVERS AGAINST HOST INADEQUACIES

In both lists the leading items could be classified as self-defensive maneuvers. The lists advised the speaker to arrive an hour early because: (1) the microphone will be broken,

(2) the lamp wil be burnt out in the projector, (3) the request for a slide projector will have been forgotten, (4) there will be no water for the speaker, or (5) all of the above. These apparently trivial items deserve further discussion.

The Broken Microphone

Case A. The microphone won't work at all, and there is no replacement available in the whole institution. This state of affairs assures that the speaker will have a sore throat by noon and, self-defensively, will increase the number of group activities to cut down "talk time," thereby leaving out some useful lecture information.

Case B. The microphone works imperfectly, crackling and spurting at unexpected intervals. This state ensures a distracted speaker who fails to evince enthusiasm. (She is just waiting for the next crackle!) This case may not matter too much, because the audience—also distracted—no longer cares what the speaker is saying.

Case C. The microphone works in such a manner that it sounds all right to the audience but produces a slight echo and reverberation to the speaker, giving her a constant ringing in the ears accompanied by acute headache. This case is the most insidious, for the speaker appears (and is) distracted but the audience can't figure out why.

Case D. The microphone works but (1) is not portable or (2) must be hand held. Either of these states limits the speaker, but compared to the previous states, they are minor.

Rule 1 for sponsors of workshops. *No other factor is as important to the success of a workshop as a well-functioning microphone.*

Audiovisual Factors

Whether the requested equipment is simply not there or just does not work hardly matters to the speaker. Good intentions of the host do not help. When it is obvious that the situation cannot be remedied, every speaker will graciously assure the host that her slides, transparencies, or films were not really essential to her presentation. Don't believe it! If they were not essential, she would not have brought them. The speaker's only recourse is to revise her planned talk so as not to require the audiovisuals, and it is difficult to revise a speech at the same time one is giving it! The result, of course, is that the speaker appears distracted. (She is—half her mind is off revising the next paragraph.)

Rule 2 for sponsors of workshops. *Have all required audiovisual hardware on hand with: (1) extra bulbs and parts, (2) a three-way adapter plug so the machine can be connected to the current, and (3) an extension cord so the machine can be placed optimally in relation to the screen.*

Incidentally, it is particularly distracting when a screen is placed on a side wall, assuring that the audience must turn away from the speaker's voice in order to see the accompanying visual material. This tactic is guaranteed to frustrate a workshop leader because:

1. Where chairs are rigid, the turning assures discomfort for participants.
2. Where chairs are movable, the shuffling of furniture will blot out the speaker's voice.

AND NOT A DROP TO DRINK!

Presence of a pitcher and glass of water may seem too trivial to mention except for the "inverse, perverse, throat tickle–water correlation." That rule states: In the presence of adequate drinking water the speaker's voice never waivers; in the absence of drinking water a throat tickle, cough, spasm, or worse inevitably occurs.

Rule 3 for sponsors of workshops. *Water is not all that expensive; if necessary the speaker will even pay to have it present.*

OTHER HOST ERRORS

While the defects listed thus far usually can be corrected by the speaker arriving early enough to complain or make suggestions, there are some host maneuvers for which there is little defense. These are discussed here in the hope that future hosts will be careful to avoid such pitfalls.

The Shifting Audience Game

A workshop speaker has a fairly short time in which to establish a productive educational relationship with an audience of relative strangers. Development of this relationship is facilitated in two ways. First, the speaker tries to show the audience that she knows what it is like to be in their particular situation. She reinforces this relationship by examples in which she shows how the subject matter she is presenting can be useful to them. In other words, her whole workshop has been composed with this particular audience in mind.

If upon her arrival the speaker finds that the makeup of the audience has been changed, she is out of luck. Suppose, for example, she expected to meet with nursing supervisors to discuss management techniques. A large portion of her material may have covered tactics and strategies to use in management of subordinate head nurses. If she arrives to find that head nurses have suddenly been included in the audience, she must revise or throw out that portion of her presentation. Similarly, if she wrote for an audience of master's prepared clinical specialists and finds the audience has been expanded to include everyone from clinical specialists to licensed practical nurses, the speaker may have to massively revise the level of the content while she talks.

Rule 4 for sponsors of workshops. *It is important to inform the speaker of the characteristics, positions, and responsibilities of the audience, and the type of participant must not be changed at the last minute so as to "fill empty chairs."*

Sometimes the change in the proposed audience takes place earlier and the speaker is informed. If this occurs after the speaker has prepared for a workshop, some form of financial remuneration is in order. I can recall numerous instances in which, after working two or more days preparing a workshop, the task had to be begun all over again upon receiving word that the audience mix had been arbitrarily changed by the host.

The Numbers Racket

A workshop can be seriously impaired if the leader plans on an attendance of 30 and arrives to find a group of 100 participants. Such an alteration in audience size will not matter too much for the lecture-discussion portions of the workshop, but it can be devastating for the group activities. Workshop speakers use different types of group activities for different size groups, and the planned activities will have been designed on the basis of the projected audience size.

Suppose, for example, the leader planned activities for work groups of ten persons with each group reporting back to the full audience. For a total audience of 30 persons, there would be three group reports, while for an audience of 100, there would be ten such reports. Not only would ten reports throw off the time allotment of the leader, but the audience would be yawning by the fifth report. (Yet no group would be content to withhold its own findings.) The leader's only recourse is to increase her group sizes, and that may not allow for the kind of interchange required by her group materials.

Rule 5 for sponsors of workshops. *Keep the participants within the agreed-upon numbers. The leader's case studies, group assignments, and discussion plans will have been designed to fit a particular audience size.*

Pinning Down the Subject Matter

In relation to the subject matter of the workshop, the host can err by being either too general or too specific. Suggested topics such as "Nursing in the 70s," "Nursing Management," or "Cardiovascular Nursing" give the speaker no idea what the host wants. Where the host is reluctant to clarify the topic, the speaker has two options: to refuse to do the workshop or to speak about anything she pleases. The speaker accepts engagements of this sort only under two conditions: (1) when she always wanted to see Daytona Beach anyway or (2) when she wants a trial run on materials being prepared for another audience. Neither of these motives are likely to give the host a particularly effective workshop.

The opposite host error is the attempt to write the workshop for the speaker. For example, if the host insists that the speaker explain changes in patterns of nursing education using the Zifferblotte model, he is robbing the audience of the chance to see *this* speaker's perspective on patterns of education. Motto: If you want Zifferblotte, get Zifferblotte!

Similarly, the host should let the speaker set her own tone and style. If, for example, the host has published the agenda with "cute" subtitles, and the speaker is a staid and serious type, she may be offended. If the host does not want the ideas and personality of *this* speaker, then he should not have contracted for this speaker.

Rule 6 for sponsors of workshops. *Tell the speaker-leader clearly and precisely what subject matter you want, but let her do it her own way.*

SELF-DEFENSIVE MANEUVERS FOR HOSTS

The speaker-leader is not the only one who needs some self-protection in the workshop business; the hosts must also protect themselves. The following principles represent some essential self-defense maneuvers for the sponsor of a workshop.

The Mack Truck Principle

The host institution must recognize that the guest speaker may be hit by a Mack truck while crossing the street to get to the auditorium. In recent years, the Mack truck theory is being supplanted by the "my plane is grounded in Albany" principle. The effect, of course, is the same: an audience of 100 and no show! For every "single star" workshop, the host needs a contingency plan. Now the truth is that there is somebody right in town, probably on staff at the sponsoring institution, who knows just as much about this subject matter as the guest speaker. The hometown person, of course, was never considered for the workshop because she failed to meet the criteria for determining an expert: (1) lives at least 100 miles away and (2) is unknown personally to the participants.

The intelligent and cautious host contacts this potential understudy well in advance of the workshop, and calling upon past favors, gets a commitment from the person to serve as substitute in an emergency. For those few times when an emergency does occur, it is very likely that the hometown audience will be shocked and delighted to find this unknown sage right in their midst.

RULE 7 FOR SPONSORS OF WORKSHOPS. *Always have a prepared back-up speaker— even if it is only yourself.*

Where you have two or three speaker-leaders instead of just one, the Mack truck principle is less crucial. The remaining speakers can be prevailed upon to speak more slowly (usually a good idea anyway) or to lengthen time periods for group activities (also a good idea).

Another Numbers Game

As mentioned, having two or more speakers gives protection against Mack truck eventualities. It also is protection against the "single deadly speaker syndrome." Indeed, only a few people are interesting, as speakers, for more than half a day. Alternating leadership refreshes an audience even better than a coffee break. In addition, since audience members are likely to respond to different approaches, having a variety of speakers ensures that more people will be pleased with the workshop.

Know Your Speaker-Leaders!

The host should never select a workshop leader sight-unseen. One cannot assume that someone who writes well will speak well, nor that someone who speaks well will be able to organize and run a workshop. Writing, speaking, and workshop organizing require different talents. One cannot assume that fame—or notoriety—confers the ability to run a workshop; some important and well-known nurses mumble or get nervous in front of audiences. In addition, some up-and-coming nurse who is relatively new on the scene may work harder at preparing and presenting a workshop than the established nurse leader.

Controlling the Agenda

The host should retain control of the workshop agenda. He has the right to examine and make suggestions concerning the day's scheduling if the schedule has been left to the speaker. If there are several speakers, the host probably will devise the schedule himself. The following timing factors are important to the success or failure of a workshop relevant to the agenda preparation.

1. Schedule a morning and afternoon coffee break, and see that the speaker does not ignore these breaks. Lots of work gets done at coffee time—meeting new people, exchanging ideas and responses.

2. Post a finishing time, and see that it is observed. Participants need to be able to arrange other obligations around workshop hours. Many will plan to see to other work duties at the close of the workshop day. They will be resentful, therefore, if you infringe on this time by ignoring the scheduled closing time.

3. Insist that the agenda alternate speaking and group activities. No participant can tolerate a whole day of lecture, sitting on the same uncomfortable chair. Even those who dislike group activities will welcome the chance that group formation gives them for moving about.

4. Control the time for evaluation activities. If evaluation is left as an optional activity at the end of the final day, many participants may neglect to fill out the forms. As the host, one has the right to review all evaluations; the speaker has the same right. One also has the right to expect evaluations from participants and to schedule time for this activity.

HOST COURTESIES

When a single speaker-leader assumes major responsibility for a workshop, it is important that the host support services facilitate the task. There are a few extra touches that a speaker will really appreciate for a workshop endeavor.

1. Make clear to participants the relationship between host and speaker. If the speaker is from another place or institution, tell the audience that the *hosts* will answer "ways and means" and orienting-type questions. Otherwise, participants inevitably bother the speaker with questions which she cannot answer: Where is the nearest bookstore? The ladies room? How many nursing students are on this campus? Where does the bus stop?

2. If you *do* have a bookstore and your speaker *does* have a recently published book, see that copies are available for purchase. Some participants get very angry with the speaker when copies are not available; they fail to recognize that the local bookstore is not the speaker's turf. (She probably cannot even find it, let alone tell participants whether or not it carries her book.)

3. Predetermine the final closing time of the last day with care. Consider local train, plane, and bus times if your audience must travel to get home. Do not let your speaker be hung with requests for different closing times. (When this happens, she cannot win. If she quits early to please travelers, some participants inevitably will complain that they didn't get their full dollar's worth. If she does not

quit early, the shuffling of "early leavers" disrupts proceedings so much that she and the remaining audience are distracted.) As host, one can help by setting some clear guidelines for program closure.

4. Remember that the speaker has been "on stage" all day and probably is exhausted. An "evening out" invitation is nice but not essential. If the host extends an invitation, he should make sure that the situation is really a social one, not putting the speaker in a position where she has to go back "on stage" for another audience.

SUGGESTIONS FOR LEADERS OF WORKSHOPS

The following suggestions are not related to educational theory or theory of instruction. Certainly, the workshop leader needs all the educational preparation she can get, but these mundane hints may be every bit as important to the success of a workshop.

1. Workshop leading is half education and half presentation. If a speaker is not a bit of a thespian, she should not conduct workshops. One major job of the workshop leader is to make the audience believe that the topic under discussion is one of vital and special importance to her and to them. If the leader finds herself unable to evince this enthusiasm for a given subject matter, then she should refuse to do workshops on that topic.

2. In lecture-discussion, the speaker must "play to the audience." This means that she must learn to read audience responses. If they miss a critical point, it should be reworded. If the audience interests lie in different aspects than those anticipated by the speaker, she must adjust her game plan. If the workshop extends over a number of days, the speaker should revise her upcoming presentation each evening on the basis of audience feedback.

3. Splitting people into work groups is

always a problem. There is no single right answer. Sometimes it is effective if people who work together solve problems together in a small group activity. More often it is desirable to split friends and cohorts so that each will be exposed to new ideas and new people. This is one of the purposes of most workshops. Nevertheless, most acquaintances will stay together unless the speaker has some scheme for distributing them over different groups. The speaker needs to have a distribution system planned in advance.

4. Work group size should be kept small enough for maximum participation, yet large enough for sharing of a variety of ideas and opinions. Groups of seven to eight are probably ideal, but constraints on group size may exist because of physical facilities or size of the total audience. Group exercises in which each group plans strategies for a single role player will be constrained by the number of roles that exists in the subsequent role play.

5. The speaker must consider the physical facilities in planning work groups. Every group *must* have its own territory in respect to acoustics. If one must choose between smaller-sized groups infringing upon each other's air space or larger groups with better acoustics, the latter is preferable. The speaker should not try to accomplish the impossible, e.g., to divide an audience into work groups in auditoriums with immovable seating.

6. Giving directions for small work group activities is a real art. The leader should pretest the clarity of her written directions, revising them until they are absolutely clear. The leader should not expect small work groups to remember verbal directions; such directions should be repeated on the printed worksheets.

7. The leader must be sensitive to her effect upon the small work groups. If her presence in a work group robs natural group leaders of their roles, then she should play a consultant role, entering groups only when members request assistance. If the leader's personality

allows a small group to accept her as a regular member, then she can feel free to participate in this manner. In any case, the small work groups are the places for participant leadership, not for further dominance by the speaker-leader.

8. No matter what principle is used to create small work groups—chance assignment, geographic or positional distribution schemes, or other systems—it is likely that at least one group will be nonproductive. The nonfunctional group occurs because of personality clashes among members or because of lack of participant leadership. This is one case in which the leader may choose to participate and impose a structure of her own on group activities.

9. Where there are several group activities in a workshop, the leader must decide whether or not to form new groups for each separate activity. If one or more groups is nonfunctional in the original grouping, she has no choice but to alter group composition for subsequent activities. If all groups happen to have worked effectively in the first group exercise, then the leader may weigh the values of keeping the same groups versus forming new groups for the second exercise.

Any group takes considerable time in negotiating its stated and unstated rules and in determining the roles assigned to and accepted by various members. Thus, retaining the same small groups eliminates renegotiating activity, allowing more time to be devoted to the assigned task. Maintaining the same groups through diverse assignments may be essential if the workshop tasks require that each subsequent exercise build upon the product of the preceding exercise. Diversity in group formation has the value of exposing each participant to new contacts, different ideas, and different methods of proceeding with group activities. It is up to the leader to determine how often new groups should be formed.

10. There must be some way for each small work group to give feedback concerning its production. One of the best ways is to reduce those results to audiovisual form. Transparencies are acceptable and creating them also provides an audiovisual preparation lesson. Plain old chart pads and crayons are better, however, because reports of various groups can be plastered on the walls for side-by-side comparison. In instances where there are just too many groups for individual reports, group reports can be placed around the walls just before a coffee break. Then participants can browse through reports while on break. This practice also gives the leader time to select out the three or four reports which she will want to discuss before the total audience. The leader, of course, selects reports for both content and contrast.

11. Review and critique of group work is the hardest part of leadership in a workshop. The typical sequence for review consists of: (a) presentation of results by a representative of the group, (b) additional comments from other ingroup members, (c) questions, comments, and evaluation by audience members, and (d) summary review and critique by the workshop leader. Even if all the key points have been made before she speaks, the leader should give her summary. At this time, she adds any vital aspects overlooked by the audience and reacts to each group's individual work. She also compares and contrasts results produced by different groups.

12. Workshop speakers should not be distressed by conflicting evaluations from participants. Approximately half of any group will prefer group activities and will claim there were not enough of them. The other half will call group activities a waste of time and castigate the speaker for not lecturing more often. A moment's reflection will make the speaker realize that there is no way to please such a group. Indeed, if results run highly in favor of either the lecture activities or the group activities, it probably reflects a defective performance in one area rather than a good performance in the other.

SUMMARY

From the perspective of the speaker-leader, then, these are some of the major points that contribute to the success or failure of a workshop. Seldom is a workshop so well planned—by both host and speaker—that it avoids each and every problem. Perhaps the highest feasible goal is to minimize errors. It may be that a different, but complementary, list of hints for workshops can be produced from the other side of the table, i.e., from the perspective of the host institution. The author would welcome the chance to read a list of "do's and don'ts" written from that perspective.

Finally, it seems necessary to comment once again on the nature of the items discussed in this article. Few of these items are inherently interesting or challenging. They, at best, are merely housekeeping chores. And items of this sort are probably those of least interest to the educator. Nevertheless, given the structure and format of the workshop mode of education, these housekeeping chores, if ignored, can detract from the intellectual and educational aspects of the endeavor. Adequate "housekeeping" alone cannot produce an excellent workshop, but poor housekeeping can assure that an otherwise well-prepared workshop will necessarily fail.

MAKING PRESS INTERVIEWS WORK FOR YOU

By Lynne Brodie Welch and C. William Welch

Reprinted with permission from *The Journal of Nursing Administration,* Volume 9, Number 5, 1979, pp. 48-49.

As a nurse administrator, you should consider the value of press interviews when something new or different is happening in your institution or when a delicate or potentially explosive situation comes up. Press interviews provide an opportunity to create a positive public image for your institution, which will encourage people to want to be associated with it. By reminding the public of your institution's unique function and services, you can engender financial support through donations, gifts, or scholarships; political support through connections with community, state, and federal leaders; and public support through a positive image in the minds of consumers and potential consumers—patients, employees, or students.

Press interviews can help you smooth troubled situations and make them work to your advantage. For instance, telling your side of a story during a strike demonstration or grievance procedure can do much to gain support for your point of view. If legal action or consumer complaints against your institution have been publicized, you should discuss the situation in a knowledgeable, competent manner, explaining your side of the situation. In this way you can help maintain your institution's credibility in the public mind.

Here are some tips to help make your press interview more effective.

PLANNING FOR THE INTERVIEW

Accept or inititate an interview only if you have something to say that is new, interesting, or newsworthy. An interview without substance will turn the journalist off, maybe for a long time. If the journalist has asked for the interview, find out why he wants to talk with you and decide whether you are the appropriate person to be interviewed. No matter how much you want to be interviewed, resist the temptation if you know that someone else has more information or expertise in the topic that is to be discussed.

It is a good idea, particularly if the journalist is on a "fishing expedition," to spend some time before the interview thinking of topics to discuss. Good subjects might be a new project or procedure at your institution, a human interest story, or some information that is not generally known about your institution. Knowing the subject in advance will give you an opportunity to do some homework and prepare information that might be needed, such as charts or statistics.

Know the journalist, his publication, and

its audience before you start the interview. If you are not familiar with the publication, get copies of several recent back issues. Reading the table of contents and a few of the articles will give you its flavor and help you adapt your presentation to the audience. Read several articles that the journalist has written so that you are familiar with his style and approach. During the interview, it does not hurt to have a copy of the publication on your desk or to mention some of the interviewer's articles. Most people respond positively to interest in their work.

Plan the time and the place for the interview. If it is to be a general discussion, it could take place over lunch or coffee. On the other hand, if you will be dealing with very specific information involving charts or other printed material, your office or a conference room is probably best. Allow extra time in your schedule; an interview often takes longer than you think it will.

You should be careful about interviewing exclusively with one publication, for its competitors may decide that you are playing favorites. To avoid hard feelings, spread out your interviews and consider releasing information to a number of publications at the same time.

THE INTERVIEW PROCESS

If you are in a new or unusual location, be sure to give the journalist good directions. If he has been looking for you for some time, you could be off to a bad start. Make your interviewer feel welcome by alerting your secretary or receptionist that he is coming. During the interview, to make sure that you have no interruptions, have your secretary intercept incoming calls. The only outgoing calls you should make are calls to get information the journalist needs at that moment. It is best for the continuity of the interview to do this toward the end of the interview.

Find out at the onset whether or not you will be able to check the article for accuracy before it is published, because this may affect how you conduct youself during the interview. Tread carefully in this area, because many journalists do not like to have their material checked by the interviewee before publication. If the journalist agrees, you may want to read over the article for accuracy. Journalists want to present accurate material, and welcome clarification of a point; however, the journalist will present the material as he sees it, not necessarily as you might present it.

You are being interviewed to tell about and sell something, so be sure to show your enthusiasm and involvement. Sell the journalist on you and your subject, and be quotable. Short, pointed statements colorfully put are far more quotable than long, drawn-out statements. If you use examples and amusing stories to make your point, you provide the journalist with something eye-catching to include in the article. Stories tend to generate interest in the subject being written about and increase the audience for the article.

Do not take chances with off-the-record information. If you do not want to see it in print, do not say it. Be alert for trick questions that may tempt you to make unwise statements. However, it is important to tell the bad news along with the good. Few subjects have no negative side, but be as positive as possible. If you do not know the answer to a question, say so, but offer to find out if you think you can.

In talking with an interviewer, think of the readers of the publication, and use technical words or abbreviations only if you know they will be generally understood. When you do use technical information, statistics, or jargon, it is wise to put the information in writing to help assure accuracy and minimize misunderstanding. Most journalists will welcome written clarification. Offer photographs for illustration if you have them, as they add to reader interest.

Even though you are the one being interviewed, you should not do all of the talking—nobody wants to listen to a monologue. You can ask the interviewer questions to sharpen the focus of the interview, suggest other avenues of interest, and clarify the subject. Be prepared to take the lead and to suggest topics for discussion or other people to interview. Not all journalists are skilled interviewers, and we all have off days; most interviewers will be grateful for the assistance.

If there is a third person present, such as a member of your public relations department, he or she should not do the talking for you, or it will appear that you are not being candid. If more than one person from your institution is to be interviewed, plan and coordinate what you will say ahead of time to avoid repetition. The interviewer does not want to hear the history of the institution twice. In group interviews, avoid getting into policy squabbles, for that reflects poorly on you and your institution and may be used to your disadvantage in the article. However, you and your colleagues should not hesitate to present differing opinions. Many times a variety of opinions is appropriate, and your institution will be seen as one that encourages individual thought.

AFTER THE INTERVIEW

Once the interview is over, follow up with any promised information promptly—journalists have deadlines. If you are able to check the article for accuracy, do so immediately and return it to the writer right away.

The interviewer will remember you better if you keep in touch by suggesting other people to interview or other topics. You will be more likely to have repeat interviews if you think of the first one as the beginning of a long relationship.

When the article is published, contact the journalist by mail or telephone to let him know that you thought it was well done or that he used an interesting approach. Such statements will further cement your relationship. You should consider using the article as a press release or reprint for additional publicity for your institution or yourself, but be sure to check into the copyright provisions.

What if something is wrong with the article? If the fault is minor, let it go. There would be little value in bringing it to the attention of the journalist or his boss. If it is a major problem, call the journalist, explain the problem, and tell him that you will write a letter to the editor containing the explanation, but you want him to know first. Then write your letter matter-of-factly. Name-calling or sarcasm will only reflect poorly on you, and will succeed in getting your name crossed off the interview list.

SUMMARY

Press interviews are a valuable public relations tool for the nurse administrator. The interview provides you an opportunity to speak to the community for the purpose of clarifying a situation, or disseminating important information about your institution. Each interview with the press should be planned with a definite focus in mind. You should be quotable, but say only those things that you would like to see in print. Keep in touch with the journalist so that you can be assured of other interviews in the future. Effective press interviews will help the public understand more about you and your institution.

REFERENCES AND NOTES

1. This model is adapted from Shannon, C., and Weaver, W. *The Mathematical Theory of Communications.* Urbana, Ill.: Copyright © 1949 by University of Illinois Press.

2. Cherry, E.G. The Communication of Information. In *Communication and Culture,* A. Smith, ed., New York: Holt, Rinehart and Winston, 1966.

3. Shannon, C. and Weaver, W. 1949.

4. Beer, S. *Decision and Control.* London: Wiley, 1966.

5. Cherry, E.G. 1966.

6. Vickers, G. A classification of systems. *General Systems* 15:3–6, 1970.

7. Cronkhite, G. *Communication and Awareness.* Menlo Park, Calif.: Cummings, 1976, pp. 283–285.

8. Cronkhite, G. 1976.

9. Borden, G.A., Gregg, R.B., and Grove, T.G. *Speech Behavior and Human Interaction.* Englewood Cliffs, N.J.: Prentice-Hall, 1969, p. 182.

10. Borden, G.A., Gregg, R.B., and Grove, T.G. 1969, p. 200.

11. Karlins, M. and Abelson, H. *Persuasion: How Opinions and Attitudes Are Changed* (2nd ed.). New York: Springer, 1970, pp. 107–132.

12. McCroskey, J.C., Larson, C.E., and Knapp, M.L. *An Introduction to Interpersonal Communication.* Englewood Cliffs, N.J.: Prentice-Hall, 1971, pp. 78–91.

13. Borden, G.A., Gregg, R.B., and Grove, T.G. 1969, p. 216.

14. Borden, G.A., Gregg, R.B., and Grove, T.G. 1969, p. 227.

15. Bettinghaus, E.P. *Persuasive Communication* (2nd ed.). New York: Holt, Rinehart, and Winston, 1973, p. 252.

16. Simons, H.W. *Persuasion: Understanding, Practice and Analysis.* Reading, Mass.: Addison-Wesley, 1976, p. 61.

17. Simons, H.W. 1976, p. 63.

18. Borden, G.A., Gregg, R.B., and Grove, T.G. 1969, p. 234.

19. Borden, G.A., Gregg, R.B., and Grove, T.G. 1969, p. 234.

20. King, R.G. *Forms of Public Address.* New York: Bobbs-Merrill, 1969, p. 22.

21. King, R.G. 1969, p. 22.

22. Borden, G.A., Gregg, R.B., and Grove, T.G. 1969, p. 241.

23. Borden, G.A., Gregg, R.B., and Grove, T.G. 1969, p. 243.

24. McCroskey, J.C., Larson, C.E., and Knapp, M.L. 1971, p. 161.

25. King, R.G. 1969, pp. 25–26.

26. King, R.G. 1969, pp. 27–28.

27. King, R.G. 1969, p. 31.

28. Borden, G.A., Gregg, R.B., and Grove, T.G. 1969, pp. 230–231.

29. Heide, W. Nursing and women's liberation—A parallel. *Am. J. Nurs.* 73(5):824, 1973.

30. Oliver, R.T. Communication and Leadership Program. Santa Ana, Calif.: Toastmasters International, 1970, p. 4.

31. Smith, O. The magic of enthusiasm. *The Toastmasters* 38(6):13, 1972.

32. Gibb, J.R. Defense Level and Influence in Small Groups. *Leadership and Interpersonal Behavior,* Petrullo, L., and Bass, B.M., eds. New York: Holt, Rinehart and Winston, 1961.

33. Gibb, J.R. Sociopsychological Processes of Group Instruction. *The Dynamics of Instructional Groups,* Henry, N.B., ed. Fifty-ninth Yearbook of the National Society for the Study of Education, Part II, 1980, pp. 115–135.

34. Reprinted with permission from the book *Parent Effectiveness Training* by Thomas Gordon. Copyright © 1970 by Thomas Gordon. Published by Dave McKay Co., Inc., pp. 41–44.

35. Gordon, T. 1970.

36. Prather, H. *Notes to Myself.* Lafayette, Calif.: Real People Press, 1970. Copyright © 1970 by Real People Press. Used with permission.

SUGGESTED READINGS

Communication Problems

Helberg, D.H. Communicating under stress. *Assoc. Op. Room Nurses* 20(11): 46–50, 1972.

McCroskey, J.C. Oral communication apprehension: A summary of recent theory and research. *Human Comm. Res.* 4(1):78–96, 1977.

Smith, C.M. Identifying blocks to communication in health care settings and a workshop plan. *J. Cont. Ed. Nurs.* 8(2):26–32, 1978.

Conferences

Cooper, S. Getting the most out of a conference. *J. Cont. Ed. Nurs.* 7(5):11–17, 1976.

Davis, L.N., and McCallon, E. Designing Learning Activities. *Planning, Conducting, Evaluating Workshops.* Austin, Texas: Learning Concepts, 1974, pp. 109–155.

Hubbard, S.M. Effective communication through oral presentation. *Oncol. Nurs. Forum* 7(2):37–40, 1980.

Hutchinson, S., and Talley, N. The group supervisory conference. *J. Nurs. Ed.* 13(9):13–17, 1974.

Mayer, G.G. and Bailey, K. Adapting patient care conferences to primary nursing. *JONA* 9(6):7–10, 1979.

Nadler, N., and Nadler, Z. Designing the Core of a Conference. *The Conference Book.* Houston, Texas: Gulf Publishing, 1977, pp. 42–66.

Nadler, L., and Nadler, Z. Linkage, Evaluation and Follow-up. *The Conference Book.* Houston, Texas. Gulf Publishing, 1977, pp. 231–247.

Palmer, M.E. Patient Care Conferences: An opportunity for meeting staff needs. *JONA* 3(2):47–53, 1979.

Plummer, E.M. The clinical conference discussion leader. *Nurs. Forum* 13(1):94–105, 1974.

Radtke, M., and Wilson, A. Team conferences that work. *Am. J. Nurs.* 73(3):506–508, 1973.

Dynamics of Communication

Costley, D.L. Basis for effective communication. *Supv. Nurse* 4(1):16–22, 1973.

Elliot, T., and Everly, G. Communication: A program design. *Supv. Nurse* 10(2):12–18, 1979.

Hasling, J. The Method of Argumentation. *The Audience, The Message, The Speaker* (2nd ed.). New York: McGraw-Hill, 1976, pp. 84–100.

Kramer, M., and Schmalenberg, C. Constructive feedback. *Nursing 77* 7(11):102–106, 1977.

Linver, S. *Speak Easy.* New York: Summit Books, 1978.

Miltz, R. Nurses improve their personal communication. *Supv. Nurse* 8(12):13–15, 1977.

Smoyak, S. The confrontation process. *Am. J. Nurs.* 74(9):1633–1635, 1974.

Veninga, R. Interpersonal feedback: A cost-benefit analysis. *JONA* 5(2):40–43, 1975.

Groups, Group Process/Exercises

Allen, F.T. Way to improve employee communications: Personnel council. *Nation's Business* 63:54–56, 1975.

Appelbaum, A.L. AHA moves toward 1980 involvement of political action committee. *Hospitals* 53(6):86–88, 1979.

Ganong, W.L., and Ganong, J.M. Reducing organizational conflict through working committees. *JONA* (1):12–19, 1972.

Hammerstand, S.M., Johnson, S.H., and Land, L.V. New graduate orientation program. *J. Cont. Ed. Nurs.* 8(5):5–11, 1978.

Miles, M.B. *Learning to Work in Groups.* New York: Teachers College Press, 1973.

Morris, K.T., and Cinnamon, K.M. *A Handbook of Verbal Group Exercises.* La Jolla, Calif.: University Associates, 1974.

Taylor, A., Rosengrant, T., Meyer, A., and Samples, B.T. *Communicating.* Englewood Cliffs, N.J.: Prentice-Hall, 1977, pp. 258–283.

Woodrow, M., and Wheat, R.P. Community forums promote health awareness. *Cross-Reference on Human Resources Management* 8(6):1–3, 1978.

Inter-Shift Reporting

Clair, L.L., and Trussel, P.M. The change of shift report: Study shows weaknesses, how it can be improved. *Hospitals* 43:91–95, October 1, 1969.

Feeley, E.M. The challenge of inter-shift reporting. *Supv. Nurse* 4(2):43–45, 1973.

Gagneaux, V., and Shaver, D.V. Distractions at nurses' stations during inter-shift report. *Nurs. Res.* 26(1):42–46, 1977.

Lavoie, D., and Foley, A. How to make change-of-shift reports more meaningful. *Nursing 73* 3(4):55–56, 1973.

Mezzanotte, E.J. Getting it together for end-of-shift reports. *Nursing 76* 6(4):21–22, 1976.

Mitchell, M. Inter-shift reports—To tape or not to tape. *Supv. Nurse* 7(10):38–39, 1976.

Wiley, L. Wadda ya say at report? *Nursing 75* 5(10):73–78, 1975.

Interviewing

Berglas, C. Employment interviews. *Supv. Nurse* 9(11):29–31, 1978.

Bermosk, L. Interviewing—A key to effective supervision. *Supv. Nurse* 4(3):46–56, 1973.

Bowden, M.S., and Carbiener, A.D. Interviewing and selecting staff: A team approach to interviewing. *Supv. Nurse* 9(11):14–26, 1978.

Cicatiello, J.S. The personal development interview. *Supv. Nurse* 6(11):15–24, 1975.

Dale, R., and Baley, K. The group interview. *Supv. Nurse* 9(11):40-44, 1978.

Kaiser, P. Ten steps to interviewing job applicants. *Am. J. Nurs.* 78(4):627–630, 1978.

Serafine, C.F. Interviewer listening. *Personnel J.* 54:398. 1975.

Welch, L.B., and Welch, C.W. Making press interviews work for you. *JONA* 9(5):48–50, 1979.

Listening

Munn, H.E. Are you a skilled listener? *Assoc. Op. Room Nurses* 25(5):994–1000, 1977.

Meetings

Doyle, M., and Straus, D. *How to Make Meetings Work: The New Interaction Method.* La Jolla, Calif.: University Associates, 1976.

Levoy, R.P. How to stretch your association meeting mileage. *Am. J. Hosp. Pharmacy* 30(11):1024–1025, 1973.

Schindler-Rainman, E., and Lippitt, R. *Taking Your Meetings Out of the Doldrums.* La Jolla, Calif.: University Associates, 1977.

Semantics and Voice

Anderson, V.A. *Training the Speaking Voice.* New York: Oxford University Press, 1977.

Deal, J. General semantics. *Supv. Nurse* 8(5):62–66, 1977.

Kell, C. Organizing and Outlining the Speech. *Fundamentals of Effective Speech Communication.* Capps, R., and O'Connor, J.R. (Eds.), Cambridge, Mass.: Winthrop, 1978, pp. 42–64.

Levenstein, A. Mind your language. *Supv. Nurse* 8:50–51, 1976.

Stone, J., and Bactiner, J. *Speaking Up: A Book for Every Woman Who Wants to Speak Effectively.* New York: McGraw-Hill, 1977.

UNIT II. WRITTEN COMMUNICATION

- *Drafting a memo*
- *Dictating letters, reports, and references*
- *Reviewing performance checklists and evaluations*
- *Approving policies, procedures, and committee minutes*
- *Improving the use of nurses' notes and care plans*
- *Sketching advertisements for vacant positions*
- *Reading job resumes*
- *Using and reading visual aids in meetings and conferences*
- *Interpreting a research article*
- *Searching the literature*
- *Coauthoring a manuscript for journal publication*
- *Maintaining a continual surveillance of relevant journals, texts, and organizational publications in your area*

Is this an exhaustive list of expected administrative and management communications? No, but its extent does emphasize the amount of time and energy that many nursing administrators and managers spend sending and receiving written messages.

Expressing yourself in writing and reading about other people's ideas and projects presents an immediate challenge to both senders and receivers of written messages. First, the sender is never totally certain who her reader will be. We assume we know who is going to read our letters, memos, and articles, but rarely can we know for certain, or actually control, who reads them. In contrast, when a sender intentionally prepares an oral or nonverbal message, this problem is less likely to occur because the sender can see or verify the audience for whom her message is intended. Second, in many written messages there is little or no opportunity for the receiver to clarify or validate her perception of the sender's message. In other words, the feedback loop between sender and receiver is delayed by time and distance, and often never really takes place at all. Consequently, the sender of a written message often only has one real chance to send a message that clearly shares or explains her thoughts. Even then, written communication is problematic because of the myriad of unique personal experiences, values, and beliefs through which the receiver perceives a message. In this unit, the reader's attention is called to this time-consuming communication mode which, despite its importance, has not been given detailed exposure in the nursing administration literature.

Chapter 4 focuses on three important aspects of the nursing and allied health literature: important literature resources to be aware of, use and dissemination of the literature in hospitals, and results of a survey of 65 nursing and health science journal editors on writing for publication. In Chapter 5 the reader's attention is narrowed to the more day-to-day components of written communication. Selections cover the writing of policies, procedures, and nursing standards, as well as making visual aids to use in meetings or workshops and drafting a memo.

4.   The Professional Literature

In this chapter, Reference Sources for Nursing *by the Interagency Council on Library
Resources for Nursing merits special attention. This listing, periodically updated by a
committee of the Medical Library Association, identifies the major literary and media
resources in nursing in the United States and
Canada. Responsible decision making by
nursing administrators and staff development
directors is based on timely information and
accurate documentation from the professional
literature. Try supplementing your selected
journal reading and literature searches with
one or two of the literature access tools listed
in this selection. Suggestions for using such
references in day-to-day practice are included
in our note at the end of the bibliography.
Also, remember that many of the prices listed
in the selection may have risen since the article
was first published.*

*In the second reading, our own article, we
ask how a group of educators who provide
instruction for the mass of practicing nurses
in short-term acute-care hospitals use and
share instructional resources and professional
journals in their immediate work setting. As
you read this survey, rate your own literature
surveillance habits against those reported. If
you value keeping abreast of the literature
and sharing such information with colleagues
and staff, have you identified these expecta-*

*tions in current job descriptions and evalua-
tion criteria? If you are not satisfied with
available literature and resource facilities in
your department or hospital library, what can
you do to direct funds toward improving this
condition or to acquire outside funds for
more journals and relevant texts?*

*Concluding this chapter is McCloskey's
survey of 65 nursing and allied health journal
editors. This selection asks editors for basic
facts and statistics about their journal's publishing practices that both novice and experienced writers will appreciate knowing.
Indeed, beginning writers and those nursing
administrators just beginning to consider
preparing a manuscript for publication review
will want to savor, reflect upon, and then
reread the text in this selection.*

*Eventually, inexperienced writers, espe-
cially those planning to climb to the heights of
academia, will also want to read Styles' "Why
Publish," and Lewis' excellent editorials "Pretentious Prose" and "What Bugs Editors."
Finally, for a refreshingly honest, sympa-
thetic account of journal article publishing
with a happy ending, you can supplement the
last selection with Perry's "The Trials and
Tribulations of a Would-Be Author." (See the
Writing for Publication section of this unit's
Suggested Readings for bibliographic details.)*

REFERENCE SOURCES FOR NURSING

Revised by a committee of the Interagency
Council on Library Resources for Nursing

This is the tenth revision of a list of reference works for nurses, including a Canadian supplement. Although it does not purport to be definitive, it will guide a nurse to discovering materials in subjects immediate to her profession. Selected sources for related disciplines and general literature are included as well. This listing may also be useful to librarians responsible for nursing libraries. Addresses for most publishers can be found in *Bowker's Medical Books in Print* and addresses for organizations in *Encyclopedia of Associations.*

Whether a student, administrator, educator, or a practitioner at any level and in any setting, whether she is researching a subject or trying to improve her skills, a nurse will find these sources helpful.

Listings are by type of publication; that is, abstract journals, bibliographies, and so forth. Thus, if a nurse were interested in home health care, she might turn to the *International Nursing Index* or *Cumulative Index to Nursing and Allied Health Literature* for periodical literature on the subject. Where to explore educational programs or research grants, nursing history, pharmacology, or legal questions, and sources for statistics are shown as well.

An effort has been made to check the most recent sources and editions; since compiling a reference book is a time-consuming task and expected dates of publication are seldom realized, works in progress are not listed.

Alternate suggestions are given for most reference sources, since the editors anticipate that some nurses must consult libraries with limited collections.

All prices cited are from 1978.

Abstract Journals

Abstracts of Hospital Management Studies. University of Michigan School of Public Health, Cooperative Information Center for Hospital Management Studies, 109 South Observatory, Ann Arbor, Mich. 48109. Quarterly, with annual cumulations. Annual subscription, $35.

Abstract of Reports of Studies in Nursing. In *Nursing Research* beginning with Vol. 9, No. 2, 1960. Indexed by author and subject in the *Cumulative Index to Nursing Research.*

Abstracts of Studies in Public Health Nursing, 1924–1957. In *Nursing Research,* 8:45–115, Spring 1959.

Medical Care Reviews (Previously titled *Public Health Economics and Medical Care Abstracts*). University of Michigan, School of Public Health, Bureau of Public Health Economics, Ann Arbor, Mich. 48109. Monthly, except September. Annual subscription, $15.

Rehabilitation Literature. Chicago, National Easter Seal Society for Crippled Children and Adults. Monthly. Annual subscription, $12.50. Review articles, book reviews, abstracts, and comments.

Resources in Vocational Education. AIM/ARM Project, Center for Vocational Education, Ohio State University, 1960 Kenny Road, Columbus, Ohio 43210. Bimonthly, $34. Abstracts research, instructional, and other materials in vocational and technical education.

Other abstract journals of interest to nurses are *Excerpta Medica, Abstracts for Social Workers, Biological Abstracts, Chemical Abstracts. Dissertation Abstracts International, Nutrition Abstracts and Reviews, Psychological Abstracts,* and *Sociological Abstracts.*

Audiovisuals

Catalogs

Educators Guide to Free Audio and Video Materials. W.A. Wittrich and J.L. Berger. 24th rev. ed. Educators Progress Service, Dept. A4A, Randolph, Wis., 53956. 1977. $10.50.

Educators Guide to Free Films. J.C. Doffer and M.F. Horkheimer, Eds. 37th ed. Randolph, Wis., Educators Progress Service, 1977. $12.75.

Educators Guide to Free Filmstrips. J.C. Diffor and M.F. Horkheimer, Eds. 29th ed. Randolph, Wis., Educators Progress Service, 1977. $10.00.

8mm Films in Medicine and Health Sciences, R.B. Benschoter, Ed. 3rd ed. Biomedical Communications Division, University of Nebraska Medical Center, 42nd and Dewey Avenue, Omaha, Neb. 68105. 1977. $9.00.

Health Sciences Video Directory. L. Eidelberg, Ed. Shelter Books, 218 East 19th St., New York, 10003. 1977. $27.50.

Index to Health and Safety Education-Multimedia. 3rd ed. The National Information Center for Educational Media (NICEM), publications available from the University of Southern California, National Information Center for Educational Media, University Park, Los Angeles, Calif. 90007. 1977. $47.00.

Index to Psychology-Multimedia. 3rd ed. 4 vols. The National Information Center for Educational Media (NICEM), publications available from the University of Southern California, National Information Center for Educational Media; University Park, Los Angeles, Calif. 90007. $109.50.

U.S. Library of Congress Catalogs: Films and Other Materials for Projection (Formerly *Library of Congress Catalog—Motion Pictures and Filmstrips*). Cataloging Distribution Service, Library of Congress, Building No. 159, Navy Yard Annex, Washington, D.C. 20541. 1973. $65.00. Three quarterly issues and annual cumulation. (Quinquennial cumulations available.)

U.S. National Library of Medicine. *AVLINE Catalog.* 1975–76. DHEW Pub. No. (NIH) 77–1295. Washington, D.C., U.S. Government Printing Office, 1977. $5.00. The catalog is arranged in subject and procurement source sections; no access by title is provided. Lists items catalogued by the National Library of Medicine (NLM) from November 1975 through December 1976 for the AVLINE (Audio Visuals on-LINE) data base. Updates for the items catalogued in 1977 will appear quarterly in the *NIM Current Catalog;* AVLINE section.

U.S. National Medical Audiovisual Center Catalog. Audiovisuals for the Health Scientist. DHEW Pub. No. (NIH) 77-506. Washington, D.C.: U.S. Government Printing Office, 1977. $4.25.

Selected Additional Publications

Anglo-American Cataloging Rules. North American Text. Chapter 12, Revised; Audiovisual Media and Special Instructional Materials. Chicago, American Library Association, 1975. $1.50 (Separately published monograph.)

Audio Cyclopedia. H.M. Tremaine. 2nd ed. Howard W. Sams & Co., Box 558, Indianapolis, Ind. 46268. 1969. $34.00.

Audio-Visual Equipment Directory, 1977–78. S. Herickes, Ed. 23rd ed. Fairfax, Va. National Audio-Visual Association, 1977. $17.00 prepaid, $18.50 billed.

Audiovisual Market Place: A Multimedia Guide— 1976–77. J.A. Neal, Ed. 6th ed. New York, R.R. Bowker, 1976. $19.95.

Developing Multi-Media Libraries. W.B. Hicks and A. Tillin. New York, R.R. Bowker. 1970. $13.95.

Library Technology Reports. Chicago, American Library Association, 1965-, bimonthly, $125.00. This periodical includes evaluations of multimedia equipment.

Management of 35mm Medical Slides. A Strohlein. United Business Publications, Inc., subsidiary of Media Horizons, 750 Third Ave., New York, 10017. 1975. $11.00.

Media: A Pocket Guide. H. Arrasjid and D.A. Arrasjid. 3rd ed. MSS Information Corp., P.O. Box 978, Edison, N.J. 08817. 1972. $8.50.

Media Equipment: a Guide and Dictionary. K.C. Rosenberg and J.S. Doskey. Libraries Unlimited, P.O. Box 263, Littleton, Colo. 80120. 1976. $11.50.

Operating Audio-Visual Equipment. E.S. Eboch and G.W. Cochern. 2nd rev. ed. Chandler Publishing, San Francisco, Calif. Orders: Harper and Row, 1968. $4.95.

Organizing Nonprint Materials. A Guide for Librarians. J.E. Daily. Part I: pp. 3–113 recommended. Marcel Dekker, 95 Madison Ave., New York, 10016. 1972. $12.50.

Planning and Producing Audiovisual Materials. J.E. Kemp, 3rd ed. New York: T.Y. Crowell, 1975. Orders: Harper & Row, $11.50.

Standards for Cataloging Non-Print Materials. 4th ed. Washington, D.C.: Educational Communications and Technology, 1975. $4.95.

Bibliographies and Book Lists

Administrator's Collection. AHA Catalog No. 1052. Chicago: American Hospital Association, Bacon Library, 1977. $2.00.

Allied Health Book List, 1977–1978. Majors Scientific Books, Inc. 8911 Directors Row, Dallas. Texas 75247. Free.

Books of the Year. In each January issue of the *American Journal of Nursing.*

Bowker's Medical Books in Print. New York: R.R. Bowker, annual. $37.50.

Brandon, A.N. "Selected List of Books and Journals for the Small Medical Library." 7th rev. *Bulletin of the Medical Library Association,* 65:191–215, April 1977. Reprints available from the Medical Library Association.

Council of National Library Associations, Joint Committee on Library Service in Hospitals. *Basic List of Guides and Information Sources for Professional and Patients' Libraries in Hospials,* 8th ed. Chicago: The Council, 1973. Single copy free from the American Hospital Association.

Medical Reference Works, 1679–1966. J.B. Blake and C. Roos, Eds. Medical Library Association, Chicago 60611. $10.00. Suppl. 1 (1967–1968), $3.75; suppl. 2 (1969–1972), $6.95; suppl. 3 (1973–1974), $4.95.

Shaffer, D.E. *Library Resources for Nurses: A Basic Collection for Supporting the Nursing Curriculum.* Dale E. Shaffer, 437 Jennings Ave., Salem, Ohio 44460. 1974.

U.S. Department of Health, Education and Welfare. *Catalog of Publications. July 1975.* DHEW Pub. No. 75-1. Washington, D.C.: U.S. Government Printing Office, 1977. $1.75.

World Health Organization. *Catalog of Publications,* 1947–1973. Suppl. 1974–1976. Available free from the WHO, U.N. Plaza, New York, 10017.

Dictionaries and Word Books

Acronyms, Initialisms and Abbreviations Dictionary: a Guide to Alphabetical Designations, Contractions, Acronyms, Initialisms, and Similar Condensed Appellations. Ellen T. Crowley, Ed. 5th ed. Detroit, Gale Research, 1976. $38.50.

Discursive Dictionary of Health Care. Prepared by the Staff for the Use of the Subcommittee on Health and the Environment of the Committee on Interstate and Foreign Commerce, U.S. House of Representatives, Washington, D.C.: U.S. Government Printing Office, 1965. $2.40.
Prepared to clarify terms used in the debate on national health insurance. Includes acronyms.

Dorland, W.A. *Dorland's Illustrated Medical Dictionary.* 25th ed. Philadelphia: W.B. Saunders, 1974. $22.50.

Duncan, H.A. *Duncan's Dictionary for Nurses.* New York: Springer Publishing, 1971. $7.50.

Garb, Solomon, and others. *Abbreviations and Acronyms in Medicine and Nursing,* New York: Springer Publishing, 1976. $6.95; $3.95, paperback.

Hinsie, L.E. *Psychiatric Dictionary.* 4th ed. New York: Oxford University Press, 1970. $22.50.

Jablonski, S. *Illustrated Dictionary of Eponymic Syndromes & Diseases & Their Symptoms.* Philadelphia: W.B. Saunders, 1969. $13.75.

Megalini, S. *Dictionary of Medical Syndromes.* Philadelphia: J.B. Lippincott, 1970. $18.

Miller, B.J. *Encyclopedia & Dictionary of Medicine & Nursing.* Philadelphia: W.B. Saunders, 1972. $10.95.

Roget's International Thesaurus. 3rd ed. New York: T.Y. Crowell, 1962. $6.95.

Skinner, H.A. *Origin of Medical Terms.* 2nd ed. New York: Hafner Press, 1970. $17.95.

Stedman's Medical Dictionary. 23rd ed. Baltimore: Williams and Wilkins, 1976. $21.95.

Steen, E.R. *Medical Abbreviations.* 3rd ed. Philadelphia: F.A. Davis, 1973. $6.00.

Tabler, C.W. *Cyclopedic Medical Dictionary.* 12th ed. Philadelphia: F.A. Davis, 1973. $9.95.

Webster's New Collegiate Dictionary. Springfield, Mass.: Merriam, 1973. $8.95–$10.95.

Webster's Third New International Dictionary. Unabridged. Springfield, Mass.: Merriam, 1976. $59.95–$75.00.

Directories

American Hospital Association. *AHA Guide to the Health Care Field, 1977* (Formerly, Part 2 of the 2nd August issue of *Hospitals*). Chicago: American Hospital Association, $25. (1978 ed. $30 to members; $37.50 to nonmembers)

American Medical Directory. 26th ed. Chicago: American Medical Association, 1974. $125.

American Men and Women of Science. 13th ed. J.C. Press, Ed. 7 vols. New York: R.R. Bowker, 1976. $300.

Catholic Hospital Association 1977 Guide Book. St. Louis: Catholic Hospital Association, annual. $10.

Directory of Medical Specialists, 1977–78. 18th ed. 2 vols. Chicago: Marquis Who's Who, 1977. $69.50.

Encyclopedia of Associations, 11th ed. Vol. 1: *National Organizations of the United States.* Detroit: Gale Research, 1977. $70.

Foundation Directory, 6th ed. New York, Columbia University Press. 1977. $35.

Health Care Directory, 77–78. C.T. Norback and P.G. Norback, Eds. Oradell, N.J.: Medical Economics Co., 1977. $150.

Health Organizations of the United States, Canada and Internationally; a Directory of Voluntary Associations, Professional Societies and Other Groups Concerned with Health and Related Fields, 4th ed. Paul Wasserman and J.K. Bossart, Eds. Anthony T. Kruzas, Associates, 1977. Available from Edwards Brothers, 2500 So. State St., Ann Arbor, Mich. 48104. $29.

International Directory of Nurses with Doctoral Degrees, Kansas City, Mo.: American Nurses' Foundation, 1973. $8.50; $6.50, paperback. Originally published in *Nursing Research.*

National Health Directory, 1977. Washington, D.C.: Science and Health Publications, 1977. $19.50.

First directory of decision makers in health and medicine at federal, regional, and state levels.

Official directories of nursing and related organizations, including voluntary organizations and governmental bureaus, are published in the April issue of *The American Journal of Nursing* and the March and September issues of *Nursing Outlook.*

Scientific, Technical and Related Societies of the United States. 9th ed. Washington, D.C.: National Academy of Sciences, 1971. $13.50.

Standard Periodical Directory. 5th ed. New York: Oxbridge Publishing Co., 1977. $75.

Ulrich's International Periodicals Directory, 1977–78. 17th ed. New York: R.R. Bowker, 1977. $57.50.

U.S. Government Manual, 1977/78. Washington, D.C.: U.S. Government Printing Office, 1977, $6.50.

Who's Who in America, 1976–1977. 39th ed. Chicago: Marquis Who's Who, 1976. $72.50.

Who's Who in Health Care. 1st ed., New York: Hanover Publications, 1977. $60.

Who's Who of American Women, 1977–1978. 10th ed. Chicago: Marquis Who's Who, 1977. $52.50.

Yearbook of International Organizations, 16th ed. Brussels: Union of International Associations. 1977. Distributed by International Publications Service, 114 E. 32nd St., New York 10016.

Webster's New World Thesaurus (Fontana, 1971, $4.95) is our favorite thesaurus and don't forget *The Nurse's Almanac* edited by H.S. Rowland (Germantown, Md.: Aspen Systems Corp., 1978, $24.95). This last reference includes brief descriptions and statistics on a wide spectrum of topics in and related to nursing. The following sections will provide nursing administrators

with a wealth of introductory comments and statistics for speeches, meetings, and reports: News Highlights, Costs of Health Care, Nursing Administrators, Professional Standards Review Organization (PSRO), Unions, Finding a Job, Nursing and the Law, Hospitals, Patient Rights, and Women Today.

In addition, administrators in staff development, continuing education, and undergraduate as well as graduate nursing education will benefit from *Lippincott's Guide to Nursing Literature* (Philadelphia: J.B. Lippincott, 1980, $10.95)— the first and only complete guide to nursing journals and references published in the United States, Canada, and Great Britain. In this book, Binger and Jensen describe professional journals, references, and resources pertinent to nurses, identify their particular usefulness to specific audiences, and highlight the special features of more than 300 publications for nurses. Also included are chapters on the "do's," "don'ts," and "how to's" of searching the literature, monitoring information in your specialty, and preparing a journal article for journal publication.

Drug Lists and Pharmacologies

American Drug Index, 1977. N.F. Billups, Ed. Philadelphia: J.B. Lippincott, 1977. $14.50.

American Hospital Formulary Service. Washington, D.C.: American Society of Hospital Pharmacists, 1976. $35.00. Looseleaf in 2 vols.; updated six times a year. $17.50 yearly supplement.

A.M.A. Drug Evaluations. 3rd ed. Littleton, Mass.: Publishing Sciences Group, 1977, $29.50.

Current Drug Handbook, 1976–78. M.W. Falconer et al., Eds. Philadelphia: W.B. Saunders, 1976. $6.50.

Drugs in Current Use and New Drugs 1977. Walter Modell, Ed. New York: Springer Publishing, 1977. $6.50.

Drugs of Choice, 1976–77. Walter Modell, Ed. St. Louis: C.V. Mosby, 1976. $28.50.

Facts and Comparisons. 1100 Oran Drive, St. Louis, Mo. 63137. Annual, updated monthly. $43.50. Suppl. $28.50. Available on microfiche from Plaza Bank, Suite 820, 2200 West Port Plaza Drive, St. Louis, Mo. 63141. $43.50.

Goodman, L.S., and A. Gilman, *Pharmacological Basis of Therapeutics.* 5th ed. New York: Macmillan, 1975. $32.50.

Guide to Drug Information. Winifred Sewell. Hamilton, Ill.: Drug Intelligence Publications, 1976. $13.00.

Handbook of Nonprescriptions Drugs, 5th ed. Washington, D.C.: American Pharmaceutical Association, 1977. $12.50.

Merck Index: an Encyclopedia of Chemicals and Drugs, 9th ed. Rahway, N.J.: Merck, 1976. $18.00.

Merck Manual of Diagnosis and Therapy. 13th ed. Rahway, N.J.: Merck, 1977. $9.75.

Modern Drug Encyclopedia and Therapeutic Index. 14th ed. New York: Yorke Medical Book, Dun-Donnelley, 1977. $34.00.

Nurse's Drug Handbook. Suzanne Loebl et al., Eds. New York: John Wiley and Sons, 1977. $10.95.

Physicians' Desk Reference to Pharmaceutical Specialties and Biologicals. 31st ed. Oradell, N.J.: Medical Economics, 1977. $11.50 (price varies with quantity purchased).

United States Dispensatory. 27th ed. Arthur Osolo and Robertson Pratt, Eds. Philadelphia: J.B. Lippincott, 1973. $30.00.

United States Pharmacopeia. 19th ed. Easton, Pa.: Mack, 1975. $30.00.

Educational Programs in Nursing

State-Approved Schools of Nursing—L.P.N./ L.V.N.

State-Approved Schools of Nursing-R.N. New York, National League for Nursing, annual. These two directories contain the fullest and most up-to-date information on schools of nursing of any publication. The League also publishes a list of all doctoral programs in nursing; separate booklets on NLN-accredited schools for master's degree, baccalaureate, diploma, associate degree, and practical nursing education; and baccalaureate programs accredited for public health nursing preparation. Should you consult a library without these NLN publications, general directories of education will include schools of nursing, for example, *Peterson's Annual Guide to Graduate and Undergraduate Study* (Princeton, N.J.: Peterson's Guides).

Histories

American Nursing by B. Kalisch and P. Kalisch (Boston: Little, Brown, 1978, $10.95) offers one of the most readable histories of American nursing that we have encountered.

Austin, A.L. *History of Nursing Source Book,* New York: G.P. Putnam's Sons, 1957. Out of print, but available in many libraries.

Clendening, L. *Source Book of Medical History.* New York: Peter Smith, 1960. $7.50.

Columbia University, Teachers College. *The Adelaide Nutting Historical Nursing Collection.* New York: The University, 1929. Out of print, but available in many libraries. A classified list of books, pamphlets, and other materials dealing with the history of nursing in America and in other countries.

Deloughery, G.L., and Griffin, G.J. *History and Trends of Professional Nursing.* 8th ed. St. Louis: C.V. Mosby, 1977. $8.50.

Dolan, J. *Nursing in Society: a Historical Perspective.* 13th ed. Philadelphia: W.B. Saunders, 1973. $10.75.

Garrison, F.H. *History of Medicine.* 4th ed. Philadelphia: W.B. Saunders 1929; reprint 1960. $19.50.

Grippando, G.M. *Nursing Perspectives and Issues.* Albany, Delmar, 1977. $9.32.

Notable American Women, 1607–1950; a Biographical Dictionary. 3 vols. Cambridge, Mass.: Harvard University Press, 1971. $75.

Nutting, M.A., and Dock, L.L. *History of Nursing.* 4 vols. (Vols. 3 and 4 edited and in part written by Miss Dock.) New York: G.P. Putnam's Sons, 1907–1912. Reprint 1974, Numarc Books, P.O. 2003, Buffalo, N.Y. 14219. $95.

Roberts, M.M. *American Nursing; History and Interpretation.* New York: Macmillan, 1954. Out of print, but available in many libraries.

Safier, G. *Contemporary American Leaders in Nursing; an Oral History.* New York: McGraw-Hill Book Co., 1977. $7.95.

Stewart, I.M., and Austin, A.L., Eds. *History of Nursing,* 5th ed. New York: G.P. Putnam's Sons, 1962. First four editions by L.L. Dock and I.M. Stewart under the title *Short History of Nursing.* Out of print.

Indexes

Abridged Index Medicus. Washington, D.C.: U.S. Government Printing Office, monthly. $31.35 ($39.20 foreign).

Each issue contains citations to articles in 10 English-language journals. *Cumulated Abridged Index Medicus.* 1970, 1971, $22.75; 1973, $24; 1975, $22; 1976, $23.

American Journal of Nursing Indexes. New York. American Journal of Nursing Co. Annual index available on request. Cumulative indexes; latest cumulation, 1971–1975, $8; 1966–1970, $6; 1956–1960, $4.50; 1951–1955, $3.90; 1941–1945, $2. Earlier cumulative indexes, dating from 1900, are now out of print but available in many

libraries.

Cumulative Index to Nursing and Allied Health Literature (Formerly, *Cumulative Index to Nursing Literature*). Glendale Adventist Medical Center, Box 871, Glendale, Calif. 91209. Bimonthly with annual cumulations. Annual subscription, $42.50 ($45 foreign). Earlier cumulations: 1956-1960 available from University Microfilms, Ann Arbor, Mich. 48106; 1961-1963, $23; 1964–1966, $28; 1967–1968, $28; 1969, $25.50; 1970, $25.50; 1971, $28; 1972, $28; 1973, $30.50; 1974, $33; 1975, $37.50; 1976, $40. Complete service, 1961 through 1978, $322. Nursing Subject Headings have been included in annual cumulations since 1971. An author-subject index to English-language periodical literature in nursing and paramedical fields. Includes book reviews, pamphlets, illustrated material, films, filmstrips, and recordings.

Education Index. New York: H.W. Wilson Co., monthly, except July and August, with annual cumulations. Price on service basis.

Hospital Literature Index. Chicago: American Hospital Association, quarterly, with annual cumulations. Annual subscription $60 ($66 foreign).

Hospital Literature Subject Headings. 1977, $10.

Cumulative Index of Hospital Literature. 1945– 1949, 1960-1964, out of print, but available in many libraries; member prices: 1950-1954, $10; 1955–1959, $17.50; 1965–1969, $30; 1970–1974, $75; Nonmember: 1950-1954, $12.50; 1955–1959, $22.00; 1965-1969, $37.50; 1970–1974,$93.75.

Index Medicus, Compiled by the U.S. National Library of Medicine, U.S. Government Printing Office, Washington, D.C. 20402. Monthly. Annual subscription, $170 ($213 foreign). Subject and author index to articles selected from more than 2,300 biomedical journals. Includes bibliography of medical reviews.

Cumulated Index Medicus. Annual. 1977 ed. in 14 vols. $202; domestic; $252.50 foreign. Annual cumulation of *Index Medicus,* Vols.

1-8 (1960-1967) originally published by the American Medical Association, now available from the Johnson Reprint Corp., Publisher, 111 Fifth Ave., New York 10003, at $1,600 per set.

Index to Public Health Nursing Magazine. 1909-1952, Pub. No. 21-1491. New York: National League for Nursing, 1974, $35.

International Nursing Index: 1966-present. New York: American Journal of Nursing Co., quarterly, with annual cumulations. Annual subscription, $40. Annual cumulations. vols. 1-5, 1966-1970, $7.50 per vol., 3 or more vols., $5 each; vols. 6-8, 1971-1973, $20 per vol. or all 3 vols. for $17.50 each; vols. 9-12, 1974-1977, $30 per vol. Indexes over 200 nursing journals, U.S. and foreign, and includes nursing articles indexed from nonnursing journals for *Index Medicus.*

Nursing Outlook Indexes. New York. American Journal of Nursing Co. Annual index published in December issue, 1957-1967; 1976-present (1968-1975 published separately). Cumulative indexes: 1958-1962, $4.50; 1953-1957, $4.

Nursing Research Indexes. New York. American Journal of Nursing Co. Annual index in final issue of each volume. Cumulative index, 1952-1963, $5.

Nursing Studies Index. Virginia Henderson and the Yale University Index staff. Philadelphia: J.B. Lippincott, 1963-1972. Vol. 4, 1957-1959, $15; Vol. 3, 1950-1956, $25; Vol. 2, 1930-1949, $28; Vol. 1, 1900-1929, $35; 4-vol. set. $85. An annotated guide to reported studies, research in progress, research, methods and historical materials in periodicals, books, and pamphlets published in English.

Social Sciences Index: Humanities Index. New York: H.W. Wilson Co., quarterly, with annual cumulations. Price on service basis (two separate indexes since 1974).

Remember, computerized searches of many of these indexes and abstract journals are now available to readers for a moderate fee through their local health science library or regional medical library. (See Sparks, 1978, p. 646, under Library/Learning Resources in the Suggested Readings for the address of the regional medical library nearest you.) For instance, data bases exist for *Hospital Literature Index, Resources in Education, Current Index to Journals in Education, Psychological Abstracts, Social Sciences Citation Index, Science Citation Index,* and *Dissertation Abstracts International.* And Medline picks up citations in *Index Medicus* plus several hundred nursing journals.

Legal Guides

Bullough, B., Ed. *The Law and the Expanding Nursing Role.* 3rd ed. New York: Appleton-Century-Crofts, 1975. $9.50.

Creighton, H. *Law Every Nurse Should Know.* 3rd ed. Philadelphia: W. Saunders, 1975. $10.50.

Nursing and the Law. The Health Law Center and C.J. Streiff, Eds. 2d ed. Rockville, Md.: Aspen Systems, 1975. $15.

Library Administration and Organization

Bloomquist, H. et al. Eds. *Library Practice in Hospitals: A Basic Guide.* Cleveland: Case Western Reserve University Press, 1972, $22.50.

International Nursing Index, Nursing Thesaurus. American Journal of Nursing Co. Issued as Part 2 of first issue of INI each year. Reprint available from the Editor, INI. $2 (French Thesaurus, $2).
    Guide to the use of nursing subject headings in the *International Nursing Index.*

Medical Library Association, *Handbook of Medical Library Practice.* 3rd ed. G. L. Annan and J.W. Felter, Eds. Chicago: Medical Library Association, 1970. (Out of print; new ed. in prep.)

National League for Nursing. *Guide for the Development of Libraries in Schools of Nursing,* 3rd ed. Pub. No. 14-1423. New York: National

League for Nursing, 1971, $1.25.

U.S. National Library of Medicine. *Medical Subject Headings.* Washington, D.C.: U.S. Government Printing Office, annually in the January issue of *Index Medicus.* Reprint available, 1977 ed., $8.

Research and Statistical Sources

For statistics compiled by the federal government consult the *Monthly Catalog of U.S. Government Publications* and the publication lists of the U.S. Census Bureau and the U.S. Public Health Service, especially its National Center for Health Statistics and the Bureau of Health Manpower.

A Brief Guide to Sources of Scientific and Technical Information. S. Herner. Washington, D.C.: Information Resources Press, 1978 (in press).

Facts about Nursing, 1976-7. Code D-60. Kansas City, Mo.: American Nurses' Association, 1977. $10.00.

Nation's Nurses, 1972. Inventory of Registered Nurses. A.V. Roth and A.R. Walden, Kansas City, Mo.: American Nurses' Association, 1974. $3.00.

Nurse-Faculty Census-1976. Pub. No. 19-1650. New York: National League for Nursing, biennial. $2.50.

Selected Federal Computer-Based Information Systems. Herner, S., and M.J. Vellucci, Eds. Washington, D.C.: Information Resources Press, 1972. $24.95.

Some Statistics on Baccalaureate and Higher Degree Programs in Nursing, 1975-76. Annual. Pub. No. 19-1649. New York: National League for Nursing, annual.

The National Referral Center for Science and Technology of the Library of Congress publishes a number of directories periodically. The selected directories listed below are available from the Superintendent of Documents, U.S. Printing Office, Washington, D.C. 20402.

Directory of Information Resources in the United States, Biological Sciences, 1972. $5.00.

Directory of Information Resources in the United States, Federal Government, with a Supplement of Government-Sponsored Information Resources, 1974, $4.25.

Directory of Information Resources in the United States, Physical Sciences, Engineering, 1971. $6.50.

Directory of Information Resources in the United States, Social Sciences. Rev. ed. 1973. $6.90.

Research Grants

Annual Register of Grant Support, 1977-78. 11th ed. Chicago: Marquis Who's Who, 1977. $52.50.

Catalog of Federal Domestic Assistance, 1976 Update. Washington, D.C.: U.S. Government Printing Office, annual. Looseleaf, $16.00.

The Foundation Directory, 6th ed. New York: The Foundation Center, 1977. $36.00.

Foundation News. New York: Council on Foundations, bimonthly. $20. Includes in each issue the Foundation Grants Index, a record of currently reported foundation grants of $5,000 or more.

Fund Sources in Health and Allied Fields. Oryx Press, 7632 East Edgemont Ave., Scottsdale, Ariz. Monthly. $95.00.

Grantsletter. Matteo Equities, Inc. 48 W. 21st St., New York 10010. Monthly. $48.00.

Grants Register, 1977-79. 5th ed. New York: St. Martin's Press, 1976. $25.00.

Handicapped Funding Directory. Research Grants Guides, P.O. Box 357, Oceanside, N.Y. 11572, 1978. $14.50.

Medical Research Funding Bulletin. Science Support Center, P.O. Box 587, Bronxville, N.Y. 10708. Trimonthly. $31.00.

U.S. National Institutes of Health. *Research Awards Index* (formerly *Research Grants Index).* 3 vols. DHEW Pub. No. 77-200. Washington, D.C.: U.S. Government Printing Office, fiscal year 1976-1977. $21.75.

Wilson, B.L., and Wilson, W.K. *Directory of Research Grants,* 1977-78. Phoenix, Ariz.: Oryx Press, 1977. $34.75.

On-Line Sources

Lockheed Information Systems. *Foundation Directory.* Current year's data, 2,500 listings, semi-annual updates. New York: The Foundation Center. $60 per on-line connect hour, $0.30 per full record printed off-line.

Foundation Grants Index. January 1973–present, 35,000 records, bimonthly updates. New York: The Foundation Center, $60 per on-line connect hour, $0.30 per full record printed off-line.

SDC Search Service. *Orbit Grants.* Current month's data, 1,500 records updated monthly. Scottsdale, Ariz.: Oryx Press. $60 per on-line connect hour, $0.35 citation record printed off-line.

Orbit SSIE. 1974–present, 400,000 records with approximtely 9,000 records updated monthly. Washington, D.C.: Smithsonian Science Information Exchange, Inc. $100 per on-line connect hour, $0.25 per citation printed off-line.

Writers' Manuals

Campbell, W.G. *Form and Style: Theses, Reports, Term Papers.* 5th ed. Boston. Houghton Mifflin, 1977. $5.50, paper.

Fowler, H.W. *Dictionary of Modern English Usage.* 2nd ed. New York: Oxford University Press. 1965. $10.00.

Manual of Style. 12th ed., rev. Chicago: University of Chicago Press, 1969. $12.50.

Strunk, W., Jr., and White, E.B. *The Elements of Style,* 2nd ed. New York: Macmillan, 1972. $4.00; $1.65, paper.

———. *Student's Guide for Writing College Papers.* Rev. 3rd expanded ed. Chicago: University of Chicago Press, 1977. $7.95; $3.45, paper.

Turabian, K.L. *Manual for Writers of Term Papers, Theses, and Dissertations.* 4th ed. Chicago: University of Chicago Press, 1973. $8.50; $3.45, paper.

CANADIAN SUPPLEMENT
(E&F = English and French available)

Audiovisuals

Canadian Department of Health and Welfare. *Film Library Catalogue.* E&F. Ottawa: Canadian Film Institute, 1975. $1.

Health Sciences Education. Mediascience Ltd., 728 Bay St., Toronto, M5G 1N5. 1973. Available on request.

Nursing Media Index—16 mm. Films. 2nd ed. Marilynne Seguin, Ed. and comp. Toronto. 1974. $12.

Sonomed. Montreal: Association des Medecines de Langue Francaise du Canada, monthly. Annual subscription, $50.

Bibliographies and Book Lists

Canadian Government Publication Catalog. Ottawa: Information Canada, monthly; with annual cumulations. E&F.

Canadian Nurses' Association. *Bibliographies.* Issued by the Association on specific topics. List available on request from 50 The Driveway, Ottawa, Ontario, K2P 1E2.

Directories

Association of Universities and Colleges of Canada. *Inventory of Research into Higher Education in Canada.* Ottawa, 1976. E&F. $3.

Canada Year Book. Ottawa: Information Canada, annual. E&F. $10 (approx.).

Canada Institute for Scientific and Technical Information. *Directory of Federally Supported Research in Universities.* Ottawa: National Research Council of Canada, 1977. E&F. $50 (approx.).

Canadian Almanac and Directory. Toronto: Copp Clark, annual. $32 (approx.).

Canadian Hospital Directory. Ottawa: Canadian Hospital Association, annual, $22 (approx.).

Canadian Medical Association. Listing of CMA committees, medical and allied health associations. Canadian Medical Association, 1867 Alta Vista Drive, Ottawa K1G 0G8. Available upon request.

Canadian Medical Directory. Toronto: Seccombe House, annual. $27 (approx.).

The Canadian Who's Who. Toronto: Who's Who Canadian Publications, triennial, $45.

The Corpus Administrative Index. Toronto: Corpus Publishers Services Ltd., bimonthly. $123 (approx.).

Corpus Almanac of Canada. Toronto: Corpus Publishers Services Ltd., annual. $33 (approx.).

National Research Council of Canada. National Science Library. Health Sciences Resource Center. *Canadian Locations of Journals Indexed in Index Medicus.* Ottawa, annual. $10 (approx.).

National Science Library. Health Sciences Resource Centre. *Conference Proceedings in the Health Sciences.* $35 for basic 1973 listing and $15 for annual supplements.

Official Directory of CNA office and provincial and territorial affiliates. Available on request from 50 The Driveway, Ottawa, Ontario, K2P 1E2.

Statistics Canada. *Universities and Colleges of Canada.* Ottawa: Information Canada, annual. E&F. $9 (approx.).

———. *Union List of Scientific Serials in Canadian Libraries.* 6th ed. Ottawa: National Research Council of Canada, 1975. E&F. $80 (approx.).

Drug Lists and Pharmacology

Canadian Pharmaceutical Association. *Compendium of Pharmaceuticals and Specialties.* Toronto, annual. E&F. $25 (approx.).

Educational Programs in Nursing

Canadian Nurses' Association. *General Entrance Requirements for Schools of Nursing and Schools of Practical Nursing.* Ottawa, annual. E&F.

Educational Programs for Nursing Personnel. Annual reprint from Canadian Hospital Association Directory. (Distributed by Canadian Nurses' Association.)

———. *Nursing Programs Offered at Canadian Universities.* Ottawa, annual. E&F.

———. *Outline of General Academic Entrance Requirements for Programs in Nursing at Canadian Universities.* Ottawa, annual. E&F.

———. *Short-term and Non-degree Courses and Institutes.* Ottawa, annual. E&F.

CNA publications are available on request from 50 The Driveway, Ottawa, Ontario, K2P, 1E2.

Histories

Association des Infirmieres Canadiennes. *Presence.* Ottawa, 1969. $3.

Canadian Nurses' Association. *The Leaf and the Lamp.* Ottawa, 1968. $3.

Gibbon, J.M., and Mathewson, M.S. *Three Centuries of Canadian Nursing.* Toronto: Macmillan, 1947. $2.

Innis, M.O., Ed. *Nursing Education in a Changing Society.* Toronto: University of Toronto Press, 1970. $3 (approx.).

Weir, G.M. *Survey of Nursing Education in Canada.* Toronto: University of Toronto Press, 1932. Available on microfilm from University Microfilms, Ann Arbor, MI 48106.

Indexes

The Canadian Education Index. Toronto: Canadian Education Association, quarterly, with annual cumulations. $50.

The Canadian Nurse Annual Index. Cumulative index, vol. 51–55, 1955–1959; vol. 56–60, 1960–1964.

Canadian Periodical Index. Ottawa: Canadian Library Association, monthly, with annual cumulations. E&F. $45.

L'Infirmiere Canadienne Annual Index. Cumulative index, vol. 51–55, 1955–1959; vol. 56–60, 1960–1964.

RADAR: Repertoire Analytique d'Articles de Revues du Quebec. Montreal: Universite Laval, bimonthly. $75 (approx.).

Legal Guides

Canadian Nurses' Association. *Compilation of Provincial Nurses' Acts and Related Legislation.* Ottawa, annual. E&F. Available on request.

Good, S.R., and Kerr, J.C. *Contemporary Issues in Canadian Law for Nurses.* Toronto: Holt, Rinehart and Winston. 1973. $7 (approx.).

———*Le Nursing et la Loi canadienne.* Montreal: Les editions HRW, 1974. $7.

Research Grants

Association of Universities & Colleges of Canada. *A Canadian Directory to Foundations and Other Granting Agencies.* 4th ed. Ottawa, 1973. E&F. $7.50 (approx.)

Research Reports: Indexes and Lists

Canadian Health Education Specialist Society. *Annotated Guide to Health Instruction Materials in Canada,* 3rd. ed. Ottawa, 1972. Annual supplements. $3 (approx.).

Canadian Nurses' Association. *Index of Canadian Nursing Studies.* Rev. ed. Ottawa, 1974. $5. Annual supplements 1975, 1976. $1 each.

National Library of Canada. *Canadian Theses.* Ottawa: Information Canada, annual. E&F. $2 (approx.).

Statistical Data Sources

Statistics Canada, Nursing in Canada: Canadian Nursing Statistics. Ottawa, annual from 1975. E&F. $1.40 (Formerly, *Countdown: Canadian Nursing Statistics* by the Canadian Nurses' Association. Annual from 1967–1974. E&F. $5.50.)

SUGGESTIONS FOR USING
REFERENCE SOURCES

Here are a few practical suggestions for incorporating some of these references into literature surveillance habits in your immediate work environment.

1. *Selecting correct headings or classification terms in abstracts and indexes is crucial. Familiarize yourself with the guide's organization and entry form. Use the thesaurus. Read all user's instructions and explanations. This simple step can save much wasted time and effort. For instance, in the* International Nursing Index, *articles related to job enrichment and job satisfaction are not indexed under these terms, but under the headings: Attitudes of Health Personnel, Hospital Personnel Administration, Personnel Satisfaction, and Personnel Management.*

2. *If you are using* Hospital Literature Index *or* Abstracts of Health Care Management Studies, *list the classifications and headings you want scanned. Then, have your secretary photocopy these selections monthly and place them in a binder for your convenient perusal. You may want to have a binder on two or three topics, for example: Licensure and Regulations, Manpower—Resources, Utilization, and Nursing Service Department—Staffing.*

3. *As a nursing administrator, you need practical information on decision-making strategies for an inservice presentation you are going to give your middle managers. Check* International Nursing Index *for the most recent books on the subject and* Hospital Literature Index. *Perhaps other departments or institutions have already done a similar type of inservice.*

4. *Finally, when delegating surveillance tasks to others, always provide clearly defined headings, subheadings or key words for scanning and retrieval.*

KEEPING UP: THE STAFF DEVELOPMENT EDUCATOR AND THE PROFESSIONAL LITERATURE

By Jane L. Binger and Ann J. Huntsman

Reprinted with permission from *Nurse Educator*, Volume 4, Number 3, May-June 1979, pp. 19–22.

How do you maintain an effective surveillance of new information and issues in your assigned area of staff development? Do you use periodical indexes and abstracts to aid your literature search? Or do you skim selected journals for appropriate articles? How often are you asked by nursing staff and management personnel to recommend a journal article or book on a particular subject?

The professional journals are a major avenue for sharing both research and nonresearch reports. Furthermore, the dissemination and use of research and creative endeavors are predominant concerns of nursing managers, educators, and clinicians[1-5]. Yet, given the importance of this subject, few recent studies are available on information resources used by educators teaching either generic nursing students or practicing nurses. The results of such a study, conducted by the authors, provide some useful information for staff development educators.

THE SURVEY

Mailed questionnaires were sent to a systematically selected random sample of staff development educators in 141 short-term acute-care hospitals in order to identify resources and related journal usage practices. These hospitals represented one-fourth of those registered by the American Hospital Association in California[6].

Sample

One hundred and ten educators replied (78 percent response) and usable results from 94 of them are summarized in this report. Thirty-four percent of the educators were titled inservice instructors, 32 percent inservice directors, and 23 percent inservice coordinators. Other titles included nurse educator, clinical specialist nursing educator, and clinical nurse educator.

Professional Characteristics

The majority of the educators are women (96 percent), between 27 and 38 years of age (55 percent), and have at least a baccalaureate degree (77 percent).

The educators bring diverse employment experiences to their assigned content areas. More than three-fourths have previously worked as staff and charge nurses. And one-fourth have an employment record including the positions of staff, charge, assistant head and head nurse, educator in a nursing program, and inservice education director.

Perceived Support and Role Expectations

A frequently held assumption of education is that it involves learning where to seek necessary information and how to use new information appropriately[7]. The human and physical environments surrounding the adult learner are also crucial to his participation in learning activities[8, 9]. Critical environmental factors include attitudes, expectations, and feelings about learning and the learner expressed by colleagues, peers, and significant others. Consequently, the educators were asked several questions about perceived attitudes and expectations in their immediate work environment.

Nearly 85 percent felt they have their immediate superior's support to pursue and use new information and professional learning in their present position. For the majority of educators, this superior was their inservice director. For those who are inservice directors, the superior commonly mentioned was the nursing service director.

Ninety-six percent indicated they are expected by those with whom they work directly (staff nurses, head nurses, and other educators) to be aware of current information and trends within their assigned area. Finally, 36 percent reported that they are asked one or more times a week for journal article or book recommendations by nursing staff or management personnel. Thirty-four percent reported they are asked one or more times a month for such information. And, unfortunately, nearly 30 percent stated they are only asked occasionally or rarely to recommend selected reading material.

LEARNING RESOURCES

Instructional resources may be classified into six categories: materials, devices, techniques, settings, content, and staff[10]. They promote and facilitate learning and have drastically increased in breadth with the trend toward self-directed, self-tested learning[11]. In this study, the educators were asked to indicate those sources that provide them with the most information for staff development. Second, they were asked to identify those surveillance methods they use to keep abreast of published professional information.

The majority of educators use a combination of methods to provide information for use in their job. For three-fourths, this combination includes reading, participation in continuing education courses and workshops, and conversation with peers and colleagues within and outside of their hospital. For a smaller number (25 percent), learning resources include formal courses and inservice staff conferences, meetings, and seminars.

Surveillance methods used for published information are summarized in Exhibit 4-1. Interestingly, nearly 40 percent of the educators use five of the six surveillance methods: systematic journal scanning, scanning periodical indexes and/or abstracts, reading book advertisements, scanning bibliographies, and reading book reviews.

Indexes and Abstracts

Since the breadth of information encompassed in nursing, education, and medicine is so great, it seemed only natural to explore the use of periodical indexes and abstracts. These reference tools assist the reader in efficiently locating information by author, title, journal, and issue. And, abstracts (abstracting journals) briefly summarize articles in addition to identifying their citations.

Reported periodical indexes and abstracts used by the educators during the last year are identified in Exhibit 4-2. Considering the educators' departmental roles, the frequent mention of *Index Medicus, International*

**Exhibit 4-1.   Information Surveillance Methods
Used by Educators (*N* = 88)**

Methods	Percent of Educators
Systematic journal scanning	95
Scanning periodical indexes and/or abstracts	47
Reading book advertisements	42
Scanning bibliographies	37
Reading book reviews	37
Scanning footnotes and references	25

Nursing Index, Nursing and Allied Health Index, and *Nursing Research Abstracts* is expected. What does seem surprising, though, is the relatively high reported use of *Current Index to Journals in Education.* Last, that nearly one-third report no use of indexes and abstracts during the last year does not seem totally surprising since a number of educators represented hospitals with fewer than 140 beds and relatively small budgets for nursing library materials and learning resources.

Professional Journals and Library Usage

The remainder of the questionnaire requested specific information on the educators' use of professional journals, specific journal sections read, identification of the persons who purchase journal subscriptions, and their use of and satisfaction with their hospital library facilities.

The eduators reported reading, either for their own learning or for use in inservice, 88 professional journals. The most frequently mentioned 19 journals are identified in Exhibit 4-3. Three trends seem especially notable. First, *Nursing Research,* the research journal of the American Nurses' Association and the National League of Nursing, was reportedly used by only 6 percent of the educators for both their own and inservice use. Second,

journals focusing on clinical topics of either a medical or nursing nature dominate the other 69 journals, each of which was mentioned by less than 5 percent. Third, more than half of the frequently mentioned journals have an administrative, educational, leadership, research, or general subject matter, rather than a clinical practice orientation.

A majority read professional journals thoroughly. Fifty-seven percent reported reading the advertisement, classified ads, letters-to-the-editor, question/answer department, editorial, news section, research briefs and articles, nonresearch articles, book reviews, and the journal article abstracts.

The educators reported that the majority of journals they use are bought by the staff development department (43 percent), the hospital library (27 percent), or jointly by the inservice department and the hospital library (23 percent). In terms of specific individuals, 35 percent of these educators personally purchase journal subscriptions for their department.

More than three-fourths reported using their hospital library facilities at least once every one to three months. More specifically, nearly 27 percent use their library at least weekly. However, 52 percent indicated they were not satisfied with the selection of nursing texts and periodicals in their library. Finally, it is encouraging to note that nearly 70 percent

**Exhibit 4-2.   Periodical Indexes and Abstracts
Used by Educators During the Last Year ($N = 90$)**

Indexes and Abstracts	Percent of Educators
Index Medicus	36.6
International Nursing Index	30
None	30
Nursing and Allied Health Index (Previously *Index to the Nursing Literature*)	26
Nursing Research Abstracts	22.2
Current Index to Journals in Education	20
Hospital Literature Index	20
Abstracts of Hospital Management Studies	13.6
Resources in Education	12.4
Psychological Abstracts	11.2
Rehabilitation Literature	7.8
Sociological Abstracts	7.8
Science Citation Index	3.3
Current Contents	3.3
Dissertation Abstracts International	2.2
Social Science Citation Index	1.1

use one or two other libraries such as community, college, or public libraries to supplement their literature search and retrievals.

IMPLICATIONS AND
RECOMMENDATIONS

The results of this study can be generalized fairly accurately to staff development educators in short-term acute-care hospitals in California and less so to similar staff development educators in other states with mandatory continuing education. Second, the results are particularly interesting due to the fact that staff development educators potentially interface with a larger segment of students—practicing nurses—than any other group of educators. They also interact with many nonnurses, and consequently are front-line disseminators of information and issues in nursing to numer-

ous other health professionals. Needless to say, the resources and information on which these educators base their practice have great import for their own professional credibility and that of nursing in general.

That the majority of these educators feel supported by their superiors both to pursue and to use new professional information is encouraging. Hopefully, this perceived feeling is, in turn, true for their students—nursing management and staff members. The expectation that it is the staff development educator's responsibility to acquire and share new information must be included in staff development job descriptions and stressed in promotion criteria.

Somewhat disappointing is the large number of educators who only reported scanning journals to maintain a surveillance of the professional literature. Other efficient, easy-to-use surveillance methods include bimonthly

**Exhibit 4-3.   Selected Professional Journals Read
by Educators at Least Once Every Three Months** (*N* = 87)

Journal Titles	Percent of Educators	
	For Own Learning	For Use in Inservice
Nursing 77	75	77
American Journal of Nursing	70	70
R.N. Magazine	40	40
Supervisor Nurse	34	37
Nurse Educator	31	29
Heart & Lung	31	22
Journal of Nursing Administration	27	20
Nursing Outlook	16	14
In-Service Training and Education	11	13
Training (The Magazine for Human Resources Development)	10	6
Hospitals (J.A.H.A.)	10	5
Journal of Continuing Education in Nursing	10	7
Nursing Clinics of North America	8	6
Critical Care Update	7	8
Hospital Topics	7	5
Nursing Digest	7	7
Nursing Research	6	6
Modern Health Care	6	2
Nursing Administration Quarterly	6	3

scanning (or having a secretary scan) relevant indexes and abstracts, using key words to search out relevant topics. A file can be kept of current book reviews, advertisements, and reference lists on subjects of your interest. Examples of files might be "Teaching Strategies," "Orientation Programs," and "Independent Learning Packets/Articles."

Educators who only scan journals may be the very people who have particularly heavy schedules and understaffing problems. They are not benefiting from aids to fast, effective journal scanning—indexes and abstracts—nor are they reaping the benefits of reading a variety of timely, appropriate articles and research on their interests in staff development or on educational or administrative concerns.

Although it is promising to note that they use other libraries in addition to their hospital library, the majority of persons surveyed are not satisfied with available nursing texts and journals in their facility. Requests for specific materials should be brought to the attention of the librarian and director of nursing service. Two suggestions for improving the scant resource situation are sharing staff development resources between hospitals and obtaining auxiliary contributions for journals and texts.

For further information on an established hospital learning resource center and a hospital library consortia, see articles by Graves and Dunavent, Sherer and Thompson, and Huntsman and Thompson in the Suggested Readings under "Library/Learning Resources."

Staff development educators and their departments are important gatekeepers of professional resources for all hospital nursing staff. They select the journals to which hundreds of other nurses in the institution will be exposed. To foster an appreciation of research in nursing, it is crucial that journals such as *Nursing Research, International Journal of Nursing Studies,* and *Research in Nursing and Health* be included in those purchased for staff development and nursing service, and that educators make visible use of them. Journal clubs and group critiques may indeed by unrealistic due to time and staffing constraints. However, the role models in the staff development department *can* be seen carrying, reading, scanning, Xeroxing, posting, and discussing professional journals.

Finally, authors with articles directed at staff development educators can note the most frequently reported journals read by the participants in this survey and submit their manuscripts to these journals. Prime examples of relevant subject matter are recent work in adult learning, management training, leadership strategies and techniques, teaching strategies, cost-effective methods of orientation, and evaluation techniques.

CONCLUSION

Now, after exploring the resources and reading habits of these educators, how do *you* compare? How do you and your peers in staff development maintain a surveillance of new information and professional issues? And what journals continually update your nursing practice?

PUBLISHING OPPORTUNITIES FOR NURSES: A COMPARISON OF 65 JOURNALS

By Joanne Comi McCloskey

Reprinted with permission from *Nurse Educator*, Volume 2, Number 4, July-August 1977, pp. 4-12.

Of the 65 articles that we reviewed on writing for publication, Joanne McCloskey's was our first choice for potential, beginning, and experienced writers alike! It will help you answer the following critical questions: Where should I submit my manuscript? What readership do selected journals attempt to reach? How long should I expect to wait for a response from a journal after I submit my manuscript? What are the common responses for a journal rejecting a manuscript? And which journals focus on solicited manuscripts, and therefore may not be the best place to submit an unsolicited (unrequested) manuscript?

The sharing of ideas and knowledge is essential to the educational process. One of the best ways to accomplish this dissemination of information is through the writing of articles and their subsequent publication. It is a way for nurse educators to share information and have ideas critiqued by peers and students in an open forum atmosphere, while promoting nursing's knowledge base and its professional image. However, the publishing process is unfamiliar to many, and this lack of knowledge can cause unnecessary difficulties in the marketing of manuscripts.

This article is intended to help the nurse-writer find her way through the maze of alternatives and procedures which lead to publication. It should help her select an appropriate journal for her work and also provide some insight into the publishing process.

It is hoped that educators in schools of nursing will share this information with their students and colleagues, and inservice educators will make the information available to the nurses they work with, thus encouraging them to contribute to the nursing literature.

Selecting a journal is one of the most important aspects of getting an article published. But the process of becoming familiar with the many available journals is time-consuming and many authors simply settle for a choice from the few they know best. Such a practice no doubt leads to the rejection of many good manuscripts: well-known journals are so popular that stiff competition forces a high rejection rate; and specialized journals have such a narrow focus that if your topic is not in their field it will not interest them. Selecting a journal knowledgeably from a wide field reduces such hazards and improves your chances for publication. Exhibit 4-4 is, essentially, a list of 65 nursing and health journals and the information about each which will facilitate an author's choice of an appropriate market for her work.

This information resulted from a survey conducted from July through December 1975. The editors of all journals (except those of state nurses' associations) listed in the 1974 *Cumulative Index to Nursing Literature* were mailed a questionnaire. Out of 106 questionnaires mailed, four were returned not delivered. Of the remaining 102, 70 went to U.S. journals and 32 to foreign journals. After a few months, 37 of the U.S. and English journals which had not responded were contacted again by a second mailing. Six months after the first mailing, 79 journals (77 percent) had returned the questionnaire including 55 U.S. journals and 24 foreign journals. Of those returned, 14 could not be included in the results. Some, like *Patient Care* and *Reports on Higher Education,* answered that they were completely staff-written; others contained only conference proceedings; a few had been discontinued; and one said it did not circulate to nurses (a remarkable statement since it was listed in the *Cumulative Index to Nursing Literature!).*

The two-page questionnaire was designed to obtain publishing information that would be useful to authors in comparing the journals. The information requested included: circulation, frequency, subscription cost, journal audience, preferred length of manuscript, number of copies to be submitted, author payment, reprints, length of time for editorial decision and publication of accepted manuscript, number of solicited and unsolicited manuscripts published each year, acceptance rates of unsolicited manuscripts, and most frequent reasons for article rejection.

Shortly before the deadline for this article, all editors involved were mailed a copy of the information they had submitted in 1975 and were asked to verify its accuracy. At this time four new journals were queried for the first time and questionnaires were mailed again to four that had not responded originally.

There are, of course, some limitations in this project. A few nursing journals are missing from the list because they did not respond: *Nursing Forum, Journal of Continuing Education, Journal of Gerontological Nursing,* and *Journal of Psychiatric Nursing.* Journals in certain fields other than nursing that nurse-authors might contribute to are not included (e.g., sociology, physiology, or medicine). Such journals might be identified by consulting the publishing directories *(The Directory of Publishing Opportunities* or *Ulrich's International Periodical Directory)* that are available in most libraries. Some information is incomplete because the respondents did not answer certain questions or, in a few cases, because the answers were incomprehensible. A fourth limitation is that specific manuscript recommendations are *not* included because this would have consumed too much space. However, most publications will furnish manuscript guidelines upon request. It is important to obtain these if they are available, since journals vary in their requirements for bibliographies, references, and illustrations.

The following discussion gives some details related to the questions asked in the survey and shares the insights gained through my interaction with the editors.

CATEGORIZATION OF JOURNALS

The table contains 42 nursing journals (including 20 foreign) and 23 health journals (including 5 foreign). They are categorized according to who reads them, since the most frequent reason for article rejection given by the editors was that authors were not familiar with the readership of the journal. On the basis of its editor's description of the audience it is published for, each journal was assigned to one of the following categories: general nursing (6 journals), specialty nursing (16), foreign nursing (18), licensed practical nursing (2), health care personnel (16 U.S. and 5 foreign) and general public (2). The categories appear in a "nursing first" order; journals are listed alphabetically in each category.

CIRCULATION

The journals vary widely in the number of readers they have, anywhere from 400 *(Zambia Nurse Journal)* to one million *(Family Health Magazine)*. For the most part, the circulation figures represent paying subscribers. Journals affiliated with organizations often have a reduced, occasionally free, subscription fee for members.

For example, *Imprint, Hong King Nursing Journal, South African Nursing Journal, National News,* and the *Journal of Allied Health* circulate free to members of the affiliating organizations. Some journals not affiliated with organizations have a controlled free circulation: *Supervisor Nurse* is free to nursing service directors, supervisors, and head nurses; *Nurse Educator* is free to nearly all actively employed nursing educators; *Emergency Medicine* is free to physicians; *Canada's Mental Health* is free to Canadian subscribers; and *Point of View*'s entire circulation is complimentary to operating room, delivery room, and emergency department personnel.

Of the nursing journals, the three with the largest circulation with a commanding margin are *Nursing 77* (400,000 subscribers, now ranking as the largest paid-circulation magazine for *any* professional group), *American Journal of Nursing* (310,000 subscribers) and *R.N.* (205,000). The enormous circulation of these popular nursing journals is reason enough to strive for publication in them. Once your article is printed you communicate with over one-third of the registered working nurses in the United States. In contrast, publication in less well-read journals may reach only 10,000 nurses (still a goodly sum in comparison with professional journals in many other

fields). Of course, if these 10,000 nurses are the very ones who can implement your idea, then it is best to choose the smaller circulation.

ORGANIZATIONAL ASSOCIATION

Knowing which organization a journal is affiliated with helps an author identify the readership, an important step in selecting the right journal. Forty-three (66 percent) of the journals surveyed are associated with organizations. The table contains only current affiliations; however, some journals which are now independent have been associated with an organization in the past. For example the now independent *Nursing Times* was affiliated with the Royal College of Nursing (the nursing association of the United Kingdom) until 1968.

The readership for journals in the "health care personnel" section is specified in cases where they did not report an organizational affiliation or when their title does not indicate the readership.

YEARLY FREQUENCY

Most journals publish monthly. Editors, not authors, choose the issue in which a certain article will appear. Although few authors consider it, some months are more desirable than others. For example, among nursing educators the October issue, coming at the beginning of the academic year when everyone is fresh, is widely read. Contrast the June issue, which no doubt gets fewer readers among tired teachers and students.

ARTICLE WORD LENGTH

The preferred length of a manuscript varies a good deal from journal to journal, but most nursing editors in this country prefer a length of 2,000 to 4,000 words (editors of foreign journals usually prefer shorter manuscripts). At 250 words per typed page, this is an 8- to 16-page article—a length that does not allow much word-wasting. Although it is unlikely that a good manuscript will be rejected because it is too long or (more rarely) too short, it is best to get a feeling for the appropriate article length of the journal. Some journals prefer short articles and some (not as many) longer ones—compare *The American Journal of Nursing* with *Nursing Research*. If you do not know the intended length, scan several copies of the journal and make a calculated guess: you may save yourself a rewrite later on.

COPIES SUBMITTED

Most journals require that you submit two copies of your manuscript: the original and a photocopy or carbon. (The journal's manuscript guidelines usually specify this.)

A manuscript should be sent to only one journal at a time. Editors invest considerable time and effort in reviewing a manuscript and naturally they do not like doing this when they suspect that another editor from another journal is doing the same. As one editor in the survey put it:

I object strongly to being sent a manuscript which has also been "farmed out" to other editors for consideration. In the past year I have accepted four articles, in one case by return of post, only to be informed that the author has decided to accept the offer of another journal.

Editors like to receive the original manuscript because then they do not immediately suspect that the same article is arriving concurrently on the desks of their competitors. It is also helpful to state in your covering letter that you have not submitted your manuscript to any other journal. For further insight into the editor's point of view concerning manuscript submission, see the entertaining August 1975 editorial, "What Bugs Editors" by Edith P. Lewis, editor of *Nursing Outlook*.

AUTHOR PAYMENT

Very few of the nursing and health journals pay their authors. When they do, it is usually for a solicited article, written exclusively for that journal.

REPRINTS

Instead of monetary payment or, in a few instances, in addition to it, some journals supply authors with free reprints—sometimes as many as 100. Although this may seem like a lifetime supply to the uninitiated, requests for reprints (especially if your article is a report of new research) can consume this pile in a few months. Since one reprint can cost anywhere from 20 cents to one dollar (depending on article length), 100 free reprints can represent considerable savings for the author. Some journals are generous in this respect, but most supply reprints only on request and at cost. A few journals do not make them available at all.

Free issues instead of free reprints may be provided. Although the list cites only those that mentioned it, most journals send authors at least one free issue of the journal containing their article.

THE WAITING PERIOD

Editors usually acknowledge receipt of manuscripts with a postcard or form letter, but then authors may not hear from them for two or more months. Most journals send manuscripts with publishing potential out to two or three readers who have expertise in the content. In some situations one unfavorable opinion can mean rejection. Smaller journals sometimes do not have an editorial board and the editor is the sole reader. The amount of time required for the editorial decision varies with the journals and can take anywhere from two weeks to six months. Based upon 51 responses to this question, I calculated an average waiting time of eight weeks. These long delays do provoke some authors to make duplicate submissions. However, the delays do not excuse the practice.

Once your manuscript is accepted you face another wait, often a much longer one, until it is actually published. Delays of six to twelve months between acceptance and publication are frequent, even common. I calculated an average of six months (based on 52 responses) between the time authors receive their acceptance notice and actually see their article in print.

One explanation for these long delays is the editorial practice of "article banks." When journals receive a large number of good articles, they may accept more than they can publish right away. Also, many editors like to put together several articles on the same topic to present a neat package for the reader. If yours is the last article to be accepted for such a series, then it will be published right away. But if it is one of the first, it will be filed in the "bank" and the wait can be a long one. And, what is worse, when the article is finally published it may be out of date. To prevent this, some editors ask authors to update a manuscript that has been "banked" for a long time. Although you can always withdraw an article if you feel you are caught in the "banking" process, the prospect of "starting over again" discourages most authors from taking such action.

SOLICITED AND UNSOLICITED ARTICLES

As the data show, journals differ greatly in the percentage of articles that they solicit. Some journals solicit all or most of their articles,

thereby reducing the chances of little known authors publishing in them. Solicited articles (requested of a particular individual by an editor) have almost 100 percent acceptance rates for all journals. *Nursing Clinics of North America,* one journal that publishes almost 100 percent solicited articles, suggests that you let them know about a subject or idea you wish to write about and they will put this information in their files for the planning of future issues.

The last column in Exhibit 4–4 reveals that unsolicited articles (those sent to a journal for consideration without previous request) have a much lower and more varied rate of acceptance. The contents page of most journals contains a statement which reveals whether the editors encourage unsolicited manuscripts. New journals, which are not yet well known, usually have higher acceptance rates.

Some journals prefer to receive abstracts or outlines of potential articles rather than review an entire unsolicited manuscript. This way the editor can tell you if he is interested in the subject and may give you some guidelines to use in writing it. However a positive response to an abstract does not guarantee acceptance of the article: the completed manuscript is usually reviewed by the editorial board (who may not have been involved in the recommendation concerning the abstract) and its acceptance greatly depends upon their recommendations. Not all editors will review abstracts, so check the journal's manuscript guidelines or ask the editor first.

One advantage to starting out with an abstract is that it *is* permissible to send the same abstract to several different journals at once. You can then compare the editors' responses and make the best choice.

REASONS FOR ARTICLE REJECTION

The editors were also asked to check their most frequent reasons for rejecting articles.

Three possible responses were listed along with a place for other reasons. Forty-five editors checked that their most frequent reason for rejecting an article was that "The subject matter is not relevant for our audience"; 38 editors checked "Poorly written"; and 25 checked "Idea not unique." As the responses show, selecting the most appropriate journal is indeed important.

The "other reasons" editors cited for rejecting articles are listed below in categories which show how many times the reason was mentioned.

1. Mentioned numerous times:
    *Subject covered recently or scheduled
    for the future*

2. Mentioned three or more times:
    *Too technical for our publication
    Content inaccurate or undocumented
    Based upon poor research design or
    faulty methodology*

3. Mentioned once or twice:
    *Nursing aspects not described well
    Content not important
    Reads as a speech not an article, and
    would be difficult to change
    Conclusion unwarranted by data as
    compiled
    Previously published elsewhere
    Case histories badly presented*

EDITORS' ADVICE

The last question in the survey asked the editors if there was any other information which they would like to pass on to authors. The most frequent response was that authors should be familiar with the journal to which they submit an article, including its focus in terms of types of articles and readership. Thus, once again, the importance of journal selection is apparent. Several editors responded that interested authors would be wise to query them first in order to ascertain their interest in the topic. (See the section on solicited and unsolicited manuscripts.) Other editorial advice and comments included:

1. Manuscripts must be well organized, look neat, and be double-spaced throughout.

2. Specifications for manuscripts are available upon request. Get them and follow them.

3. Start with a thorough search of the literature.

4. Outline before writing, particularly if you are an inexperienced writer.

5. If content is controversial, document the sources and recognize opposing views.

6. Ask friends to critique before submitting.

7. Write in a straightforward fashion; avoid sounding pompous or pedantic.

8. Use the active voice whenever possible.

9. Keep information concise, relevant, and up-to-date.

10. Double-check figures and totals.

11. Furnish your name, address, and phone number as well as your job title and affiliation.

12. Encourage any potential nurse-authors whom you know!

Readers may want to supplement this section with Binger's 1979 survey of nursing journal editors, which highlights frequently observed writing weaknesses in manuscripts submitted for publication review and gives practical hints for correcting two common writing weaknesses: overly formal and pedantic writing and poor organization.

In summary, a nurse-author will be published more frequently if she sends her manuscript to a *carefully* chosen journal. This article attempts to facilitate this selection process. It also provides some insight into the publishing process of nursing journals.

This survey includes by far the majority of current nursing journals. However, don't forget such new arrivals to the nursing literature as Professional Nurse, Nursing and Health Care, Nursing Administration Quarterly, Nursing Leadership, Western Journal of Nursing Research, Research in Nursing and Health, Critical Care Quarterly, CE Focus, Cancer Nursing, Nursing Law and Ethics, *and* Geriatric Nursing. *Also,* Journal of Continuing Education in Nursing, Journal of Gerontological Nursing, *and* Nephrology Nurse *provide excellent publication vehicles for nurses interested in writing in these specialties.*

For readers without present access to journals mentioned in this selection, remember that any health professional in the United States may obtain health science literature through his or her local public library if such literature is not available in nearby locations. The interlibrary loan system is sponsored by the National Library of Medicine in Bethesda, Maryland. It particularly helps nurses in rural and small hospitals with poor to nonexistent library facilities obtain timely journal articles. Phone your local library and ask about this valuable outreach program.

Right now, though, why not take a few minutes to jot down a few ideas for a manuscript outline? We're waiting to see your name and ideas in print!

Exhibit 4-4. Publication Data on 65 Nursing and Health Journals

General Nursing	CIRCULATION	ORGANIZATIONAL ASSOCIATION	YEARLY FREQUENCY	ARTICLE WORD LENGTH	COPIES SUBMITTED (incl. original)	AUTHOR PAYMENT	REPRINTS	TIME FOR EDITORIAL DECISION	TIME FOR PUBLICATION OF ACCEPTED MANUSCRIPT	SOLICITED ARTICLES PER YEAR	UNSOLICITED ARTICLES PER YEAR	ACCEPTANCE RATE UNSOLICITED ARTICLES
A.J.N.	310,000	Amer. Nurses	12X	1500–2500	2	$20/pp or	100 free for exclusively prepared material	Several Weeks	2–18 Months	35%	65%	5–10%
Nursing Clinics of North America	38,000	None	4X	3600	1	None	100 free & 1 Journal		6 Months	Nearly 100%	"2 out of 65"	Rare
Nursing '77	400,000	None	12X	1500–2500	1	$100–$350 Article	Not Supplied	6–8 weeks	6–12 Months	Most	Some	5%
Nursing Digest	12,000	None	4X	—	—	$7/pp				102 Reprinted	Does not accept original manuscripts	
R.N.	205,000	None	12X	2000–2500	2	$50–$200 Article	At Cost	2–3 Weeks	3 Months	Most	Many	10%
The Nurse Practitioner: A Journal of Primary Nursing Care	2,000	None	6X	2,500–3250	2	None	2 Journal Copies Free	6–8 Weeks	Varies	10	10–20	

Specialty Nursing

AORN Journal	27,719	Assoc. of Operating Room Nurses	13X	3,000	2	None	At Editor's Discretion	1-6 Months	2-12 Months	25	75	60%
Cardiovascular Nursing	120,000	American Heart Association	6X	3,000	2	None	Not Supplied	4-6 Weeks	5-6 Months	Most (5-6)	Few	12-20%
Heart and Lung: The Journal of Critical Care	54,000	Amer. Assoc. of Critical Care Nurses	6X	3,750	2	None	At Cost	4-6 Weeks	5-6 Months	50	50	40%
Imprint	40,000	National Student Nurses' Association	4X	1,500-2000	2	None	Some Free	2 Months	12 Months	1/3	2/3	50%
Journal of Neurosurgical Nursing	2000	Amer. Assoc. of Neurosurgical Nurses	4X	Varies	2	None	At Cost	2-3 Months	12 Months	Publishes Mostly Manuscripts of Members Presented at Annual Meetings		
Journal of Nurse-Midwifery	2,500	Amer. College of Nurse-Midwives	4X	2500-5000	2	None	At Cost in orders of 100 or up	3 Months	6-9 Months	---	40-50	50%
Journal of Nursing Administration	18,000	None	10X	Varies	3	$10/pp	At Cost	4-6 Weeks	6-10 Months	25	50	35%
Journal of Nursing Education	3,300	None	9X	2,000-3,000	2	None	At Cost	6 Weeks	6-12 Months	Few	Most	40%

Speciality Nursing	CIRCULATION	ORGANIZATIONAL ASSOCIATION	YEARLY FREQUENCY	• ARTICLE WORD LENGTH	COPIES SUBMITTED (incl. original)	AUTHOR PAYMENT	REPRINTS	• TIME FOR EDITORIAL DECISION	• TIME FOR PUBLICATION OF ACCEPTED MANUSCRIPT	• SOLICITED ARTICLES PER YEAR	• UNSOLICITED ARTICLES PER YEAR	• ACCEPTANCE RATE UNSOLICITED ARTICLES
JOGN Nursing	18,000	Nurses Assoc. of Amer. College of Obstetricians & Gynecologists	6X	2,500–5,000	1–4	None	At Cost	3–6 Weeks	2–12 Months	13	27	65%
Maternal Child Nursing Journal	1,000	Graduate Faculties of Depts. of Mat. & Ped. Nos. Univ. of Pitts.	4X	2,500–5,000	2	None	100 Free	3–6 Months	3–9 Months	Few	Most	75%
MCN, The American Journal of Maternal Child Nursing	25,000	None	6X	2,500–3,250	2	None	100 Free	6 Weeks	Up To 1 Year	10	50	25%
Nurse Educator	24,000	None	6X	2,500–5,000	2	None	At Cost	6–8 Weeks	3–10 Months	10–12	10–12	30%
Nursing Outlook	28,000	National League For Nursing	12X	2000–4000	2	None	100 Free	6–8 Weeks	4–6 Months	15	85	10%
Nursing Research	7,000	Amer. Nurs. Assoc. and National League for Nurs.	6X	5,000	3	None	At Cost	6 Months	12 Months	Few	60	33½%

Occupational Health Nursing	12,000	12X	3,000	2	None	At Cost	1 Month	3 Months	30	20	50%
Supervisor Nurse	77,000	12X	2,000–4,000	2	$50/Art.	At Cost	2–8 Weeks	4–8 Months	32%	48%	75%
Foreign Nursing											
International Nursing Review	4,000	6X	1,500–3000	2	None	50 Free	1–2 Months	Varies	33⅓%	66⅔%	Not Available
Australia Australasian Nurses Journal	18,000	11X	2,000–3000	1	Australian 5 Cents/Line	At Cost		Nearest Issue	Any worthwhile paper		
Australian Nurses Journal	14,000	12X	2,000–2,500	1	"Variable"	At Cost		2–3 Months	20	45	40%
Canada Canadian Nurse	85,000	12X	1,000–2,500	2	Honorarium	At Cost	3–12 Weeks	2–5 Months	Some	Most	25%
England Midwife, Health Visitor & Community Nurse	22,000	12X		2	By Arrangement	At Cost	3 Months	6 Months			
Midwives Chronicle	19,000	12X	1,000–2,000	1	"Based on Length"	At Cost	1 Week	Varies	Some	Most	75%
Nat News	5,000	8X	No Regulations	1	Varies	At Cost	2–4 Weeks	6–12 Weeks	Not Available	Not Available	Not Available

Foreign Nursing	CIRCULATION	ORGANIZATIONAL ASSOCIATION	YEARLY FREQUENCY	ARTICLE WORD LENGTH	COPIES SUBMITTED (incl. original)	AUTHOR PAYMENT	REPRINTS	TIME FOR EDITORIAL DECISION	TIME FOR PUBLICATION OF ACCEPTED MANUSCRIPT	SOLICITED ARTICLES PER YEAR	UNSOLICITED ARTICLES PER YEAR	ACCEPTANCE RATE UNSOLICITED ARTICLES
Nursing Mirror	56,684	None	Weekly	2,000	1	By Negotiation	Not Supplied	"As long as possible"	Varies	Half	Half	40%
Nursing Times	55,000	None	Weekly	1,500–2000	2	By Negotiation	At Cost	Up to 4 Weeks	3–6 Months	50	10	50%
Occupational Health	3,000	Royal College of Nursing	12X	1,500–2,000	2	By Negotiation	6 Journal Copies Free	2 Weeks	2 Months			
Hong Kong Hong Kong Nursing Journal	4,000	Hong Kong Nurses Association	2X	3,000	2	A Silver Spoon	10–20 Free		1 Month	Most	Few	
India Christian Nurse	1,500	None	6X	300–500	2	None	A Few Journal copies free	1 Month	2 Months	2		
The Nursing Journal of India	14,000	Trained Nurses' Assoc. of India	12X	2000	2	None	On request at cost	1 Month	2–3 Months	Few	Most	50–60%
Jamaica The Jamaican Nurse	4–5,000	Nurses' Assoc. of Jamaica	3X	2,500 Maximum	2	None	2 Copies free	3 Months	3 Months	15	5	Most
Rhodesia The Rhodesian Nurse	1,000	Rhodesia Nurses' Assoc.	4X	250	2	None	Free	2 Months	3–5 Months			
South Africa S.A. Nursing Journal	37,332	South African Nursing Assoc.	12X	2,000	2	R 12,50–R 15,00/1000 Words	At Cost	2 Months	Depends	1/3	2/3	70%

Journal	Circulation	Sponsor	Frequency	Word Length	Copies	Page Charges	Reprints	Review Time	Time to Publication			
New Zealand New Zealand Nursing Journal "Kaiziaki"	9,000	New Zealand Nurses' Assoc.	12X	No Preference	1	None		Few Days	1-2 Months	Few	Most	Most
Zambia Zambia Nurse Journal	400	Zambia Nurses' Assoc.	3X	6,000-7,500		None		1 Month	1 Month			
LPN Journals												
Journal of Practical Nursing	50,000	Nat. Assoc. for Practical Nurse Educ. and Service, Inc.	12X	800-2,500	2	Usually None	3 Journal copies free	6-8 Weeks	2-12 Months	Most	Some	35-40%
Nursing Care	65,000	Nat. Federation of LPNs	12X	1500-2500	2	$20/pp	2	1 Month	6 Months	12	50	50%
Health Care Personnel												
American Lung Assoc. Bulletin	40,000	Amer. Lung Assoc.	10X	2,000-2,500	2	None	A "reasonable number" free	1 Month Maximum	2-6 Months	60	10	10%
Emergency Medicine	125,500	None	12X	No restriction	1	None	100 free on request	1 Month	3 Months	Most are staff written		
Family Planning Perspectives	29,000	Planned Parenthood Fed. of Amer.	6X	4,000	2	None	25 Free	1 Month	4 Months	Most	Some	10%
Hospital and Community Psychiatry	17,500	Amer. Psychiatric Assoc.	12X	2,000-2,500	2	None	5 Journal copies free	2-3 Months	9-12 Months	Few	Most	25%

Health Care Personnel

	CIRCULATION	ORGANIZATIONAL ASSOCIATION	YEARLY FREQUENCY	ARTICLE WORD LENGTH	COPIES SUBMITTED (incl. original)	AUTHOR PAYMENT	REPRINTS	TIME FOR EDITORIAL DECISION	TIME FOR PUBLICATION OF ACCEPTED MANUSCRIPT	SOLICITED ARTICLES PER YEAR	UNSOLICITED ARTICLES PER YEAR	ACCEPTANCE RATE UNSOLICITED ARTICLES
Hospital Formulary	25,000	None (for medical and Pharmacy personnel)	12X	2,000–4,000	2	None	Free on request	1 Month	6 Months	70	20	50%
Hospital Forum	10,241	Assoc. of Western Hospitals	12X	1,500–2,000	2	None	"Depends"	2 Weeks	2 Months	6	30	20%
Hospital Progress	16,000	Catholic Hosp. Assoc.	12X	2,500–3,000	2	By Agreement	By Agreement	2–3 Months	4 Months	Varies	Varies	
Hospitals, Journal the Amer. Hosp. Association	75,000	Amer. Hosp. Assoc.	24X	2,000–2,500	3	Usually None	2 Journal copies free	2–3 Months	6–12 Months	188	62	20%
In-Service Training and Education	16,000	None	4X	2,500	2	None	2 Journal copies free					
Journal of Allied Health	2,500	Amer. Society of Allied Health Prof.	4X	3,000	3	None	6 Free	2 Months	3–18 Months	5	27	55%
Journal of School Health	11,000	Amer. School Health Assoc.	9X	4,000 Maximum	3	None	1 Journal copy free	2 Months	3–6 Months	0	100	25%

Journal												
MH	7,000	National Assoc. for Mental Health	4X	3,000	2	None	At Cost	3 Weeks	6–12 Months	14	18	12%
Modern Healthcare	52,000	None (for Hosp. & Nsg. Home Management)	12X	600–800	1	Only on commissioned articles	None	Varies	Varies	Most are staff written		50%
P.A. Journal —A Journal for New Health Practitioners	2,800	None	4X		2	None		1–2 Months			30	50%
Point of View	37,500	Ethicon, Inc. (for OR, DR, ED Personnel)	4X	1,000–1,500	2	$75–$150/ Article	Free	4–6 Weeks	18–24 Months	Few	Most	90%
Public Health Reports	18,000	U.S. Public Health Service	6X	3,000	4	None	100 Free to senior author	3–4 Months	6–8 Months	10	80	45%
Foreign												
Canada's Mental Health	24,000	Minister of National Health & Welfare	4X		2	None	7 Journal copies free	3–6 Months	3–6 Months		Most	
Canadian Journal of Public Health	5,000	Canadian Public Health Association	6X	1,000–1,500	2	None	At Cost	Varies	18 Months		50	90%
Dimensions in Health Service	13,000	Canadian Hosp. Assoc.	12X	3,000	2	None	A few journal copies free	2–6 Months	2–6 Months	55	20	75%

Health Care Personnel	CIRCULATION	ORGANIZATIONAL ASSOCIATION	YEARLY FREQUENCY	ARTICLE WORD LENGTH	COPIES SUBMITTED (incl. original)	AUTHOR PAYMENT	REPRINTS	TIME FOR EDITORIAL DECISION	TIME FOR PUBLICATION OF ACCEPTED MANUSCRIPT	SOLICITED ARTICLES PER YEAR	UNSOLICITED ARTICLES PER YEAR	ACCEPTANCE RATE UNSOLICITED ARTICLES
England The Chest, Heart and Stroke Journal	6,000	The Chest, Heart and Stroke Assoc.	4X	2,500	2	By Negotiation	At Cost	1-3 Months	3-6 Months	Most	Very Few	Very Few
World Hospitals	2,500–3,500	International Hospital Federation	4X	3,000–5,000	2		At Cost	1-3 Months	3-12 Months	6	18	67%
General Public												
Family Health Magazine	1,000,000	None	12X	1,000–3,000	1	Depends on length & content	At Cost	6 Weeks	Varies	Most	Few	Very Low
Life and Health	100,000	None	12X	750–3,000	1	$50-$150/Art.	2 Journal copies free	1 Month	Indefinite	Half	Half	10%

● In most cases data are approximate, **not** exact
Blank spaces represent **unanswered** questions
pp in author payment column = printed page

5. Essentials in Day-to-Day Writing and Reading

The first selection in this chapter offers the reader interesting answers to the following practical questions: How can policies and procedures for a hospital be organized for efficient and effective usage by hospital personnel and management alike? Who coordinates the policy and procedure system in the hospital and what type of background does this person bring to the task? What steps are involved in taking a policy from its first draft form to a completed policy signed by the appropriate departmental heads and staff? And what circumstances does Okorafor view as critical to the success or failure of an ongoing policy and procedure program?

The next reading is highly recommended for all nursing personnel involved with writing nursing practice standards, personnel evaluation instruments, quality assurance tools for both retrospective record audit and concurrent review, and care plans. Bloch defines such frequently used terms as criteria, stand-ards, *and* norms *and then clarifies their use in audit instruments by developing a hypothetical model for the reader. Readers may want to take a few notes on the differences between a* criterion *and a* standard, *although these two words are often used interchangeably in the* professional literature. *Also note the challenges involved in creating reliable and valid methods to measure the criteria you develop.*

Next, Corts identifies the major types of visual aids that can be used in meetings, conferences, and speeches. He also teaches the reader how to create his or her own visual aids and select the most appropriate one for a given audience. Note the appropriateness of chart pads and felt-tip pens for brainstorming sessions and reporting back on task groups in large workshops and meetings. These simple pens and pads of newsprint are being used at some of the most expensive workshops and conferences in the United States.

Last, Swift's classic article on the thoughts and steps involved in writing and rewriting a memo will assist readers trying to simplify their writing style. If you are getting negative feedback on your memos or just want to improve this frequently used administrative communication tool, read this selection and then follow the same steps on your next memo. We have both used this process repeatedly to improve our own memo writing and agree that the rewards and satisfaction far outweigh the investment in time.

HOSPITAL POLICIES AND PROCEDURES: EVEN THE SYSTEM NEEDS A SYSTEM

By Helen I. Okorafor

Reproduced, with permission, from *Hospitals*, October 1, 1978, Volume 52, Number 19, pp. 107–112.

A hospital needs written policies and procedures to provide organizational coherence, effectiveness, and efficiency; to provide effective controls and guidance; to provide means for implementing creative and constructive changes; and to sustain performance.

Another important advantage of an effective policy and procedure system involves meeting many of the requirements of hospital regulatory agencies, such as the Joint Commission on Accreditation of Hospitals (JCAH), state health departments, and others. Almost all regulatory bodies demand to examine a hospital's policy and procedure manual during their inspections or surveys of the hospital. In addition, the increasing demands presented by third-party payers and government agencies necessitate development of an effective policy and procedure system.

Review of the pertinent literature and discussion with some responsible personnel from hospitals that have effective policy and procedure systems provide the following recommendations:

- Responsibility for development and coordination of a policy and procedure system should be assigned to one person who can devote a block of time—4 to 12 hours per week—to this responsibility.

- A form for documentation of the policies and procedures and a binder for the pages should be designed. A looseleaf or similar binder that permits easy removal and insertion of pages in the correct sequence is preferred.

- An introductory policy that describes the policy and procedure system should be formulated, and all personnel should be informed about it.

- High priority should be given to typing, duplication, and distribution of copies of policies, and a distribution list should be established.

- Existing policies and procedures should be critiqued, changed if necessary, and written in the proper format for formal approval and distribution in the new system for the policy and procedure manual.

- Section numbers should be assigned to policies, and a table of contents and an index should be included in the manual.

The policy and procedure manual should be easy to understand, to interpret uniformly, and to retrieve. The first policy or procedure that is written should meet an existing need, and subsequent ones should be added as needs arise. Hospitals should follow through on development of policies and procedures, sustain interest in them, and explain them continually.

The policy and procedure system at Wishard Memorial Hospital, Indianapolis, became effective in December 1976. Since that time, approximately 300 policies and procedures have been implemented.

Responsibility for the development and the coordination of the hospital's policy and procedure system is assigned to an administrative assistant who is an RN and who has a master's degree in hospital and health administration. She also is responsible for ensuring that the hospital complies with the standards and the regulations of hospital regulatory bodies, including the JCAH and the Indiana State Board of Health. Assigning these two responsibilities to one person has worked very well for the hospital.

For example, at Wishard Memorial Hospital, approximately 80 percent of all deficiencies noted during 1976–1977 by the JCAH, the Indiana State Board of Health, and the Food and Drug Administration (FDA) have been corrected by formulating and enforcing pertinent new policies. (All of the deficiencies noted by the FDA have been corrected through this approach.)

The coordinator is able either to formulate policies and procedures to meet standards and regulations when they are strictly administrative or to recommend that they be formulated by appropriate departments, services, or committees. A hospital should consider using a coordinator who has both an administrative and a clinical background, because hospital policies and procedures cover both clinical and administrative aspects of operation.

The design of Wishard Memorial Hospital's policy and procedure form was based on two important considerations:

1. A unit that is given the opportunity to contribute to the development of a policy, especially when the policy affects that unit, will be more likely and more willing to enforce the policy when it becomes official.

2. Most hospital regulatory bodies require coordination among affected units in the development of policies. For example, the JCAH requires that all nursing policies and procedures be formulated with the cooperation of the medical staff, the hospital administration, and any other affected units of the hospital.

At Wishard Memorial Hospital, a policy may be recommended by a department or a clinical service through the department head or the clinical chief, a committee or a task force through the chairperson, any member of the administrative staff, and the administrator and/or medical director.

All recommended policies are submitted in draft form to the policy/procedure coordinator for review. The coordinator reviews them for appropriateness, completeness, content, and typographical errors. The coordinator tries to solve any problems with the recommender. However, if a problem involves units other than the recommender's unit, the coordinator advises the recommender to solve the problem with the affected units or she holds a meeting for all of the affected units in order to solve the problem. When the draft has been corrected, the recommended policy is typed in the proper form, returned to the recommender for his signature, and resubmitted to the coordinator.

The recommended policy then is ready for review and concurrence signatures by all department heads, chiefs of services, and administrative staff members whose units will be affected by the policy. Any problems that are identified by these reviewers must be resolved before the policy is sent to the administrator and/or medical director for approval. This concurrence process satisfies the need to involve key personnel in the formation of policies and procedures and the requirement of regulatory bodies that departments cooperate in developing the policies that affect them.

Certain policies that are initiated by the medical director and/or administrator need not go through this process. Instead, the draft is submitted to the coordinator for review, retyping into the proper form, and return to the medical director and/or administrator for approval.

Wishard Memorial Hospital is a city/county hospital that has an unusual organizational structure. The hospital administrator is responsible to the medical director who also is the superintendent of the hospital. The administrative approval that makes the policies and procedures official is given by the administrator "and/or" the medical director—that is, a few policies will require approval signatures from both the medical director and the administrator. In general, however, the medical director gives administrative approval for policies that deal with patient care, and the administrator gives approval for general operational/personnel policies. Final review of all policies is conducted by the governing body. In hospitals that do not have medical directors, the administrators should give approval for all policies.

Any revision of, deletion in part of, or addition to a policy requires that a new policy be formulated. Deletion of an entire policy requires that a new policy be formulated and that a notice explaining, justifying, and ordering the deletion be distributed. All new policies are reviewed each month.

Wishard Memorial Hospital's policies are numbered first according to the cost center numbers for the departments or services to which the policies apply and then according to their order of issuance. For example, in policy 950-1, the "950" identifies the department—hospital administration—and the "1" identifies the consecutive issuance number in the aggregate number of policies issued for that department.

The policy and procedure manuals are three-ring, three-inch-thick red binders in which the policies are filed by department and, within each department, by the consecutive numbers. The first section of the manuals includes the policy indexes, which are updated and distributed each month.

Each department head, chief of clinical service, and administrative staff member has a policy and procedure manual, but he receives copies of only those policies and procedures that affect his unit. Thus, he does not have to sort through impertinent information.

The success or failure of a policy and procedure system depends on several circumstances, especially the following:

- The ability and the willingness of the coordinator to make the system work. The coordinator must enjoy policy and procedure formulation and must enjoy working with people as individuals and in groups.

- The level of support given to the coordinator and to the policy and procedure system by the hospital administration.

- The level of support given to the coordinator by department heads and chiefs of clinical services. The support of these key personnel depends on the extent to which they perceive the need for the system.

Many hospitals have found that the implementation of a policy and procedure system not only accomplishes the objectives of the policies and procedures that are formulated but also results in more effective management by forcing decision making on policy and procedure questions that previously have been unresolved. In addition, effective policy and procedure systems can help hospitals meet the requirements of accrediting and licensing agencies and regulatory bodies.

Readers who are interested in an even more detailed, step-by-step approach to policies and procedures will want to read Wright's "A Lesson in Procedure Writing." Wright's article supplements Okorafor's description of the Wishard Memorial Hospital policy and procedure system by taking the reader paragraph by paragraph through a sample procedure on drawing arterial blood gases. Potential problems in certain procedure sections are highlighted. The importance of indexing a procedure under various key terms is stressed in order to facilitate a nurse's quick, easy retrieval of the written procedure.

CRITERIA, STANDARDS, NORMS—
CRUCIAL TERMS IN QUALITY ASSURANCE

By Doris Bloch

Reprinted with permission from *The Journal of Nursing Administration,* Volume 7, Number 9, September, 1977, pp. 20–30.

As nursing administrators, clinical specialists, and educators spend more and more time drafting in-house audit and evaluation tools and then sharing them with nurses in other hospitals by documentation in professional journals, the correct use of terms becomes critical. This reading provides straightforward definitions of key concepts for those writing nursing practice standards, care plans, and clinical evaluation tools, as well as quality assurance audit criteria, norms, methods of measurement, and time frames[12].

The establishment of Professional Standards Review Organizations (PSROs) in 1972, as authorized by Public Law 92-603, greatly increased efforts among health care providers to evaluate and upgrade the quality of care. As quality assurance efforts have progressed, many individuals and groups have found it necessary to define certain terms pertinent to the task. (See Exhibit 5-1 for a sample of definitions.) Such proposed definitions have similarities; however, differences are equally evident. The need for clarifying and redefining many terms is not merely a case of semantics; clear and correct usage is a necessary foundation for the conceptual soundness of work based on these definitions.

The major concern in this article is with the terms crucial to health care evaluation: *criterion, standard,* and *norm.* The American Nurses' Association, the American Medical Association, PSROs, and combinations of nurses and physicians in hospitals and other health care agencies are working to develop criteria, establish standards, and determine norms.

It is the purpose of this article, therefore, to stimulate thinking and spark discussion.

There is a need for such rethinking, because, in my opinion, confusion exists regarding some definitions—especially in respect to "criterion" and "standard." These terms are commonly misapplied: "Standards" of medical and nursing care are now being developed nationwide under the label "criteria." The many developers, therefore, of such "criteria" are not fully aware that they are in actuality developing standards. The current application of the concept "standard" in some systems is not its optimum interpretation. This is especially true where "standard" refers to the proportion of patients (or records) who must "meet a criterion"—always stated at 100 percent or 0 percent, depending on a desirable or undesirable nature. Note that this application will not strengthen present standards, which are, of necessity, crude. An elusive, fruitless

Exhibit 5-1. Definitions of Terms

Criterion

- A quality, attribute, or characteristic of a variable that may be measured to provide scores by which subjects of the same class can be compared in relation to the variable [13]

- Criteria are defined by the PSRO Manual as predetermined elements against which aspects of the quality of a health service may be compared. They are developed by professionals relying on professional expertise and on the professional literature. In a general sense, criteria may be thought of as specific statements of health care that reflect nursing values. For the purpose of this manual, criteria are statements of structure, process, or outcome that can be measured [14]

- Specified elements of medical care considered appropriate or relevant to each diagnosis or condition [15]

- A variable selected as a relevant indicator of the quality of nursing care. A satisfactory criterion for quality of nursing care must not only be relevant, but must also be capable of yielding a range of scores or values. It must be sensitive to changes in or variations in the effectiveness of nursing care [16]

- Identifiable elements of care used to judge the appropriateness of that care [17]

- Medical care criteria are predetermined elements against which aspects of the quality of a medical service may be compared. They are developed by professionals relying on professional expertise and on the professional literature [18]

- A standard or model that can be used in judging [19]

Standard

- Agreed-upon level of excellence; established norm [20]

- The *desired* achievable (rather than the *observed*) performance or value with regard to a given parameter [21]

- The desired level of compliance with criteria or norms. Standards sometimes refer to criteria that have been validated by outcomes evaluation [22]

- The word "standards" carries the connotation that there is one score or one value on a variable that must be obtained if the quality of nursing care is to be judged to be satisfactory. The word "criterion" should not be used in this sense [23]

- The degree of adherence to the defined criteria [24]

- Professionally developed expressions of the range of acceptable variation from a norm or criterion [25]

Norm

- A statistical description of the central tendency of the observed values of a selected parameter, along with a measure of the variability of the values, taken from an adequate sample of corresponding studies. The central tendency may be expressed as an arithmetic mean (average), a geometric mean, a median, a mode, or a range of values within which can be found one or more of these statistics [26]

- Empiric measures of performance such as length of stay by diagnosis [27]

- A statistical average [28]

- Medical care appraisal norms are numerical or statistical measures of usual observed performance [29]

**Exhibit 5-2.   Criterion, Standard, Norm—
The Model: Exposure to Radiation at the ABC Hospital**

Criterion; or Criterion Variable; or Parameter	Method of Measurement	Standard	Critical Time	Norm
Exposure to radiation	Film badge	Less than 1250 millirems per quarter (3 months)	End of quarter	12 millirems per quarter

*rem="Roentgen Equivalent Man"

search for improved standards may ensue—elusive and fruitless because we will be searching in the wrong place.

As a model, let us consider the use of the terms as they relate to a hypothetical example in the area of radiation exposure. Exhibit 5-2 and the ensuing figures are a progressive revelation; information will be added in an incremental technique, so that Exhibit 5-2 the basic chart, is gradually enlarged as the definitions progress. This basic chart first names the variable (or criterion): "Exposure to radiation" (on the part of x-ray technicians at a hypothetical hospital). It goes on to identify a standard of maximum safe exposure, based on best current scientific knowledge, namely 1,250 millirems per quarter; where a millirem is the unit of measurement used to measure radiation exposure, as "gram" is used to measure the variable "weight." The column labeled "Norm" indicates that x-ray technicians at this hypothetical hospital have been found in past experience to receive an average of 12 millirems of radiation per quarter, well below the upper limit expressed by the standard. The column labeled "Critical Time" indicates that measurement or data collection takes place at the end of each quarter. The "Method of Measurement" column has been added to point up the importance of considering this issue for each criterion to be used in evaluation of care. In the radiation example, measurement is carried out through a so-called

film badge. It is worn by the person exposed to radiation and it records the radiation cumulatively.

The radiation example was purposely chosen because the variable is measurable and quantifiable. It is expected to serve to enhance understanding of the less easily measured criteria that of necessity must be used in the evaluation of the quality of health care.

CRITERION: DEFINITION AND ISSUES

On the basis of the previous example and certain definitions already proposed (see Exhibit 5-1), the following is submitted:

A criterion (or criterion variable or parameter) is the value-free name of a variable believed or known to be a relevant indicator of the quality of patient care (or medical care or nursing care).

With this definition, it is now possible to proceed from consideration of radiation exposure to matters more specifically related to patient care. Exhibit 5-3 lists some representative criteria.

It is essential to note that "criterion," in this conceptualization, refers only to the description or "name" of a variable (for example, "temperature"), *not to presence or absence, quantity, or value judgment.* Thus, even such specifications as "knowledge of all medications" and "incision free from infection" would

Exhibit 5-3.　Criteria: Examples

Criterion; or Criterion Variable;
　or Parameter

Exposure to radiation

Length of hospitalization
Systolic blood pressure
Temperature
Level of medication knowledge
　(or specified in more detail):
　Level of knowledge of types
　　of medications
　Level of knowledge of side effects
　　of medications
　Other
Amount of Pain
Condition of incision
Survival

move the statements out of the criterion category and into the realm of standards, because they go beyond the neutral naming of the variable (such as level of medication knowledge, condition of incision) to embody a quantity or value judgment (knowledge of *all* medications; *free from*—or *zero*—infection).

Criteria are developed by experienced practitioners for specific populations, such as patients after appendectomy, patients with chronic pain, or patients who are bedridden. (It may, of course, be necessary in many cases to be more explicit by further specifying parameters of the population, such as age, sex, or mental state.) The reader is to assume that the hypothetical criteria, standards, and so forth in this article refer to some defined population(s).

STANDARD: DEFINITION AND ISSUES

Again, on the basis of the radiation exposure model (Exhibit 5–2) and existing definitions

**Exhibit 5-4.　The Relationship
　　　　　between Criteria and Standards**

Criterion; or Criterion Variable; or Parameter	Standard
Exposure to radiation	Less than 1,250 millirems* per quarter (3 months)
Length of hospitalization	5 days
Systolic blood pressure	100–140
Temperature	98.0°–99.9°F
Level of medication knowledge (or specified in more detail):	Total score above 75%
Level of knowledge of types of medications	Score 100%
Level of knowledge of side effects of medications	Score above 75%
Other	Other
Amount of pain	Score below 3 Pain medication taken less than 4 times in 24 hr
Condition of incision	Score 0
Survival	Alive

*rem = "Roentgen Equivalent Man"

(see Exhibit 5-1), the following definition is proposed:

A standard is the desired and achievable level (or range) of performance corresponding with a criterion (or criterion variable or parameter), against which actual performance is computed.

Hypothetical examples in the area of patient care are presented in Exhibit 5-4 to illustrate the relationship between criteria and standards.

Standards will, of course, be set at different levels, depending on the population to which they are addressed. A pulse rate standard for a newborn infant, for example, would certainly differ from that for a post-surgical adult. The examples in Exhibit 5-8 are presented for the purpose of illustration, are purely hypothetical as stated previously, and are assumed to apply to some specified population.

Items such as length of hospitalization and temperature will probably require no further clarification—both are easily measurable. On the basis of some scientific knowledge; experience, or value judgment, a numerical value can be specified as the standard. However, for the knowledge or pain examples, typical parameters in the evaluation of nursing care, the reader may exclaim in exasperation. Who knows of a nice, neat instrument for measuring medication knowledge or pain that would produce nice, neat scores?

Logic, then, dictates a new column, as it is clearly impossible to designate a standard for a criterion variable without having some means—no matter how crude—for measuring the variable. The "Method of Measurement" column is therefore added to the basic chart and illustrated in Exhibit 5-5.

Again, length of hospitalization, temperature, and so forth present no difficulty; the KOM test, however, does. The state of the art is such that we have no KOM test, nor PSE Scale, nor an IIS; and, therefore, no specific score can be cited as in the standards column.

(These examples were chosen for precisely that reason.)

Assume, for the moment, that there *were* instruments available for administration, capable of being objectively scored. A standard could then be specified, just as in the case of systolic blood pressure. At this point in time, admittedly, the specifications of such a standard would seldom be based on scientific evidence; it would be a matter of value judgment. For example, consider the impact of the following: "We believe that a patient being discharged from the hospital after first diagnosis of diabetes should know the names of *all* his medications and should know *perfectly* how and when to take them" (score 100 percent on both items); "but we would be satisfied if the patient had a *good* understanding of what the medication is supposed to do, as well as a *good* knowledge of the *major* side effects to watch for" (score approximately 75 percent on both items).

As there are no scientific underpinnings for such standards at this time, different individuals and groups would undoubtedly establish somewhat different standards relative to a criterion such as medication knowledge. Surely one would like patients to achieve a 100 percent score on all components of the hypothetical test, but that is not a realistic expectation. It may also be surmised, however, that the experts who set radiation exposure standards—although they have scientific methods of measurement—similarly lack adequate scientific evidence to designate a maximum safe level of exposure; and that their standards are based, at least in part, on value judgments. Ideally, standards are, of course, set on the basis of scientific evidence, and if such evidence is available, it should be noted with precise referencing. This was done for the model criteria sets developed by the American Nurses' Association[30].

Exhibit 5-5. The Need to Specify Method of Measurement (Hypothetical Methods Included)

Criterion; or Criterion Variable; or Parameter	Method of Measurement	Standard
Exposure to radiation	Film badge	Less than 1,250 millirems* per quarter (3 months)
Length of hospitalization	Number of days	5 days
Systolic blood pressure	Sphygmomanometer	100–140
Temperature	Oral thermometer	98.0°–99.9°F
Level of medication knowledge (or specified in more detail):	KOM test (Knowledge of Medications Test)	Total score above 75%
Level of knowledge of types of medications	KOM test, Part A	Score 100%
Level of knowledge of side effects of medications	KOM test, Part B	Score above 75%
Other	Other	Other
Amount of pain	PSE scale (Pain Self-evaluation Scale)	Score below 3
	Count of amount of pain medication taken	Pain medication taken less than 4 times in 24 hr
Condition of incision	IIS (Infection Indicato Scale)	Score 0
Survival	Alive/deceased	Alive

*rem = "Roentgen Equivalent Man"

Exhibit 5-6.   The Need to Develop Methods of Measurement

Criterion; or Criterion Variable; or Parameter	Method of Measurement	Standard
Exposure to radiation	Film badge	Less than 1,250 millirems* per quarter (3 months)
Length of hospitalization	Number of days	5 days
Systolic blood pressure	Sphygmomanometer	100–140
Temperature	Oral thermometer	98.0°–99.9°F
Level of medication knowledge (or specified in more detail):		†
Level of knowledge of types of medication		Patient knows the names of *all* medications to be taken after discharge
Level of knowledge of of medication		Patient knows the *major* side effects of each medication
Other		Other
Amount of pain		Patient has little or no pain
	Count of amount of pain medication taken	Less than 4 times in 24 hr
Condition of incision		Infection: absent
Survival	Alive/deceased	Alive

*rem = "Roentgen Equivalent Man"
†Too broad a criterion to permit establishment of a standard

If a valid, reliable, and objectively scored instrument to measure a criterion (variable) were available, standards could be specified in quantitative terms, no matter how subjective and value-laden they might tend to be. In the absence of such an instrument, however, a standards statement becomes quite crude. Note how this revision is depicted in Exhibit 5–6.

These examples of standards are presented merely to make a point, not as well-developed statements worthy of emulation. *The reader should note that the criterion (variable) is measured, not the standard. The standard is some value, specified by experts, against which reality can be compared when the criterion variable is measured.*

NEEDED: METHODS OF MEASUREMENT

In Exhibit 5–6, standards equate more closely with reality than was (purposely) done in Exhibit 5–5, and with it, all the hypothetical methods of measurement have disappeared, leaving quite a number of blank spaces. These must be filled in by those who develop criteria.

Since quality assurance programs do not purport to do research, it is not expected that methods of measurement reach a high level of sophistication. However, principles from the fields of instrument development, observation, interviewing, and so forth should be applied. Measurement of the variable will of necessity have to be carried out in a softer-than-research manner, but methods of measurement should nevertheless have a reasonable degree of reliability and validity. In some cases a simple question may suffice. For the criterion "amount of pain," for example, a standard question (such as "Please tell me how much pain you have right now") scored on a simple scale might be sufficient. Such simple approaches should be developed and tested.

For the criterion "condition of incision," a simple yes or no dichotomy might be specified (such as "infection absent" or "infection present") in the place of the hypothetical IIS. The method of measurement could include clearly specified guidelines to indicate to the observer which observations constitute the absence or presence of infections.

To show that such a yes/no dichotomy is not different *in principle* from the hypothetical, multiple-score IIS, an illustration is presented in Exhibit 5–7.

CRITICAL TIME

Another important aspect becomes apparent as the chart in this article develops—critical time[31]. It is not feasible to specify standards without concurrent specification of a time frame to indicate at what point the standard is to be applied. Criteria, however, are independent of time, as well as value-free(see Exhibit 5–8).

Specification of a time frame, commonly done, does not present any major problems. Although standards may well be written to apply to various times during a patient's hospitalization (or thereafter), if data are collected by retrospective record audit, they can be collected at any time after the specified "critical time."

OTHER CONCEPTUALIZATIONS OF STANDARD

It is necessary to raise another issue at this point because of current interpretation by a number of groups[32, 33]. These interpretations are "screening" or "chart review standards." They are set at the level of 100 percent in cases where the goal is the attainment of a desirable condition and occasionally at 0 percent where the goal is the absence of an undesirable condition. (For example see Exhibit 5–9.)

Exhibit 5-7.   Using a Yes/No Dichotomy

Criterion	Measuring Instrument	Standard
Condition of Incision	IIS (Infection Indicator Scale) (range of scores: 0–10)	Score: 0
Condition of Incision	Infection Observation Guide* Infection present: Redness Tenderness Exudate Infection absent: No redness No tenderness No exudate	Infection absent

*Again, this example of the observation guide is presented merely to make a point, not as a well-developed tool ready for use

This means that when records for a certain category of patients are screened, *all* records that fail to meet the specified "screening criterion" (or, in the conceptualization discussed in this article, "fail to meet the specified standard") are to be pulled for further study.

Translated into the conceptualization as understood and described in this paper, the example in Exhibit 5-9 would read as in Exhibit 5-10.

There is a fundamental—and, I believe, important—difference between the two interpretations. In this writer's interpretation, a *"standard" is some value assumed by the criterion variable* (such as knowledge: 75 percent of perfect; or conditions of incision: infection absent). *It is not a proportion of patients (or their charts) who should meet the standard.* In the interpretation described here, the 100 percent "screening standard" is implied, rather than spelled out. The standard implies that *all* patients should attain that standard; it is assumed that *all* records of persons not meeting the standard be examined to ascertain the reason why it was not met. Exhibit 5-11 might help to clarify this point.

The issue might be clarified further in another way. Let us compare a patient care example with the radiation exposure model (see Exhibit 5-12).

The model clearly implies that 100 percent of the persons wearing the film badge should receive less than 1,250 millirems of radiation per quarter; there is no need to specify "100 percent." However, depending on the seriousness of the condition represented by the criterion (for example, survival; condition of incision; level of knowledge), frequency of occurrence, and possibly other circumstances, an agency could decide to sample randomly the cases that do not meet a particular standard, rather than to examine 100 percent. In other words, if 25 percent (say 15 a week) of all surgical patients in some hypothetical hospital develop an incisional infection, it may not be feasible to study each case. A thorough examination of the care given to a 33 percent sample (five infection patients) may be sufficient. This sample could pinpoint the problem, enabling faster action to eliminate it. Yet, every patient is expected to meet the standard, to be free from infection after surgery. Thus,

Exhibit 5-8.   The Need for Specification of a Time Frame (Critical Time)

Criterion; or Criterion Variable; or Parameter	Method of Measurement	Standard	Critical Time
Exposure to radiation	Film badge	Less than 1,250 millirems* per quarter (3 months)	End of quarter
Length of hospitalization	Number of days	5 days	Discharge
Systolic blood pressure	Sphygmomanometer	100–140	24 hr postoperatively
Temperature	Oral thermometer	98.0°–99.9°F	2 days postoperatively
Level of medication knowledge (or specified in more detail):		†	
Level of knowledge of types of medication		Patient knows the names of *all* medications to be taken after discharge	At or before discharge
Level of knowledge of side effects of medications		Patient knows the *major* side effects of each medication	At or before discharge
Other		Other	Other
Amount of pain		Patient has little or no pain	3 days postoperatively
	Count of amount of pain medication taken	Less than 4 times in 24 hr	3 days postoperatively
Condition of incision		Infection; absent	5 days postoperatively
Survival	Alive/deceased	Alive	At discharge

*rem = "Roentgen Equivalent Man"
†Too broad a criterion to permit establishment of a standard

Exhibit 5-9. Screening or Chart Review Standards

Screening Criterion	Chart Review Standard	Critical Time
Pulse rate 60–90 beats per minute	100%	By third postoperative day

Exhibit 5-10. Application of Screening Standards to Example

Criterion	Method of Measurement	Standard	Critical Time
Pulse rate	Palpation at radial artery	60–90 beats per minute	By third post-operative day

in the growing chart, "Sample for In Depth Review" has been added to address this issue (see Exhibit 5–15); it will be discussed later.

NORM: DEFINITION AND ISSUES

The concept "norm" appears to be more easily understood and less subject to confusion than either "criterion" or "standard." It clearly refers to the empirically established current state, relative to the criterion under consideration (see Exhibit 5–1). A definition is therefore proposed as follows:

A norm is the current level or range or performance corresponding with a criterion (or criterion variable or parameter) and is determined by descriptive study of "the here and now" in a given population, region, institution, group, and so forth.

It should be noted that norms are not developed—norms are determined by empirical study. It would appear that the determination of norms in nursing is a long way into the future, since a fantastic amount of study would be required. While some data are available for the specification of norms on a number of medical criteria (such as informa-

Exhibit 5-11. Clarification of Screening Standard Application

Criterion	Standard	Critical Time	Sample for in Depth Review (Implied)
Survival (after appendectomy)	Alive	At discharge	All (100%) records of patients not alive at discharge
Birth weight	Greater than 2,500 g	At birth	All (100%) records of infants with a birth weight of 2,500 grams or below

Exhibit 5-12.   Application of Screening Standards to Radiation Model

Criterion	Method of Measurement	Standard	Critical Time
Exposure to Radiation	Film badge	1,250 millirems per quarter	End of quarter
Condition of Incision	Infection Observation Guide: Infection Present: Redness Tenderness Exudate Infection Absent: No redness No tenderness No exudate	Infection: absent	5 days postoperatively

tion relative to the average length of hospitalization after different types of surgery, by hospital, geographic area, and even medical provider), the specification of nursing norms will first require the development of numerous, reliable methods for the measurement of the many relevant criterion variables. How else would it be possible to determine the current extent of patients' "level of preoperative anxiety," "level of motivation," or "amount of pain"?

Be that as it may, Exhibit 5-13 is presented to delineate the relationship between criteria, standards, and norms. The development of the hypothetical norm entries proved to be quite difficult for the criteria that are not easily quantified; if a method of measurement were available, a hospital could conceivably do a study and find, for example, that the patients' average knowledge of side effects is about 30 percent of the total possible effects. Without a method of measurement, norms are difficult to spell out, even hypothetically.

In the "Norm" column, the entry for the criterion "condition of incision" also proved

to be problematic. If there were available a numerical "degree of infection" scale, the answer would be simple—on a scale from 0 to 5, the infection norm might be a number such as 2. In the absence of such quantification methods, however, even a hypothetical average is difficult to specify. If the majority of patients have no infection, the norm is probably "infection absent." It clearly is not feasible to think of determining norms until adequate methods of measurement are available. This problem led to the addition of the "Evaluation: Standard Not Met" column (Exhibit 5-14). An institution should know what percentage of their patients meet the designated standard. Thus an evaluator can instantly determine to what extent the specified standards are met and whether there is an improvement over time.

A final column to augment the basic chart has been labeled "Sample for In-Depth Review" (Exhibit 5-15).

Based on the criticality of the criterion, the proportion of patients not meeting the corresponding standard, and possibly other con-

Exhibit 5-13. Relationship of Criteria, Standards, and Norms

Criterion; or Criterion Variable; or Parameter	Method of Measurement	Standard	Critical Time	Norm
Exposure to radiation	Film badge	Less than 1,250 millirems* per quarter (3 months)	End of quarter	12 millirems per quarter
Length of hospitalization	Number of days	5 days	Discharge	6 days
Systolic blood pressure	Sphygmomanometer	100–140	24 hr postoperatively	110
Temperature	Oral thermometer	98.0°–99.9°F	2 days postoperatively	99.8°F
Level of medication knowledge (or specified in more detail):		†		
Level of knowledge of types of medications		Patient knows the names of *all* medications to be taken after discharge	At or before discharge	60% (of names of medications)
Level of knowledge of side effects of medications		Patient knows the *major* side effects of each medication	At or before discharge	30% (of side effects)
Other		Other	Other	Other
Amount of pain		Patient has little or no pain	3 days postoperatively	Little pain
	Count of amount of pain medication taken	Less than 4 times in 24 hr	3 days postoperatively	2 times in 24 hr
Condition of incision		Infection: absent	5 days postoperatively	Absent
Survival	Alive/deceased	Alive	At discharge	Alive

*rem = "Roentgen Equivalent Man"
†Too broad a criterion to permit establishment of a standard

Exhibit 5-14.   Evaluation: Standard Not Met

Criterion; or Criterion Variable; or Parameter	Method of Measurement	Standard	Critical Time		Evaluation Standard Not Met‡
Exposure to radiation	Film badge	Less than 1,250 millirems* per quarter (3 months)	End of quarter	12 millirems per quarter	
Length of hospitalization	Number of days	5 days	Discharge	6 days	70%
Systolic blood pressure	Sphygmomanometer	100–140	24 hr postoperatively	110	15%
Temperature	Oral thermometer	98.0°–99.9°F	2 days postoperatively	99.8°F	30%
Level of medication knowledge (or specified in more detail):		†			
Level of knowledge of types of medications		Patient knows the names of *all* medications to be taken after discharge	At or before discharge	60% (of names of medications)	55%
Level of knowledge of side effects of medications		Patient knows the *major* side effects of each medication	At or before discharge	30% (of side effects)	75%
Other		Other	Other	Other	Other
Amount of pain		Patient has little or no pain	3 days postoperatively	Little pain	20%
	Count of amount of pain medication taken	Less than 4 time in 24 hr	3 days postoperatively	2 times in 24 hr	25%
Condition of incision		Infection: absent	5 days postoperatively	Absent	25%
Survival	Alive/deceased	Alive	At discharge	Alive	1%

*rem = "Roentgen Equivalent Man"
†Too broad a criterion to permit establishment of a standard
‡Percent of patients (or records)

Exhibit 5-15. Sample for In-Depth Review

Criterion; or Criterion Variable; or Parameter	Method of Measurement	Standard	Critical Time	Evaluation Standard Not Met‡	Sample for In Depth Review§
Exposure to radiation	Film badge	Less than 1,250 millirems* per quarter (3 months)	End of quarter	12 millirems per quarter	
Length of hospitalization	Number of days	5 days	Discharge	6 days	70%	50%
Systolic blood pressure	Sphygmomanometer	100–140	24 hr postoperatively	110	15%	100%
Temperature	Oral thermometer	98.0°–99.9°F	2 days postoperatively	99.8°F	30%	100%
Level of medication knowledge (or specified in more detail):		†			
Level of of types of medications		Patient knows the *all* medications to be taken after discharge	At or before discharge	60% (of names of medications)	55%	25%
Level of knowledge of side effects of medications		Patient knows the *major* side effects of each medication	At or before discharge	30% (of side effects)	75%	25%
Other		Other	Other	Other	Other	Other
Amount of pain		Patient has little or not pain	3 days postoperatively	Little pain	20%	25%
	Count of amount of pain medication taken	Less than 4 times in 24 hr	3 days postoperatively	2 times in 24 hr	25%	25%
Condition of incision		Infection: absent	5 days postoperatively	Absent	25%	50%
Survival	Alive/deceased	Alive	At discharge	Alive	1%	100%

*rem = "Roentgen Equivalent Man"
†Too broad a criterion to permit establishment of a standard
‡Percent of patients (or records)
§Percent of patients (or records) not meeting standard

siderations, a given institution might specify what proportion of those records not meeting the standards should be examined in depth to pinpoint reasons for failure. For example, the criterion "survival" is of such utmost importance that 100 percent of cases not meeting the standard "alive at discharge" should be examined. The criterion "condition of incision" is certainly of importance to state of health, but of distinctly lesser degree than survival. In the hypothetical example (Exhibit 5–15), a rather large proportion of patients (25 percent) do not meet the standard of absence of infection, and therefore a hypothetical decision to examine only 50 percent of these records has been made. Then, in the case of the knowledge examples, such a large proportion of patients (between 55 and 75 percent) do not meet the standard that a 100 percent review might be completely unmanageable. Further, the effort would probably not be cost effective, thus eliciting a decision to sample only 25 percent of those records.

It should be noted that the entries in the "Sample for In Depth Review" column are not a consistent 100 percent (or 0 percent) as in the "Chart Review Standard" column in some other systems. In this suggested column the entries would be determined by an institution itself on the basis of its particular findings and circumstances.

EPILOGUE

This article evolved from a belief that the terms "criterion" and "standard" are often misapplied, and that standards are at the present time being developed under the label "criteria." The concept "criterion" is interpreted here as the name of a variable. A variable must be identified and named (1) before a method of measurement can be developed and (2) before a standard can be established for it.

The naming and listing of criteria or criterion variable for patient outcomes is probably somewhat simpler than standard setting since criteria are value-free. In contrast, the setting of standards corresponding with such outcome criteria for the numerous possible patient populations will be a long, painstaking effort. Ideally, such standards are based upon scientific evidence, but this will not be possible in a large number of cases; standards will often have to be set on the basis of value judgment and professional experience. The American Nurses' Association, in developing its model criteria sets, has made a valiant effort to use scientific evidence as a basis for standard development[34]. Such standards are subject to change, of course, as more, updated, and new scientific evidence becomes available. Continuous reevaluation of standards will therefore be necessary.

A largely neglected area is the matter of measurement of the criterion variable (witness the blanks in the progressive chart). Each criteria set must be formulated to include a column that specifies "method of measurement." The omission of measurement methods may well constitute the greatest inadequacy in current efforts to evaluate the quality of patient care through outcome evaluation.

The model presented in this article is different from those currently in wide use throughout the country. It may be valuable for retrospective record audit, concurrent review, and "Medical Care Evaluation Studies" (terminology used in the PSRO system). The reader is challenged to compare the usefulness of the various approaches.

USING VISUAL AIDS

By Paul R. Corts

From R. Capps and J.R. O'Connor (Eds.), *Fundamentals of Effective Speech Communication*, Copyright © 1978. Reprinted by permission of Winthrop Publishers, Inc., Cambridge, Mass.

Although the following discussion of the use of visual aids was intended for speechmakers, we include it in this unit on written communication because visual illustrations are as valuable an aid to written texts as to oral presentations.

You are probably familiar with the old saying that a thousand words cannot a picture make. Or put another way, one picture is worth a thousand words. This familiar saying is especially appropriate when considering the use of visual aids in relation to speechmaking.

Just as we can say that one picture is worth a thousand words, we can also say that a thousand words amplifying a picture can make that picture worth still more. In other words, visual aids should never overshadow the speaker or the speech, but should rather serve to assist the communication process with the dissemination of information through another sense, the visual. A careful blending of the visual with the oral actually complements both and represents an extremely high order of effective and efficient communication.

One of the most valuable uses of the visual aid is its ability to specify material. A visual presentation is consistently more accurate and reliable than an oral description. This is especially true when dealing with large numbers or large amounts of information and it is often true in making comparative analyses. A visual aid can deal with many numbers by putting them semipermanently in front of the audience visually. This is often more effective than a speaker orally communicating those numbers, which are either easily forgotten by an audience or readily run together. Neither of these unfortunate circumstances occurs when large amounts of information are placed in the nature of well-chosen visual aids.

Modern rhetorical theorists, who stress the need for communication and the avoidance as much as possible of even the chances for miscommunication, stress the value of *precise* communication, which is made possible through the use of visualization. The process of defining terms, of making certain that those spoken to are receiving a communication as intended by the one speaking, is enhanced by the assistance that a visual aid can give to the oral presentation. Modern communication, which is so heavily laden with information dissemination either exclusively, or as a part of a persuasion process, has special needs for the visualization process.

The use of the visual sense in no way detracts from the speaker when visual aids are properly used. In fact, the supporting visual material can free the speaker from the sheer drudgery of merely communicating precise data. The visual aid can actually disseminate the crucial information. This chapter describes basic visual aid types and some general rules to follow in using these materials.

TYPES OF VISUAL AIDS

Chart

The typical chart is used to describe relationships existing among various entities. The most frequently used chart is probably an organizational chart, which shows the nature of the relationship between the various parts. In the example provided (Exhibit 5-16) you see an organizational chart with lines demonstrating different types of relationships that exist. This type of chart is frequently used in business and professional speaking. This is often called a "line-staff" chart.

Graph

Graphs are generally used to aid in disseminating large amounts of information. A graph is also a helpful device to use when making comparisons between or among sets of data. Different types of graphs range from a very simple line graph to a more complex picture graph. In the accompanying examples you will find illustrations of a line graph, a pie graph, and a picture graph (Exhibits 5-17, 5-18, and 5-19). The line and pie graphs are relatively easy to draw. The most complex of the graphs, the picture graph, can be easily and professionally done with the use of com-

ADMINISTRATIVE ORGANIZATION OF
DEPARTMENT OF ECONOMIC SECURITY

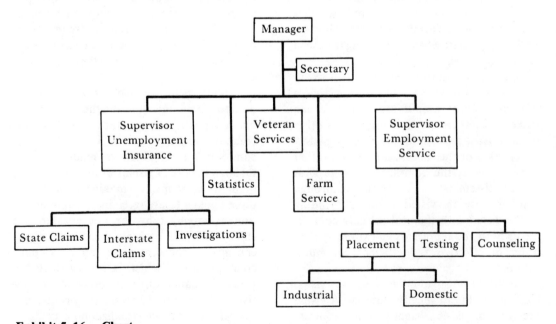

Exhibit 5–16.   Chart

mercial materials that are available in most college bookstores. When using a graph to make a comparison, be certain that the graph is highlighted properly to emphasize your intended comparison.

Diagram

Diagrams can range from a very simple explanation to an extremely complex series of interrelationships. The basic purpose of a diagram is to demonstrate through the visual sense as clearly as possible the interrelationships of various parts to a whole (Exhibit 5-20). A very effective diagram can be created through the use of plastic transparency mate-

rials, which can be laid one on top of another. This process is referred to as a transparency overlay and allows a speaker to demonstrate interrelationships of parts to the whole by starting with a very simple diagram on one plastic transparency and then, without removing the first simple diagram, laying another transparency immediately on top of the first. The second transparency will give additional dimensions. This process can be repeated with three, four, or even more transparencies laid one on top of another. Through these steps a complex interrelationship is built which allows the viewer to see, step by step, the explanation which you are making orally.

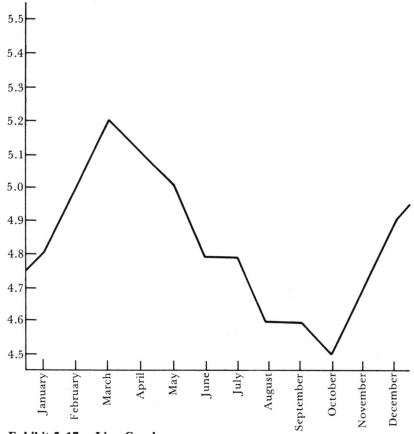

PERCENT OF PROFESSIONAL WORK FORCE UNEMPLOYED IN 1978

Exhibit 5-17.   Line Graph

GENERAL FUND BUDGET DOLLAR

Where It Comes From

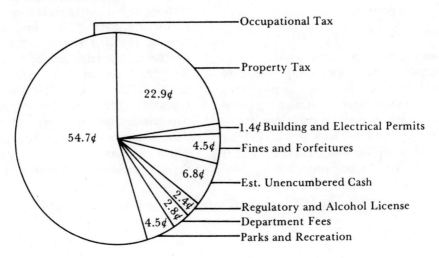

Where It Goes

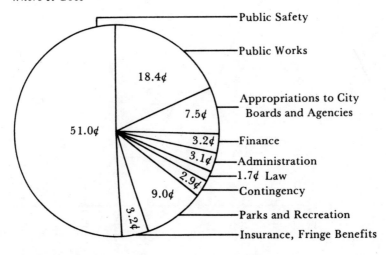

Exhibit 5-18.   Pie Graph

Maps

A map is considered a special type of visual aid because of the various functions that a map visually serves. Maps may be used simply to indicate geographical boundaries. However, a map can become very complex when other dimensions are added to simple boundary demarcations. Exhibits 5-21 and 5-22 provide examples of a simple map and a more complex dimensional map.

Object

Sometimes it is convenient for you to use a real object. To incorporate the use of a real object as a part of your speech, if the object is too large itself, you may use a model which is prepared on a scale to the original. Often an object used as a part of a demonstration has the capacity to be taken apart and put back together so that procedures can be explained in the speech and demonstrated visually with

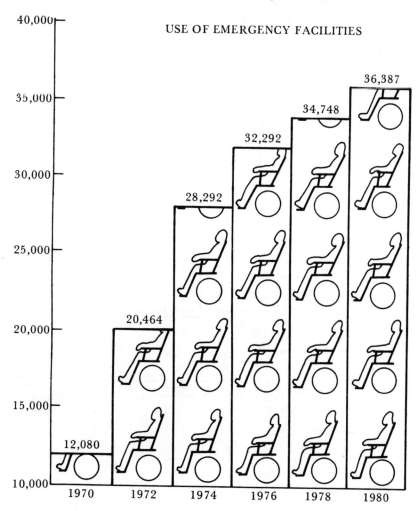

Exhibit 5–19.   Picture Graph

WALL SUPPORT FOR BRICK VENEER HOME

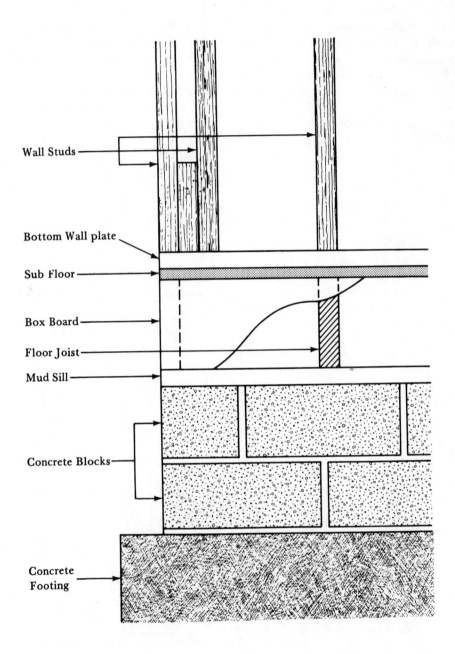

Wall Studs

Bottom Wall plate

Sub Floor

Box Board

Floor Joist

Mud Sill

Concrete Blocks

Concrete
Footing

Exhibit 5–20.   Diagram

the use of the real object. For instance, if a speaker were making a presentation on the structural aspect of automobile safety, he could use a small model automobile as a real object to demonstrate numerous points in oral presentation. A demonstration can also use a model or real object that may not be taken apart and put back together, but that may simply expose items on the inside that are not normally seen. This type of object used in a demonstration is referred to as a "cutaway." In either case, this can be a very useful and practical visual aid to a speech/demonstration.

Cartoon

The success of humor in presenting a speech has always been recognized as an especially good gift. A cartoon can assist a speaker with a visual exaggeration that will create humor. This device can be very successful in disseminating information or in persuading. Not everyone is capable of preparing a cartoon to use as a visual aid in his or her speech, but for those with an artistic touch the use of cartoons can make a fine contribution to an otherwise dull oral presentation (Exhibit 5-23).

Print

Many speakers would not recognize that a simple visual aid with nothing more than letter print has the potential for being a very successful visualization. However, lettering and printing words on a posterboard for the sake of saying, "I have a visual aid," will not automatically make a successful presentation. The use of creative lettering coordinated with the oral presentation of a speech can make a success. Type styles, letter size, the dimensions of letters, spacing, and the use of stencils are all important items to consider when preparing a print visual aid. Professional lettering is available in most college book stores and art supply stores in a variety of type styles that allow lettering to be made by rubbing over a carbon letter with a pencil, causing the letter to stick on a posterboard at the desired location. Through the use of this professional

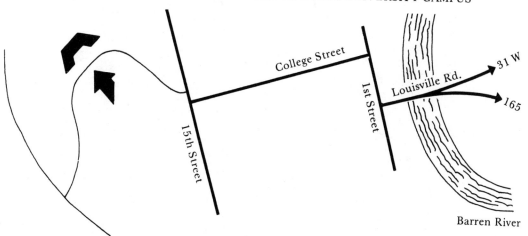

LOCATION OF CENTER FOR FINE ARTS ON STATE UNIVERSITY CAMPUS

Exhibit 5–21.   Simple Map

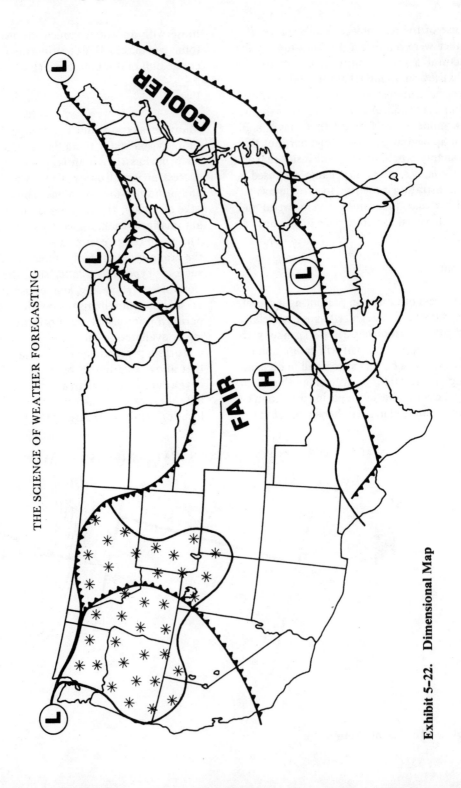

THE SCIENCE OF WEATHER FORECASTING

Exhibit 5-22.   Dimensional Map

adhesive lettering, one can make a very attractive print visual aid.

Photo, Slide, Filmstrip, or Film

Prepared photos, slides, filmstrips, or films are sometimes available and can be used as effective visual aids. Snapshot photos would rarely be appropriate for speaking situations because of their small size. An 8 × 10 photo might be appropriate for a very small audience if the picture did not have too much detail. Small photos could be transferred to a slide for projection or the speaker could use an opaque projector. However, because of the possible problems involved, beginning speakers should not attempt to use regular photos if any alternative is available. Already prepared slides, filmstrips, or films can be projected to the appropriate size, but the speaker should

be aware that film-related visual aids sometimes overpower the speaker. Usually a small amount of film, filmstrip, or slides is sufficient. The beginning speaker should be on guard to keep the audience's primary attention focused on the speaker and the speech, not on the visual aid.

Any type of film, whether a motion picture, a filmstrip, or a slide, is a picture; but a picture can also be shown if it is in print form. As you research for your speeches and find pictures in magazines or books which you believe would be useful visual aids to accompany your oral presentation, keep in mind that most pictures can be reproduced and enlarged in the classroom through the use of an overhead opaque projector.

The most important consideration in using the visual aids discussed here is to be aware of their potential for overpowering the speaker.

A Good Speaker Is........

- on time
- prepared
- organized
- well-groomed
- pleasant

Exhibit 5–23. Cartoon

The speaker must carefully plan his visuals so that they will supplement his own performance and add to the total communication act.

MEDIA FORMS

Posterboard and Felt-Tip Pen

The value of the posterboard and a felt-tip pen is the easy availability of the materials and the relative ease of preparation. If you use this form, be sure to use a large posterboard and make your lettering or drawing large enough to be easily seen by the entire audience. This media form is also especially useful because of its adaptability for almost any visual aid type. Even photos can be mounted on posterboard with print elaboration.

Flip charts (or chart pads) and felt-tip pens should be mentioned here. These are pads of large pieces of paper that can either be taped to the wall, hung on heavy duty screws on an office wall, or clipped onto metal easels manufactured for that purpose. They are excellent for workshops, group brainstorming, and task force work. They provide efficient note pads for meetings and conferences for two reasons: first, large amounts of information can be placed on a chart pad prior to the meeting; second, they provide a visible demonstration of progression of the group's work. Afterward, the charted information can easily be typed directly from the sheets into minutes or conference proceedings. Some of the most prestigious conferences we have attended have included much use of inexpensive newsprint chart pads. Pads of higher-grade paper with lines are nice for conference notes that will be reused.
We have found white drafting tape to be the least damaging to windows or painted walls. "Nontoxic" felt pens will be less likely to cause headache when you are using them for several hours, as in a workshop.

Transparency—Overhead Projector

A transparency is a sheet of clear acetate, normally 8½ × 11 in size, which is used with an overhead projector to project an image onto a screen or wall. Lettering or drawing can be done directly onto the clear acetate sheet with a felt-tip pen. Through special equipment, a transparency can photographically reproduce material from a printed page or a hand-prepared document. The transparency and overhead projector can also team up for an effective on the spot presentation which can be used in place of a chalkboard. The transparency has several advantages. First, a speaker can write on the transparency while continuing to face the audience. Second, colors can be used on the transparency, which will enliven the presentation. Third, the speaker can move quickly and easily from one acetate sheet to another without erasing the board or boggling with a large and sometimes cumbersome posterboard. Fourth, the transparency provides the option for using an overlay technique, which permits the speaker to have a multidimensional presentation by placing one acetate sheet over another to provide step by step completion of a visual aid.

Photo, Slide, Filmstrip, or Film

Film-related visual aids taken specifically for a speech usually require careful planning and setting development, which simply is impossible for many speakers. This media preparation form should not be confused with already produced and available photos, slides, filmstrips, or films which constitute a visual aid type. Photos, slides, filmstrips, or films are visual aid media forms and can be used to display other visual aid types. A chart, graph, or diagram, for instance, could be prepared in slide form for presentation or it could be prepared on a posterboard or transparency.

Opaque Projection

Through the use of an opaque projector, most visual aid types can be projected onto a screen or wall. The opaque projector will project an image from a printed page, a photo, picture, chart, or any reasonably flat, unidimensional object. It usually requires no preparation by the speaker since it simply projects an already produced image. Because of the noise associated with this projector, a beginning speaker should carefully plan use of the equipment so that use of this aid does not detract from the speaker. An opaque projector, in contrast to the overhead projector, requires a darkened room, which can also be distracting to the audience.

Audio

Although this selection is entitled "Using Visual Aids," audio aids are usually considered in conjunction with the visual. Beginning speakers seldom use audio aids but it is a media form you should be familiar with. Cassette audio tapes and small cassette players make this audio aid easily accessible. The change of pace for the audience in hearing another voice can also help hold attention and increase audience interest. A brief oral excerpt from a personal interview is an example of how an audio aid could be used in a speech. If you use an audio aid, be certain the tone quality is clear and that the volume is appropriate for the speech setting.

RULES FOR PREPARATION AND PRESENTATION

Choose Material Carefully

If you are creating a visual aid that must be placed on some type of object, first decide if you will use posterboard, plastic transpar-

ency, film, or some other type material. In dealing with an object for a model for demonstration, carefully choose the particular type of object or the appropriate type of model. Regular bond paper is never an acceptable material to use for a visual aid for an audience the size of a typical class. Bond paper is usually too small in size, too flimsy to stand up, and too thin to be opaque. Even in using posterboard, you should be cautioned about its tendency to bend, and its lack of solidity. Many speakers make excellent plans for using visual aids to accompany speeches only to find that the posterboard visual aid will not stand where it is placed and there is no equipment available to assist in holding the flimsy cardboard. Similarly, if a speaker plans to use film or a transparency which requires projection, the speaker should be aware that projectors are extremely noisy and that projection light bulbs frequently burn out, even in the middle of the speech. A speaker who prepares a very fine visual aid for projection, but who is unable to be heard because the projector makes more noise than the speaker, will not present a successful speech. However, these are really simple problems that can be easily accommodated if the speaker plans in advance, is aware that these problems may arise, and has a prepared plan for coping with these problems if they develop.

Check the Size

A visual aid, to be successful, must surely be large enough to be easily seen from any part of the audience. A visual aid with small finely detailed print, which forces members of the audience to strain in an effort to see it, will not aid the speaker, but will instead detract from the overall success of the speech. If possible, check visual aids for size in the actual situation in which the visual aids will be used. It is easy to be mistaken on size if you rely solely on your imaginative judgment.

Rehearse with the Equipment

If the visual material requires some type of special equipment, take all precautions to make certain that the equipment can be available for the particular session. Become familiar with the operation of the equipment so that a smooth transition can be made in the speech. If there are particular problems associated with the use of the equipment, such as noisy or clumsy operation, you should determine through advance preparations and trial runs the effective ways of coping with these problems. If you are inexperienced at using the equipment, don't trust your imagination but actually rehearse with the equipment.

Be Clear

Many visual aids fail to be effective and successful because the audience cannot understand the visual aid. In preparing visual material you will do well to remember that a small amount of information presented within a large framework represents the most successful approach. Considerable open space on a visual aid is important so that a listener can easily and quickly grasp a very specific but limited amount of information from the visual aid. The purpose is defeated if the audience is forced to study considerable minutiae. A simple visual aid will be more effective than an overly complex visual presentation.

Be Creative

Not everyone is an artist, but everyone has the potential for presenting a respectable, legible, neat, and colorful visual aid. In preparing visual materials, it is important to remember some of the crucial elements affecting the visual such as color, shape, size, and dimension. These elements, appropriately selected in composing a visual aid, can help the nonartist produce a highly artistic presentation.

Keep Talking

In using a visual aid a speaker should make every effort to continue speaking to the audience while using the visual aid—rather than turning and speaking to the visual aid itself. Of course, it is a standard rule that the speaker should never turn his back to the audience. This is especially important when projection of the voice is crucial in a large room. Generally, the visual aid should be completed before the speech so that the speaker can devote attention to speaking rather than working on completion of the visual aid. A period of silence in the speech will distract the audience attention from the speaker and allow the visual aid to usurp the speaker's central role.

Don't Let the Aid Become the Speech

It is easy for an inexperienced speaker to rely too much on a visual aid to support a speech. The temptation to let the visual aid be the most important factor in the speech is especially overpowering for an inexperienced speaker who finds it more comfortable to let visual material, prepared in advance, replace the speaker as the communicator. A successful visual aid simply must not become the speech.

To avoid this problem, keep the visual aid itself relatively simple and keep your presentation of the aid straight and to the point. As you first show the visual aid, orally introduce it with a comment such as "In this graph we can see that. . ."; or "This map locates . . ."; or "This mock-up shows . . . ." Then, while continuing to face the audience as directly as possible, briefly describe orally the essential elements of the visual aid stressing the major point to be seen in the aid. Having completed the use of the visual aid for its intended purpose, quickly and gracefully remove it from the sight of the audience so that it will not be a competing stimulus as you continue your speech. As you are physically removing the visual aid, continue the oral presentation of your planned speech.

The amount of time devoted to a visual aid should be related to the total speech. For instance, if you are giving a ten-minute speech and using three visual aids, each aid should normally consume no more than thirty seconds, approximately one-twentieth of the total speech. Excluding a normal introduction and conclusion of a ten-minute speech, three such visual aids would represent approximately one-sixth of the speech.

SUMMARY

Visual aids can be useful additions to effective speechmaking. While they should never over-shadow or replace the speech itself, visual presentations provide informative, interesting, and supportive material for the speech.

Basic visual aid types include charts, graphs, diagrams, maps, objects, cartoons, print, photos, slides, filmstrips, or films.

Media forms used to present visual aids include posterboard and felt-tip pen, transparency for overhead projector, and some types of film, opaque projection, and audio.

In preparing and presenting visual aids, the speaker should choose material carefully, rehearse with the aid, and be clear and creative in its presentation. The speaker should always continue speaking while presenting the aid. It is also very important that the visual aid not become the speech.

Although these rules should appear easy to follow, the beginning speaker will find that the biggest problem connected with using visual aids is the difficulty of doing two things at once: speaking while handling an aid. Careful advance preparation, full familiarity with the aid, and rehearsing with the aid can help you use visual aids successfully to make your speech more fully communicative.

CLEAR WRITING MEANS CLEAR THINKING MEANS...
By Marvin H. Swift

Reprinted by permission of the Harvard Business Review. "Clear Writing Means Clear Thinking Means..." by M.H. Swift (January-February 1973).

This selection from the Harvard Business Review *quickly and sensitively walks a reader through the process of writing and rewriting one of administrators' and managers' most common channels of written communication— the memo. The last page is especially worth noting. Indeed, clarifying and refining our writing is important, but how often do we try to improve and clarify our THINKING?*

If you are a manager, you constantly face the problem of putting words on paper. If you are like most managers, this is not the sort of problem you enjoy. It is hard to do, and time consuming, and the task is doubly difficult when, as is usually the case, your words must be designed to change the behavior of others in the organization.

But the chore is there and must be done. How? Let's take a specific case.

Let's suppose that everyone at X Corporation, from the janitor on up to the chairman of the board, is using the office copiers for personal matters: income tax forms, church programs, children's term papers, and God knows what else are being duplicated by the gross. This minor piracy costs the company a pretty penny, both directly and in employee time, and the general manager—let's call him Sam

Edwards—decides the time has come to lower the boom.

Sam lets fly by dictating the following memo to his secretary:

TO: All Employees

FROM: Samuel Edwards
       General Manager

Subject: Abuse of Copiers

It has recently been brought to my attention that many of the people who are employed by this company have taken advantage of their positions by availing themselves of the copiers. More specifically, these machines are being used for other than company purposes.

Obviously, such practice is contrary to company policy and must cease and desist immediately. I wish therefore to inform all concerned--those who have abused policy or will be abusing it--that their behavior cannot and will not

be tolerated. Accordingly, anyone
in the future who is unable to
control himself will have his
employment terminated.

If there are any questions about
company policy, please feel free
to contact this office.

Now the memo is on his desk for his signature.
He looks it over; and the more he looks, the
worse it reads. In fact, it's lousy. So he revises
it three times, until it finally is in the form that
follows:

To: All Employees

From: Samuel Edwards
       General Manager

Subject: Use of Copiers

We are revamping our policy on the
use of copiers for personal matters. In the past we have not
encouraged personnel to use them
for such purposes because of the
costs involved. But we also
recognize, perhaps belatedly, that
we can solve the problem if each
of us pays for what he takes.

We are therefore putting these
copiers on a pay-as-you-go basis.
The details are simple enough . . .

Samuel Edwards

This time Sam thinks the memo looks
good, and it *is* good. Not only is the writing
much improved, but the problem should now
be solved. He therefore signs the memo, turns
it over to his secretary for distribution, and
goes back to other things.

FROM VERBIAGE TO INTENT

I can only speculate on what occurs in a writer's mind as he moves from a poor draft to a
good revision, but it is clear that Sam went
through several specific steps, mentally as
well as physically, before he had created his
end product:

- He eliminated wordiness.
- He modulated the tone of the memo.
- He revised the policy it stated.

Let's retrace his thinking through each of
these processes.

Eliminating Wordiness

Sam's basic message is that employees are not
to use the copiers for their own affairs at
company expense. As he looks over his first
draft, however, it seems so long that this simple message has become diffused. With the
idea of trimming the memo down, he takes
another look at his first paragraph:

It has recently been brought to my
attention that many of the people
who are employed by this company
have taken advantage of their
positions by availing themselves
of the copiers. More specifically, these machines are being
used for other than company purposes.

He edits it like this:

Item:	"recently"
Comment to himself:	Of course; else why write about the problem? So delete the word.
Item:	"It has been brought to my atten- tion"

Comment:	Naturally. Delete it.
Item:	"the people who are employed by this company"
Comment:	Assumed. Why not just "employees"?
Item:	"by availing themselves" and "for other than company business"
Comment:	Since the second sentence repeats the first, why not coalesce?

And he comes up with this:

Employees have been using copiers for personal matters.

He then proceeds to the second paragraph. More confident of himself; he moves in broader swoops, so that the deletion process looks like this:

Obviously, such practice is contrary to company policy and ~~must cease and desist immediately. I wish therefore to inform all concerned--those who have abused policy or will be abusing it--that their behavior cannot and will not be tolerated. Accordingly, anyone in the future who is unable to control himself will have his employment terminated.~~ will result in dismissal.

The final paragraph, apart from "company policy" and "feel free," looks all right, so the total memo now reads as follows:

To: All Employees

From: Samuel Edwards
        General Manager

Subject: Abuse of Copiers

Employees have been using the copiers for personal matters. Obviously, such practice is contrary to company policy and will result in dismissal.

If there are any questions, please contact this office.

Sam now examines his efforts by putting these questions to himself:

Question:	Is the memo free of deadwood?
Answer:	Very much so. In fact, it's good, tight prose.
Question:	Is the policy stated?
Answer:	Yes. But it sounds foolish.
Question:	Why?
Answer:	The wording is too harsh; I'm not going to fire anybody over this.
Question:	How should I tone the thing down?

To answer this last question, Sam takes another look at the memo.

CORRECTING THE TONE

What strikes his eye as he looks it over? Perhaps these three words:

• Abuse . . .
• Obviously . . .
• . . .dismissal. . .

The first one is easy enough to correct: he substitutes "use" for "abuse." But "obviously" poses a problem and calls for reflection. If the policy is obvious, why are the copiers being used? Is it that people are outrightly dishonest? Probably not. But that implies the policy is not obvious; and whose fault is this? Who neglected to clarify policy? And why "dismissal" for something never publicized?

These questions impel him to revise the memo once again:

To: All Employees

From: Samuel Edwards
        General Manager

Subject: Use of Copiers

Copiers are not to be used for
personal matters. If there are
any questions, please contact this
office.

REVISING THE POLICY ITSELF

The memo now seems courteous enough—at least it is not discourteous—but it is just a blank, perhaps overly simple statement of policy. Has he really thought through the policy itself?

Reflecting on this, Sam realizes that some people will continue to use the copiers for personal business anyhow. If he seriously intends to enforce the basic policy (first sentence), he will have to police the equipment, and that raises the question of costs all over again.

Also, the memo states that he will maintain an open-door policy (second sentence)—and surely there will be some, probably a good many, who will stroll in and offer tò pay for what they use. His secretary has enough to do without keeping track of affairs of that kind.

Finally, the first and second sentences are at odds with each other. The first says that personal copying is out, and the second implies that it can be arranged.

The facts of organizational life thus force Sam to clarify in his own mind exactly what his position on the use of copiers is going to

be. As he sees the problem now, what he really wants to do is put the copiers on a pay-as-you-go basis. After making that decision, he begins anew:

To: All Employees

From: Samuel Edwards
        General Manager

Subject: Use of copiers

We are revamping our policy on the
use of copiers.

This is the draft that goes into distribution and now allows him to turn his attention to other problems.

THE CHICKEN OR THE EGG?

What are we to make of all this? It seems a rather lengthy and tedious report of what, after all, is a routine writing task created by a problem of minor importance. In making this kind of analysis, have I simply labored the obvious?

To answer this question, let's drop back to the original draft. If you read it over, you will see that Sam began with this kind of thinking:

• "The employees are taking advantage of the company."

• "I'm a nice guy, but now I'm going to play Dutch uncle."

∴ I'll write them a memo that tells them to shape up or ship out."

In his final version, however, his thinking is quite different:

• "Actually, the employees are pretty mature, responsible people. They're capable of understanding a problem."

• "Company policy itself has never been crystallized. In fact, this is the first memo on the subject."

- "I don't want to overdo this thing—any employee can make an error in judgment."
∴ "I'll set a reasonable policy and write a memo that explains how it ought to operate."

Sam obviously gained a lot of ground between the first draft and the final version, and this implies two things. First, if a manager is to write effectively, he needs to isolate and define, as fully as possible, all the critical variables in the writing process and scrutinize what he writes for its clarity, simplicity, tone, and the rest. Second, after he has clarified his thoughts on paper, he may find that what he has written is not what has to be said. In this case, writing is feedback and a way for the manager to discover himself. What are his real attitudes toward that amorphous, undifferentiated gray mass of employees "out there"? Writing is a way of finding out. By objectifying his thoughts in the medium of language, he gets a chance to see what is going on in his mind.

In other words, *if the manager writes well, he will think well.* Equally, the more clearly he has thought out his message before he starts to dictate, the more likely he is to get it right on paper the first time round. In other words, *if he thinks well, he will write well.*

Hence, we have a chicken-and-the-egg situation: writing and thinking go hand in hand; and when one is good, the other is likely to be good.

REVISION SHARPENS THINKING

More particularly, rewriting is the key to improved thinking. It demands a real open-mindedness and objectivity. It demands a willingness to cull verbiage so that ideas stand out clearly. And it demands a willingness to meet logical contradictions head on and trace them to the premises that have created them. In short, it forces a writer to get up his courage and expose his thinking process to his own intelligence.

Obviously, revising is hard work. It demands that you put yourself through the wringer, intellectually and emotionally, to squeeze out the best you can offer. Is it worth the effort? Yes, it is—if you believe you have a responsibility to think and communicate effectively.

Readers who write a large number of memos may want to consider printing their own memo form. On the bottom third of the piece of paper, list actions, responses, or expectations that you frequently request in memos. Phrases like "read, initial, and route to __," "read and respond," and "reply needed immediately," along with a variety of others can then be checked instead of individually written time after time. Such printing can usually be done inexpensively and allows you to spend your time in more important communication modes.

REFERENCES AND NOTES

1. Abdellah, F. Overview of nursing research 1955-1968, part 1. *Nurs. Res.* 19:6-17, 1970.
2. Taylor, S. Bibliography on nursing research 1950-1974. *Nurs. Res.* 24:207-225, 1975.
3. Gortner, S., and Nahm, H. An overview of nursing research in the United States. *Nurs. Res.* 26:10-29, 1977.
4. Lindeman, C. Delphi survey of priorities in a clinical nursing research. *Nurs. Res.* 24:434-441, 1975.
5. Lindeman, C., and Krueger, J. Increasing the quality, quantity, and use of nursing research. *Nurs. Outlook* 25:450-454, 1977.
6. American Hospital Association. *American Hospital Association Guide to the Health Care Field.* Chicago: AHA, 1976, pp. 25-43.
7. Pearson, N., and Butler, J. (Eds). *Learning Resource Centers: Selected Readings.* Minneapolis, Minn.: Burgess, 1973.
8. Houle, C. *The Inquiring Mind.* Madison, Wis.: University of Wisconsin Press, 1961.
9. Knowles, M. *The Adult Learner: A Neglected Species.* Houston, Texas: Gulf Publishing, 1973.
10. Seiberg, I. *A Handbook of Standard Terminology and a Guide for Recording and Reporting Information about Educational Technology.* Washington, D.C.: U.S. Dept. of HEW, National Center for Education Statistics, 1975. (Document No. NCES 76-7057), p. 6.
11. Meredith, G. Evaluation of attitudes toward learning resources in higher education. *Perceptual and Motor Skills* 44: 1093-1094, 1977.
12. The author wishes to acknowledge the assistance given by a number of individuals who, without having any responsibility for the thoughts expressed here, have each played a role in the formulation of the ideas presented. Dr. Betty Hagen helped to lay the foundation with the definitions she presented at an ANA Nursing Research Conference in 1972. Dr. Susan Gortner and Dr. Norma Lang made valuable comments. Mrs. Joan Rebsch and Mr. John Schmadl of the Quality Assurance Committee, Maryland Nurses' Association, District V, critiqued a draft of the paper and made helpful suggestions from outside the ivory tower.
13. American Nurses' Association. *A Plan for Implementation of the Standards of Nursing Practice.* Kansas City: ANA, 1975, p. 28.
14. American Nurses' Association. *Guidelines for Review of Nursing Care at the Local Level.* Final Report of contract HSA 105-74-207 with the Office of Professional Standards Review and the Bureau of Quality Assurance. DHEW HSA-76-3004, 1976, p. 13.
15. Decker, B., and Bonner, P. *PSRO: Organization for Regional Peer Review,* Cambridge, Mass. Ballinger, 1973, p. 341.
16. Hagen, E. Appraising the Quality of Nursing Care. American Nurses' Association, *Report of the Eighth Nursing Research Conference.* Albuquerque, N.M., March 15-17, 1972, p. 1.
17. National Academy of Sciences, Institute of Medicine. *Advancing the Quality of Health Care: Key Issues and Fundamental Principles.* Washington, D.C.; NAS, 1974, p. 28.
18. U.S. Department of Health, Education and Welfare. *PSRO Program Manual.* Rockville, Md.: Office of Professional Standards Review, 1974, p. 16.
19. Zimmer, M.J. Guidelines for development of outcome criteria. *Nurs. Clin. N. Am.,* 9(2):318, 1974.
20. ANA, 1975, p. 30.
21. Commission on Professional and Hospital Activities. *CPHA Definitions.* Ann Arbor: CPHA, 1974.
22. Decker, B., and Bonner, P. 1973, p. 341.
23. Hagen, E., 1972, p. 1.
24. National Academy of Sciences, 1974, p. 28.
25. U.S. Department of Health, Education and Welfare, 1974, p. 16.
26. Commission on Professional and Hospital Activities, 1974.
27. Decker, B., and Bonner, P. 1973, p. 341.
28. National Academy of Sciences, 1974, p. 28.
29. U.S. Department of Health, Education and Welfare, 1974, p. 16.
30. ANA, 1976.
31. ANA, 1976.
32. ANA, 1976.
33. Smith, A.P. (Ed.). *PEP Workbook for Nurses.* Chicago: JCAH, 1974.
34. ANA, 1976.

SUGGESTED READINGS

Assessment/Audit Tools

Barba, M., Bennett, B., and Shaw, W.J. The evaluation of patient care through use of ANA's Standards of Nursing Practice. *Supv. Nurse,* 9(1):42-54, 1978.

Bell, D.F. Assessing education needs: Advantages and disadvantages of eighteen techniques. *Nurse Educator* 3(5):15–21, 1978.

Hegedus, K. A patient outcome criterion measure. *Supv. Nurse* 10(1):40–45, 1979.

McCaffrey, C. Performance checklists: An effective method of teaching, learning and evaluating. *Nurse Educator* 3(1): 1–13, 1978.

McMorrow, G. An emergency room audit for a small hospital. *Supv. Nurse* 9(8):33–35, 1978.

Nodal, M. Facets of retrospective chart audit. *Supv. Nurse* 9(5):58–63, 1978.

O'Rourke, M.W. The California Nursing Practice Act: A Model for Implementation. San Francisco: California Nurses' Association, 1976.

Plaszcznski, L. A systematic approach to leadership selection. J.O.N.A. 9(3):6–15, 1979.

Documentation

Bartos, L.T., and Knight, M.R. Documentation of nursing process. *Supv. Nurse* 9(7):41–43, 46–48, 1978.

Billings, C.V. Documentation—the supervisor's dream. *Supv. Nurse* 9(10):16–17, 20, 1978.

Blount, M., et al. Documenting with the problem-oriented record system. *Am. J. Nurs.* 78(9): 1539–1542, 1978.

Colton, M.R. A note on professional record keeping. *Supv. Nurse* 9(8):56–58, 1978.

Hoover, J.J. Record keeping. *J. Cont. Ed. Nurs.* 9(3):25–47, 1978.

Knutson, K.E., and Robertson, P.A. The disciplinary conference letter. *Supv. Nurse* 7(3):10–11, 1976.

Library/Learning Resources

Binger, J.L., and Jensen, L. *Lippincott's Guide to Nursing Literature.* Philadelphia: Lippincott, 1980.

Cooper, S.S. The bulletin board as a learning resource. *J. Cont. Ed. Nurs.* 6(3):51–55, 1975.

Cooper, S.S. The nursing literature. *J. Cont. Ed. Nurs.* 1(3):35–42, 1970.

ERIC: Educational Resources Information Center. *J. Cont. Ed. Nurs.* 6(3):5–16, 1975.

Glatt, C.R. How your hospital library can help you keep in nursing. *Am. J. Nurs.* 78(4):642–644, 1978.

Graves, K.J., and Dunavent, K.M. Hospital library consortia: A vital component of hospital-wide education. *J. Cont. Ed. Nurs.* 9(5):22–25, 1978.

Henderson, V. Library resources in nursing: Their development and use. *Int. Nurs. Rev.* 15:264–274, 236–246, 1968.

Huntsman, A.J., and Thompson, M.A. Self paced learning requires careful planning. *Cross Reference* 7(2):1–3, 1977.

Sherer, B., and Thompson, M. The process of developing a learning center in an acute care setting. *J. Cont. Ed. Nurs.* 9(1):36–44, 1978.

Sparks, S.M. Letting the computer do the work. *Am. J. Nurs.* 78(4):645–647, 1978.

Taylor, S.D. How to search the literature. *Am. J. Nurs.* 74(8):1457–1459, 1974.

Nurses' Notes

Walker, V.H., and Selmanoff, E.D. A study of the nature and uses of nurses' notes. *Nurs. Res.* 13(2):113–121, 1964.

Nursing Care Plans

Jackson, C., Edmandson, V., and Green, D.R. Promoting written care plans. *Supv. Nurse* 9(8):43–47, 1978.

Mayers, M.G. *A Systematic Approach to the Nursing Care Plan.* New York: Appleton-Century-Crofts, 1972.

Mayers, M.G., and the nursing staff of El Camino Hospital. *Standard Nursing Care Plans* Volumes I–III. Stockton, Calif. K.P. Medical Systems, 1974.

Wilson, B.S. Medication error policy. *Supv. Nurse* 9(5):53–54, 56, 1978.

Wright, M.L. A lesson in procedure writing. *Supv. Nurse* 8(4):26–27, 1977.

Problems in Written Communication

Allred, H.G., and Clark, J.F. Written communication: Problems andpriorities. *J. Business Comm.* 15(2):31–36, 1978.

Professional Reading

Bennett, J.B. and Weiher, R.L. The well read manager. *Harvard Business Rev.* 50(4):134–146, 1972.

Binger, J. Perceived learning needs and resources of undergraduate and diploma program directors. *J. Nurs. Ed.* 18(6):3–7, 1979.

Binger, J., and Huntsman, A. Inservice educators as users of instructional resources and professional journals. *Nurse Educator* 4(3):19–22, 1979.

Binger, J., and Momotuk, L. What's your "nursing literature quotient"? *Imprint* 25(3):38, 40, 42, 1978.

Claus, K.E., and Binger, J.L. How directors of nursing service use and share the nursing literature. *J.O.N.A.* 8(11):17–21, 1978.

Cooper, S.S. Reading and continuing education. *J. Cont. Ed. Nurs.* 6(4):3–4, 1975.

Cooper, S.S. The nursing literature. *J. Cont. Ed. Nurs.* 1(3):35–42, 1970.

Richter, L., and Richter, E. Nurses in fiction. *Am. J. Nurs.* 74(7):1280–1281, 1974.

References

Creighton, H. References. *Supv. Nurse* 10(1): 68–69, 1979.

Cuthbert, B.L. Please list three names... *Am. J. Nurs.* 77(10):1596–1599, 1977.

Smith, A.P. How to make sure your next resume isn't an obituary. *Training* 14(5):63–66, 1977.

Reference Sources

Bernstein, T.M. *Miss Thistelbottom's Hobgoblins.* New York: Farrar, Straus and Giroux, 1971.

Flesch, R. *The Art of Readable Writing.* New York: Collier Books, 1949.

Gunning, R. *How To Take the Fog Out of Writing.* Chicago: Dartnell, 1964.

Payne, L.V. *The Lively Art of Writing.* New York: New American Library, 1965.

Prentice-Hall Editorial Staff. *Common Secretarial Mistakes and How to Avoid Them.* Englewood Cliffs, N.J.: Prentice-Hall, 1963.

Stone, W., and Bell, J.G. *Prose Style* (3rd ed.). New York: McGraw-Hill, 1977.

Strunk, W., and White, E.B. The Elements of Style (2nd ed.). New York: Macmillan, 1972.

Research Reports—Grant Proposals

Berthold, J.S. Nursing research grant proposals. *Nurs. Res.* 22(4):292–299, 1973.

Daniel, W.W., and Longest, B.B. Some practical statistical procedures. *J.O.N.A.,* 5(1):23–27, 1975.

Fleming, J.W., and Hayter, J. Reading research reports critically. *Nurs. Outlook* 22(3):172–175, 1974.

Geitgey, D.A., and Metz, E.A. A brief guide to designing research proposals. *Nurs. Res.* 18(4):339–344, 1969.

Gortner, S.R. Research grant applications: What they are not and should be. *Nurs. Res.* 20(4):292–295, 1971.

White, V.P. *Grants: How To Find Out about Them and What To Do Next.* New York: Plenum Press, 1975.

Writing for Publication

Binger, J. Writing for publication: A survey of nursing journal editors. *J.O.N.A.* 9(1):50–52, 1979.

Binger, J., and Jensen, L. Aids for Writers. *Lippincott's Guide to Nursing Literature.* Philadelphia: Lippincott, 1980. Pp. 259–266.

Burkhalter, P. So you want to write! *Supv. Nurse* 7(6):54–56, 1976.

Carnegie, M.D. The referee system. *Nurs. Res.* 24(4):243, 1975.

Cooper, S.S. Pointers for prospective authors. *J. Nurs. Ed.* 10(3):2–7, 1971.

Coraluzzo, K. Clarity and precision in writing and selecting a title. *J. Cont. Ed. Nurs.* 8(3):83–84, 1977.

Coraluzzo, K. Organizing your paper and various formats. *J. Cont. Ed. Nurs.* 8(2):45–49, 1977.

Kolin, P., and Kolin, J. *Professional Writing for Nurses in Education, Practice, and Research.* St. Louis: Mosby, 1980.

Lambert, R.D. (Ed.). Perspectives on publishing. *Annals of the American Academy of Political and Social Science. Vol. 421.* Philadelphia: American Academy of Political and Social Science, 1975.

Lewis, E.P. Pretentious Prose. *Nurs. Outlook* 22(7):431, 1974.

Lewis, E.P. The term paper. *Nurs. Outlook* 25(11):691, 1977.

Lewis, E.P. What bugs editors. *Nurs. Outlook* 23(8):491, 1975.

Maxwell, M. The agony and the ecstasy: How to successfully write and publish your paper. *Oncol. Nurs. Forum* 7(3):41-47, 1980.

McCaskey, D.S. Technical writing: The importance of reader interest. *J. Technical Writing and Comm.* 3:217–221, 1973.

Mirin, S. *The Nurse's Guide to Writing for Publication.* Wakefield, Mass.: Nursing Resources, 1980.

Mullins, C. *A Guide to Writing and Publishing in the Social and Behavioral Sciences.* New York: Wiley, 1977.

O'Connor, A.B. *Writing for Nursing Publications.* Thorofare, N.J.: Charles B. Slack, 1976.

O'Farrell, E.K. Write for the reader, he may need to know what you have to say. *J.O.N.A.* 4(5):49–53, 1974.

Perry, S.E. The trials and tribulations of a would-be author. *Supv. Nurse* 9(1):13-16, 1978.

Powell, S., Roskoski, L., and Ostmoe, P. Writing for publication: A group approach. *Nurs. Outlook* 27(11):729–732, 1979.

Stuart, G.W., Rankin, E.D., and Sundeen, S.J. Getting a book published. *Nurs. Outlook* 25(5):316–318, 1977.

Styles, M.M. Why publish? *Image* 10(2):28–33, 1978.

UNIT III NONVERBAL COMMUNICATION

As effective communicators we should be aware of the messages being exchanged verbally and nonverbally by you and other individuals, groups, and the environment, however, this state of awareness is difficult to achieve and maintain. The practical challenge is to become more sensitive to various messages and channels of communication in order to interact with other people more productively. By becoming more conscious of the messages that you are sending, you gain greater control over your ability to communicate ideas, feelings, and moods that you intend to exchange with others. Similarly, as you become more sensitive to all the messages being sent by other people in your environment, you become more skilled at interpreting the intended meanings that others are attempting to send.

Remember, we send messages, not meanings, when we communicate. Messages evoke feelings, ideas, and actions in a receiver; the meaning resides in the receiver, not the message. Indeed, it is the multitude of verbal and nonverbal messages coupled with the unique nature of human beings that makes communication so complicated and such a challenge. Two ways to meet this challenge are to have an awareness of communication and then to develop skills relevant to this phenomenon.

In this unit, different aspects of nonverbal communication are highlighted. Although important nonverbal messages include the use of time, touch, smell, space, appearance, body motions, choice of words, eye behavior, and the way in which we send vocal cues, the selections focus primarily on the latter six types.

The first reading in Chapter 6 accents the role of the nursing administrator in the design and construction of a nursing unit in order to send messages of caring, warmth, and efficiency via the hospital's environment. Historically, nursing administrators have rarely, if ever, been included on committees to plan and design the physical environment of their units in a hospital. Furthermore, nonverbal messages sent by the use of space, color, lighting, and interior design in a nursing unit or office are usually not covered in discussions of nonverbal communication in texts and journal articles. We have included Grubbs and Short's selection because we think nursing administrators of the 1980s will want to use such environmental cues to communicate with staff, patients, and the public. The second reading describes the complexities involved with developing skill in sending and reading nonverbal messages.

Selections in Chapter 7 pose the questions: Are you fully aware of nonverbal messages that you frequently send and receive? Specifically, how aware are you of other people's first impressions of you, of the nonverbal messages your appearance sends to those around you, of the status and power your office conveys to visitors to your organization?

6.   Symbolism in Communication

Nursing administrators and managers who want to help fashion the nonverbal messages sent via objects, lighting, color, use of space, and structure and design in their department or hospital will enjoy the first reading in this chapter. Grubbs and Short's "Nursing Input to Nursing Unit Design" describes the process of designing and constructing a nursing unit. It will help readers translate their ideas and feelings about the needs, functions, and messages of nursing into language that planners and architects can understand.

The second selection, "The Ability to Send and Receive Nonverbal Signals," addresses the question: Are we literate nonverbally? The complexity of developing nonverbal skills is illustrated by outlining the ramifications of trying to sensitize and train people to send and receive nonverbal messages more accurately. The advantages of training methods like feedback, modeling, coaching, and role playing in addition to such instructional modes as lectures and readings to enhance nonverbal skills are weighed against the disadvantages. The reading closes by describing four necessities for the learner who wishes to improve this complex art and skill: motivation, a positive attitude, an understanding of this communication process, and experience (or practice and feedback).

This chapter will benefit nursing educators or clinical specialists about to develop a workshop or short talk on an aspect of nonverbal communication. Readers interested in an in-depth discussion of the effects of environmental or physical nonverbal messages on staff and patients may want to supplement these readings with "The Effects of the Environment on Human Communication" in Nonverbal Communication in Human Interaction *(see "Environment" in the Suggested Readings). Here, Knapp classifies the environment into six perceptions: formality, warmth, privacy, familiarity, constraint, and distance. Although we learn that research has not really shown how combinations of these perceptions influence us, we do know that personal judgments of our surroundings affect the way we feel and respond within ourselves and to others.*

NURSING INPUT TO NURSING UNIT DESIGN

By Judy Grubbs and Stephen J. Short

Reprinted with permission from *The Journal of Nursing Administration,* Volume 9, Number 5, May 1979, pp. 25–30.

As you read this overview of the steps involved in the design and construction of a nursing unit, reflect on the role that nursing administration plays in this process in your hospital. Does a representative of nursing administration describe the functions and needs of nursing when plans are being discussed for the improvement or creation of nursing units and patient rooms? If not, how can you, as a nursing administrator, involve nursing in this process in order to actively influence nonverbal messages being sent to staff, visitors, and patients?

The desire to create an ideal nursing unit motivates all architects and nurses initiating a nursing unit design process. The success of the project can be increased with strong nursing input throughout the design process. If nurses serve as active design team members, there is more likelihood that their voices will be heard, and the final nursing unit design will better satisfy nursing's needs.

The nurse involved in the design process has a dual role as nursing service's representative and as a patient advocate. To participate effectively, she must be educated in the architectural design process from the architect's perspective.

This article presents an overview of the nursing unit design process to provide the nurse administrator with some basic knowledge of the process and appropriate nurse participation in each phase.

As with any design process, the architectural design of the nursing unit, whether for new construction or renovation, involves moving from a set of objectives to a solution that satisfies those original objectives. Each objective creates a set of design problems that must be solved by the design team.

In the typical design process, it is often difficult to ensure a complete, thorough, and balanced review of the many possible solutions to the problems identified. Traditionally, architects work with, and seek the approval of, a small group of people who are actively involved in the development, review, and approval of final design solutions. The limited perspective that results reflects the viewpoint of the few people who provide the primary inputs.

Nursing administration's goal is to provide the architect with educated guidance in identifying objects and developing solutions. This goal can be met by assigning a nurse to the design team to serve as a link between the nursing staff and the architect. The nurse liaison should be able to anticipate the level of concern the architect faces at each design phase and help to plan appropriate solutions to problems as they arise. Well-prepared and relevant nursing input stands a greater chance of being incorporated into the architect's final design.

Responsibilities of the nurse liaison may include:

- Coordination of nursing and, in some cases, patient involvement in the decision-making process.
- Gathering of various kinds of data to furnish information that will facilitate decision making.
- Generation of innovative ideas and suggestions based on nursing beliefs about patient care.
- Interpretation of terminology and professional concerns among the architect, nurses, and physicians.
- Monitoring of the design and construction phases to ensure consistency with original concepts.

However the role of nurse liaison is structured, it is important to remember that nurses' impact on the physical plan is related to how well their professional functions and needs are articulated.

LONG-RANGE PLANNING CONSIDERATIONS

Nursing involvement in the design process requires awareness of the long-range goals of the hospital and the particular impetus for the building project. In an increasingly regulated health care environment, a long-range planning study is a mandatory precursor to an architectural project.

Projects ranging from redesignation of a few beds to entire replacement of facilities are subject to review through a certification-of-need process. A hospital can no longer build a new modern nursing unit to compete for patients but must demonstrate inadequacies in existing units to justify the cost. The new unit must be based on a community's needs for beds and must demonstrate savings in operational costs through more efficient design. Design efficiency can result in cost savings through lower nurse/patient ratios, fewer transfers, and reductions in transport time involving ancillary staff or equipment. The liaison nurse may be involved in collecting data to convince review agencies of the need and economies of the project.

Hospital administrators and governing boards decide to add or update nursing units for a variety of reasons. Basically two sets of planning pressures and considerations exist. There are those related to marketing and maintaining a competitive edge, such as:

- Improving the image and appearance of the hospital
- Attracting patients through improved accommodations
- Maintaining community support
- Competing with nearby hospitals
- Maintaining the physician base
- Attracting new physicians

The second set of planning considerations, more easily justified to planning agencies, relates to changes in the type of patients and services. These considerations include:

- Increasing bed flexibility for changing patient types
- Instituting a new level of care such as acute rehabilitation
- Providing for more acutely ill patients requiring constant observation
- Improving access to key diagnostic and treatment departments
- Responding to cost containment pressures by designing units with greater productivity ratios and lower maintenance costs

Exhibit 6-1. Architectural Thinking

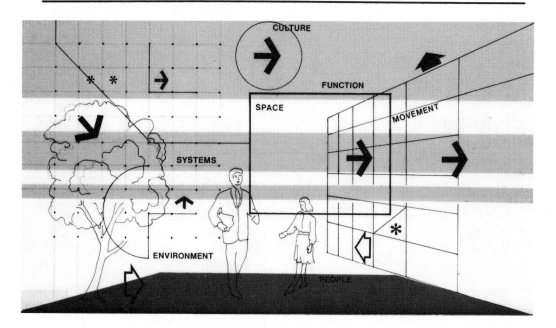

- Adapting to changes in nursing care delivery and medical technology
- Instituting automation and mechanization of hospital operations

Planning needs and considerations for the particular project must be evaluated and incorporated at each phase of the design process to guarantee that the goals of the hospitals are met, and that the project will be approved by government agencies.

DESIGN CONSIDERATIONS

In attempting to meet design objectives within the framework of long-range hospital goals, the architect identifies and shuffles many additional variables (see Exhibit 6-1). In nursing unit design, one of the major considerations is the type of nursing unit. Each unit calls for specific design solutions that balance the needs of patients, staff, and physicians.

For each project phase the architect must accomplish a particular set of objectives. The process involves soliciting input from appropriate hospital staff, balancing those expressed desires with regulatory and structural realities, and developing alternative solutions to be approved by the hospital.

PROJECT PHASES

The phases proceed from the general to the specific; nursing input must do likewise. In the early phases broad planning concepts are determined based on the philosophy of the hospital and the type of patients to be designed. Each phase adds a new layer of planning criteria, which dictate more detailed information of the design (see Exhibit 6-2).

Protocol Development Phase

In the first phase the roles of project team

Exhibit 6–2.   Project Phases.

PROTOCOL
|||||||
   PLANNING
   ||||||||
      SPACE PROGRAM
      ||||||||||
         SCHEMATICS
         ||||||||||||
            DESIGN DEVELOPMENT
            |||||||||||||||
                  CONSTRUCTION DOCUMENTS
                  |||||||||||||||||||||
  BIDDING
  CONSTRUCTION
  EVALUATION

TIME ⟶

members are defined and the decision-making process is clarified. Many hospitals set up a group empowered to make final decisions. These representatives may advise on specific issues for a particular department, or on major issues pertaining to the entire building project. They may advise as a group, or individually.

Regardless of the process by which input is received, or the level at which it is provided, the roles of project team members remain the same. A representative from the hospital's board of trustees is responsibile for assuring that the project fits within the hospital's goals and is financially feasible. The medical staff provides information on changes in health care delivery and medical techniques, and recommendations for layout and scope of services. Administration, with the assistance of department heads, reviews plans in terms of functional efficiency and ability to provide the service.

To carry out the nursing advisory role, one nurse representative can serve as the funnel through which recommendations from the nursing department are communicated to the administrator and the architect. Within the nursing department subcommittees can be created to research and develop design concepts and architectural solutions to achieve functional goals. The ultimate responsibility for resolving issues and making final decisions rests with the administrator, unless the Board of Trustees designates someone else. This responsibility includes decisions pertaining to cost versus function tradeoffs and determining whose input is valuable throughout the design process. A good relationship with hospital administration is crucial to maintaining an active nursing role.

Planning Study Phase

The objectives of this phase are to clarify the hospital goals and projected utilization of the nursing unit, and to determine the anticipated scope of services and operating philosophy. The key is the concept of care, not details of design. Nursing's most salient contributions will be presentation of data that describe the patient population and the system of delivering nursing care. What kind of patients will be in the unit? How will the nurses be organized to deliver care? What type of support systems will be used?

In answering these questions, categorizing major design concepts in terms of "mandatory" versus "desired" is helpful. Many good concepts may be disregarded if the decision-making group is not convinced of the advantages to the hospital. The nursing committee or the nurse liaison can review other nursing unit layouts and systems through site visits, literature reviews, and in-house operational studies to prepare for adequate documentation of requests. Nursing's concerns center on delivering patient care, but the planning committee also addresses issues of cost, revenue, physician marketing, and operational efficiency. Escalating building costs mandate

thorough planning to develop the most functional and cost-effective alternative.

Space Programming Phase

This phase involves converting design concepts into a space program. The space program is a written and graphic record of space needs that serves as a communication tool between the hospital and the architect. The specific content and format of a space program is dicated by the type of project and style of the architect. It may include a written narrative describing the goals, utilization figures, and concepts relevant to the total nursing unit, but the traditional space program lists the types of rooms or areas needed within the unit, and the sizes, quantities, and requirements of each.

The format may resemble that in Exhibit 6-3.

Spaces or rooms within the unit are listed for use by categories of persons or functions for which they will be used (for example, the public, patients, nurses, physicians, support services). Federal and state codes dictate requirements pertaining to both the size and inclusion of some areas, but there is opportunity to add rooms and arrange their location in relation to each other based on the concepts developed in the planning phase.

The architect prepares the project budget

Exhibit 6-3.   A Portion of a Typical Space Program for a Nursing Unit

Room/Area	Quantity Requested	Sq. Ft. per Area	Total Sq. Ft.	Requirements
Office	3	100	300	Close to classroom
Waiting area	10	15	150	Family waiting
Classroom	2	200	400	Expand to large room
Single patient rooms	16	130	2080	Close to nursing station
Double patient rooms	4	160	640	For longer-stay patients

from the space program. With the cost of hospital construction ranging from $100 to $150 per square foot, the architect will economize on space by suggesting deletion of rooms, sharing of space, and multiple use of rooms. There is less chance that a particular space will be eliminated or reduced if its priority has been well established with facts. Storage space is frequently lost during space programming due to lack of persuasive justification.

Schematic Design Phase

In the next phase a schematic design of the general layout of the unit is developed based on the space program. The architect's first focus will be on the location of the nursing unit within the building and interdepartmental relationships. The flow of persons and materials to and from the nursing unit determines the location of corridors, elevators, and other types of circulation systems.

After the unit's location in the building is determined, attention turns to intradepartmental relationships of spaces and flow patterns. The nursing staff's description of the unit is prepared in terms of performance requirements, which communicate goals for the architect in designing the unit. These include consideration of persons in the area, activities, circulation patterns, functional relationships of spaces, privacy versus openness, visual and acoustical needs, and control and monitoring requirements. Usually the nurses on the unit and the architect will work together to develop multiple schemes and options.

Here again, research of other units and site visits often help broaden the choice of options. Clearer design parameters make it easier to develop alternatives and evaluate the designs for best "fit" within the original intentions.

Design Development Phase

Once decisions are made regarding location and basic unit configuration, the architect begins to determine design details for each room and test the functional efficiency of the schemes developed. It is not uncommon for rooms and corridors to be relocated at this phase as additional concerns from the mechanical or structural engineers are considered. Nursing reaction to these changes may or may not be requested. The nurse liaison must assert her expectations that nursing input continue.

While the building's exterior and structural system design is being developed, other architectural team members are drawing up the details of each room in terms of equipment, surface finishes, light, noise level, climatic requirements, and furnishings. Details and requirements mentioned at earlier phases must be reiterated, as they may have been set aside.

Information about the effect of the sensory environment on the patient, if shared with the architect, will lead to more creative and satisfactory design solutions. There is a paucity of articles on environmental stimuli relevant to nursing unit design. The nurse must extrapolate what little information is available and work with the architect to develop new solutions. For example, studies on sleeplessness or sensory deprivation can serve to stimulate design discussions on how to avoid such negative phenomena. Techniques used at this phase range from overnight hospital stays by the architect to building mock-up patient rooms.

Construction Documents, Bidding, and Construction Phases

The subsequent phases leading to completion of the project usually require minimal nursing input. The architect will work out the final details with the structural, mechanical, and electrical engineers. As they identify problem areas, design decisions must often be reevaluated and modified. When this occurs, it is important that the project architect be sensitive to the intent of the original design. If significant architectural or functional change is required, particularly in patient-related areas, it should be reviewed and verified by nursing as an acceptable solution. The construction documents phase consumes months of time as a team of draftsmen and architects prepares sets of detailed drawings. These guide the contractor to direct the subcontractors in constructing the facility.

During the bidding phase, competitive bids are taken and construction prices are negotiated and firmly established before construction proceeds. Significant changes may occur in the form of materials and equipment substitution. These substitutions are often necessary and may be proposed as cost-saving methods. Of critical importance is whether a substitution is truly appropriate at all levels of consideration: construction cost, operating cost, life span, appearance, and function. Once again, nursing input can play a pivotal role in assuring that the final decision is responsive to nursing needs.

During the construction phase, hospital staff, including nursing, direct attention to planning the move and select furnishings. In the meantime, the contractor, who has not been educated to the original goals and concepts, will make changes that will have direct affect on the appearance and functioning of the unit, such as location and type of fixtures. Nursing usually has no contact with this key decision maker unless it is requested. Follow through by the nursing liaison is crucial throughout the construction phase. Weekly meetings or tours of the construction site are two methods for assuring continued participation. These methods may also relieve some of the inevitable opening-day dissatisfaction that occurs as time and cost considerations separate the outcome from the original design concepts.

Evaluation Phase

A postoccupancy evaluation of the nursing unit can serve several valuable purposes. Essentially, the evaluation consists of an objective assessment of how well the unit functions or meets original design goals. The architect can use the information to modify subsequent design programs. The evaluation process can educate hospital personnel who were not on the design team as to the original concepts for unit function. The problems identified can guide changes that may be required in the hospital systems or remodeling within the unit.

The process for conducting a postoccupancy evaluation can follow any number of research methods, including observations of how spaces are used or interviews of persons occupying the spaces. Objectivity can be enhanced by using nursing or architectural students to carry out the evaluation.

If the design goals were clearly identified in the early phases of the design process, the evaluation serves to complete the feedback loop. Consistency with original design concepts means success; inconsistency results in learning, so the evaluation effort is rewarding whatever the outcome.

CONCLUSION

While this overview of a typical architectural design process seems to move logically from phase to phase, the entire process is made up of many complicating factors, several of which have been mentioned. As each phase begins, another layer of constraints is added. Consequently, it is critical that the nursing staff be kept apprised of the entire process and specific objectives for each phase so that problems can be anticipated and solved. With better knowledge of the dilemmas faced by the architect and the constraints faced by the hospital administrator, the nurse can become a valuable participant in the design process.

THE ABILITY TO SEND AND RECEIVE NONVERBAL SIGNALS

By Mark L. Knapp

Reprinted, with permission, from M.L. Knapp, *Nonverbal Communication in Human Interaction* (2nd ed.). New York: Holt, Rinehart and Winston, 1978, pp. 83-113.

How skilled are you at sending and receiving nonverbal signals? What training methods are currently being used to instruct people to communicate feelings of relaxation, confidence, and genuineness, or to read messages of hostility, shyness, and anxiety? Read on to learn more about this communication mode in which many highly trained health care professionals are still illiterate.

The subject of nonverbal communication has received a great deal of attention in the last decade. Elementary, secondary, and college students are exposed to entire courses devoted to an understanding of nonverbal behavior; adults can purchase any number of books and pamphlets at local newsstands which, with varying degrees of fidelity, introduce readers to this fascinating world without words. Thus, it is reasonable to assume that contemporary Americans are not nonverbally "illiterate." However, as we look around, we readily note that there are some people who seem to be more sensitive to nonverbal cues than others; some people seem more proficient at expressing their feelings and attitudes nonverbally. And, it is eminently clear that the ability to send and receive these nonverbal cues accurately, like verbal cues, is essential for developing social competence—whether it is in the office, the courtroom, the barroom, the bedroom, or whether we want to effectively bridge gaps in social class and/or culture. If we accept the premise that one's ability to communicate nonverbal messages is important and that some are more effective than others, we might legitimately ask: How did these people become effective? and Can the same ability be developed in others?

While the foregoing questions seem simple enough, there are many related questions that add to the complexity of the issue and prohibit any easy, uncomplicated answer. First, are we talking about sending ability or receiving ability? If you are proficient at sending, does this automatically mean you will also be a sensitive decoder of nonverbal cues? Immediately, then, we are faced with the question of whether we are talking about a single skill or several separate skills. The issue is inherent in most of the following questions too—even though the singular form of the word *ability* is used throughout. Second, are we talking about an ability that manifests itself with a particular channel (face, space, voice, touch) or an ability related to various combinations of channels—for example, facial plus vocal cues? Third, are we talking about an ability that applies to all nonverbal messages or just specific types—for example, messages for specific emotions (angry, sad), messages for general affect (pleasant, unpleasant), or attitudinal messages (dominant, submissive)? Fourth, are we talking about an ability for which there are common standards for judging success? For instance, are we looking for similarities between the intended message sent and the message understood by the receiver? Are we comparing one's performance against norms developed from others? Or are we applying different standards for different age and cultural groups? Fifth, can we measure this ability by one or many methods—physiological, verbal, paper-and-pencil methods, nonverbal response forms, self-reports, and the like? Sixth, are we talking about an ability that transcends specific situations or one that applies to many situations—public, versus private situations? posed versus spontaneous situations? meeting a course requirement versus defending yourself in court? And finally, are we talking about an ability that transcends different communication partners? That is, will we manifest a similar level of competence in interactions with superiors, subordinates, peers, intimates, strangers?

The preceding is an almost staggering list of questions, and the answers, as we might expect from a relatively new field of study, are limited. With any area of study, the researchers first tackle questions related to the nature of the phenomena; then, training and skill development programs can be established and grounded on these findings. First, though, we must briefly look at some conventional methods of developing social skills—with a special concern for nonverbal skill development.

METHODS FOR DEVELOPING NONVERBAL SKILLS

Most of the ability we now have in sending and receiving nonverbal signals is derived from "on-the-job training"—with the job, in this case, referring to the process of daily living. In short, we learn (not always consciously) nonverbal skills by imitating and modeling ourselves after others and by adapting our responses to the coaching, feedback, and advice of others. This feedback is not necessarily "about" our behavior but often takes the form of a response to our behavior. Feedback, then, may refer to a person who says. "Well, you don't *look* happy" or, without making such a statement, your partner may just respond to you as a person who isn't happy. Through feedback we increase our awareness of ourselves *and others*—for example, "Can't you see I don't like you!" We not only learn what behaviors to enact, but how they are performed, with whom, when, where, and with what consequences. Naturally, some of us have more and better "helpers" than others; some of us seek help more than others. You can practice nonverbal sending and receiving frequently, but without regular, accurate feedback you may not improve your ability.

Although our primary focus has been on interpersonal feedback, we also know that audience feedback to public speakers can alter nonverbal behavior if it is perceived. Speaker fluency, utterance rate, length of speaking, voice loudness, stage fright, eye gaze, and movement may all be affected by perceived positive or negative audience feedback[1]. One study sugests that the sex of the person observing is not as crucial a variable in accurately perceiving nonverbal audience feedback as the sex of the audience members [2]. Female audience members' attitudes were more often judged accurately than males'. The question of sex differences in sending and receiving ability will be examined in more detail.

So, one source of developing your nonverbal skills resides in the feedback you receive from others and your sensitivity and receptivity to it. Ironically, some feedback will be in the form of subtle nonverbal cues—the very thing you are trying to learn. Nevertheless, situations that provide you with an opportunity for feedback and interpersonal "coaching" will certainly be preferred over situations where feedback is minimal, coaching is inhibited, and your receptivity to feedback is low.

Another popular method for teaching any social skill is through role playing. Usually a situation is presented and the learner attempts to behave in a manner that would approximate his or her behavior if this situation actually occurred. In Stanislavsky's method of teaching acting, for instance, students may improvise various kinds of walks—walking impatiently, walking to pass time, walking to annoy people living in an apartment below you, and so on. L.A. Longfellow's game "Body Talk: A Game of Feeling and Expression" is a modified role-playing experience [3]. Players try to communicate various emotions listed on cards using either the hand, the head, or the whole body and a condition called "interpersonal," which allows the player to use another person and sounds—but not words. Accuracy in communicating feelings such as love, hate, loneliness, hope, anger, shyness, and the like and accuracy in interpreting the communications of others enables you to "win" the game—and I suppose, theoretically improve your nonverbal skills. But, we don't know. Role playing and other exercises that make the learner an active participant are familiar fare in sensitivity groups and body-awareness workshops[4]. Some even contend that participants in such groups make great gains in their sensitivity to their own and others' nonverbal behavior. Objective data are difficult to obtain, but some people undoubtedly learn much from such experiences. Most of the evidence for the effectiveness of these workshops, however, is derived from testimony given by the participants. Thus, we must wonder about those

participants who chose not to testify; and of those who testified, how much of their self-perceived learning was due to the reduction of cognitive dissonance—that is, how much of the positive evaluations about role playing a mother comforting a child, touching others, baring your body to strangers, and the like is due to a need to justify the time, effort, and psychological output expended?

Various media have also been used in nonverbal skill development. Several well-known scholars in nonverbal behavior have found videotaped playbacks to be useful in developing nonverbal awareness—Birdwhistell, Scheflen, Ekman. Ekman, in a relatively short, six-hour training program, has been able to train nurses to accurately identify micromomentary facial expressions. Jecker, Maccoby, and Breitrose claim success in improving the accuracy with which teachers could judge student "understanding" from short films[5]. The training consisted of four sessions of approximately two hours each during which the attention of the trainees was focused on the gestures and facial expressions that accompanied "understanding." Teachers were tested on one series of films prior to the course, trained with another set of films, and posttested with still a third set of films. Control groups receiving no training did not improve in their recognition of these cues. Davitz found that accuracy in identifying emotions from tape-recorded speeches with "neutral" content could be improved by training.

Michael Argyle has reported a method of developing nonverbal skills[6]. Groups of two to five people interact in front of a larger group. Different group members are asked to record only one aspect of verbal and nonverbal behavior—for example, eye gaze, length and number of utterances, interruptions and pauses, facial expressions, and the like. The data from each observer are then assembled, and the whole interaction process is discussed.

Finally, some educators and trainers argue for the value of lectures and reading assignments. Certainly the development of any social skill is somewhat mediated by the amount of knowledge obtained in these ways. However, it is difficult to teach people about nonverbal behavior by spoken and written words alone. Second, it is difficult to learn any social skill without practice at the skill itself. P. Ekman and V.W. Friesen's *Unmasking the Face* is an attempt to minimize these problems[7]. The book contains many photographs of facial expressions which serve as models for various expressions of emotion—including blends. Test photos are provided for analyzing one's skill at decoding various expressions. In addition, specific methods for analyzing one's encoding ability are also given. Readers are given detailed instructions for making visual records of their own expressions, for obtaining reactions from people who view the photos, for interpreting these reactions from others, and for correcting any errors in encoding.

It should be obvious by this time that there have been few attempts to scientifically measure the degree of improvement derived from various training methods designed to develop nonverbal skills. It is difficult to say what works and what does not. Of course, training programs have a variety of goals. Some may wish to refine a very specific movement or expression; others may want to work on larger, coordinated clusters of behavior. And, it is reasonable to assume that different training methods may be necessary for optimum learning of different nonverbal signals—that is, can we develop skills in vocal behavior in the same manner as emblems or proxemics? For now, we must rely on generalities. Ultimately, the development of your nonverbal skills will depend on the following: (1) *Motivation:* The more you desire to learn nonverbal skills, the greater your chances of doing so. Often this will develop when you feel such skills will help improve the nature of your career or personal life. (2) *Attitude:* People enter learning situations with productive or unproductive attitudes—for example, "I *can* do this" versus "I can't do this" or "This will be fun" versus "This will be tedious." You may be highly motivated, but unproductive attitudes toward the learning situation will inevitably lessen the learning outcome. (3) *Knowledge:* The development or refinement of any skill is partly dependent on an understanding of the nature of that skill. True, we seem to unconsciously obtain a lot of nonverbal knowledge from watching others as we develop. Some of this knowledge we have is only known to ourselves when we hear or read about it from another source. This "consciousness-raising" may be an important ingredient in making future nonverbal adaptations. (4) *Experience:* Skills cannot be learned in isolation. With the proper guidance and useful feedback, practice will assist you in developing nonverbal skills. The greater the variety of one's expriences, the greater the opportunities for increased learning. Any given experience may provide useful information for future skill development even if you are ineffective in that particular situation.

Students frequently ask me whether all these attempts to learn about and develop skills in nonverbal communication will have negative consequences. They wonder whether we will know "too much" about others for our own good, whether those who have this information might use it to manipulate others for self-serving ends. Consider a parallel case in the area of study known as "persuasion." We could also be fearful of learning too much, and we have seen how some people have tried to control and manipulate others without regard for their welfare, as in brainwashing. Unfortunately, there are people with misguided intentions found in any area of study. However, we have been studying persuasion for over two thousand years and it does not appear that anyone has become so sophisticated that he or she invariably succeeds in persuading anyone in any situation. Furthermore, it is the nature of human adaptation to change behavior when it becomes unproductive. If people who know more about nonverbal behavior are using it "against" others, I suspect it will not be long before we see attempts to expose these activities and, if that does not stop it, behavioral changes will follow.

SUMMARY

Developing nonverbal skills is an area which is just beginning to receive scientific exploration, and few firm conclusions are forthcoming. We seem to have a pretty good grasp of various methods for developing social skills in general, but specific procedures for developing specific nonverbal skills have received little attention. We have reviewed training methods such as feedback, modeling, coaching, roleplaying, sensitivity groups, films and video tapes, observational experience lectures, and readings. At present, we can only say that nonverbal skill development will accrue with a strong desire or motivation to improve, with positive and productive attitudes toward the learning situation, with an adequate understanding of the knowledge related to nonverbal behavior, and with guided experience and practice in a variety of situations.

If you would like a more comprehensive discussion of nonverbal behavior after reading this short selection on developing skills in interpreting and sending nonverbal messages, try other chapters in Knapp's near-classic Nonverbal Communication in Human Interaction. *This book reviews current theory and research on the effects of personal space and territory, physical appearance and dress, and physical behavior, along with the effects of touching, facial, vocal, and eye behavior on human interactions.*

7. Are You Saying What You Think You're Saying?

*Beginning this chapter is Brothers' straightforward solution to inter-
view and first impression nervousness. To create a positive image at
your next important interview or meeting, try using Dr. Brothers'
five simple rules: (1) Do your homework on the people with whom
you will be talking, (2) Don't smoke, (3) Don't be late, (4) Get the
individual's name right and use it more than once, and (5) Don't talk
too much or interrupt! Pay particular attention to this author's
advice on active listening and your physical appearance during initial
encounters with potential employers and coworkers—these individuals' first impressions of you may last a lifetime.*

*The second reading tackles physical appearance, a major nonver-
bal message that poses a double challenge for nursing administrators
along with other health care professionals. First, public opinion
expects you to maintain physical fitness, good nutrition, and a
healthy appearance simply because of the line of work you are
in—health care! Second, if you are like many of the nursing administrators whom we have met, your time is very valuable. You do not
care to spend countless hours organizing your wardrobe, fixing your
hair, and matching accessories to outfits, let alone spending your
days off doing these things. Yet, looking successful and well groomed
can often make an initial impression which, in times of budget cuts
and increasing environmental controls, you may want as positive as
possible.*

In an excerpt from her book The New Executive Woman, *Williams offers suggestions and advice on how to dress to make the most
of your appearance professionally. Although the discussion does not
focus on clothes for women employed in a traditionally uniformed
discipline, the author's observations are, nevertheless, totally
appropriate to the dressing needs of female nursing administrators.*

Readers will enjoy the opening remarks on the lack of role models for female executives and the problems this has fostered. Also, how can you use clothes, colors, and accessories to create a successful image? Finally, find out how to develop a coordinated wardrobe without spending hours a month shopping. Even if you are not interested in improving your own appearance, you may want to read this selection to find out what graduate students in administration and education are reading to improve their appearance in order to compete for jobs like yours *in nursing management and administration. (Molloy's* Dress for Success *offers similar observations for the well-groomed male administrator.)*

"Your Office: Creating and Controlling Your Territory," *another excerpt from Williams' book, is last. After this selection, try to answer honestly the following questions: What feelings and moods does your office or work area convey to those with whom you meet there? Have you used colors, space, and lighting to increase your feelings of relaxation during hectic days when you hold all calls and take a minute to rejuvenate yourself? Finally, what objects have you displayed in your office to develop your image as a health care professional? Excellent visual cues include your diploma in a sedate frame; mementos given to you by your staff; current copies of* Journal of Nursing Administration, Nursing Administration Quarterly, Supervisor Nurse, Hospitals *and* Harvard Business Review; *and books on the various management functions and related administrative tasks, such as Riehland Roy's* Conceptual Models for Nursing Practice *(Appleton-Century-Crofts, 1974), and Berman and Weeks'* The Financial Management of Hospitals *(Health Administration Press, 1976) as well as Kolin and Kolin's* Professional Writing for Nurses in Education, Practice and Research, *(Mosby, 1980), Schmeid's* Maintaining Cost Effectiveness, *(Nursing Resources, 1979), and Polit and Hungler's* Nursing Research: Principle and Methods. *(Lippincott, 1978).*

MAKING A GOOD FIRST IMPRESSION

By Joyce Brothers

From *Cosmopolitan,* Volume 186, Number 1, January 1979, pp. 162–165. Copyright ©1978 by Dr. Joyce Brothers. Reprinted with permission of Simon & Schuster, a Division of Gulf & Western Corporation.

How hospital administrators, other nurses, physicians, and community members perceive you initially can strongly influence their opinions about you thereafter. Dr. Joyce Brothers' helpful hints can enhance your use of nonverbal messages given by appearance, timing, body actions, and eye contact to make a first impression of confidence.

The word *halo* is associated with saints by most people. But not by psychologists. Psychologists are well aware that what we call the *halo effect* has nothing to do with goodness or godliness, but with first impressions. And unfortunately, first impressions are not always good impressions. Take Lynda Mae . . .

Jackson was the new office manager. On his very first day, Lynda Mae caught his attention. She was flitting around the office, chatting with everyone and disrupting the routine. When she did settle down at her desk, she was constantly on the telephone.

From that day on, Lynda Mae could do nothing right as far as Jackson was concerned. He saw everything she did much more negatively than he would have otherwise. His first impression of her created a halo effect that radiated out to color his opinion of everything she did in the future. If Lynda Mae had only known about the halo effect, she could have neutralized the effects of her behavior by telling Jackson that she had been asked to collect money for the annual office picnic and that this had absorbed all her efforts that day.

The halo effect can be positive or negative. Whichever it is, it radiates out in all directions from the inital effect or impression. At its best, it helps make people think we are even better than we are.

If you are given the responsibility of rating someone on his intelligence or ability and the first time you meet that person he impresses you positively, you are likely to rate him high in other positive traits that may not be related at all to that first impression. You are likely to give him credit for being more efficient, kind, and courageous than if your first impression had been poor.

The halo effect is a key factor in the make-or-break moments of your life—in first encounters, in job interviews, business lunches, sales presentations, the first time the boss invites you home to dinner. All are crucial moments when the halo effect can determine success or failure.

There are give basic rules that will help you create a positive halo for yourself during these encounters.

1. *Do your homework.* If you are meeting new people, try to find out something about them. If they are prominent in business or one of the professions or the arts, look them up in *Who's Who.* If you have access to a library with the *New York Times* on microfilm, check the index and see if the man or woman you are to meet is mentioned there. People are very flattered when someone tells them, "I will never forget how impressed I was when I heard you were an Eagle Scout and a member of Byrd's expedition to the Pole." Or, "How is your daughter, the CPA, doing these days?" Or, "I have to tell you that I read a speech you gave before the Rotary Club in 1970—and I think it changed my life." This kind of flattery is very easy to take. And it will get you everywhere.

2. *Don't Smoke.* I don't smoke myself, so perhaps I feel a little more strongly about this rule than some people. But many people today have given up cigarettes so recently that it makes them uncomfortable when others smoke in their presence. And many feel very strongly that cigarette smoke is a pollutant and they resent being exposed to it. So if you are a smoker, restrain yourself at this first meeting when the halo effect is in operation. At the very least, it is a good idea not to be the one who lights up first.

3. *Don't be late.* Many people believe that it is fashionable to arrive anywhere from 20 minutes to an hour after the appointed time for a social engagement, but in business it is a black mark if you show up late. It is not only discourteous, but it makes people believe that you do not value their time, and that is a sure way to create a completely negative halo effect.

4. *Get the name right and use it more than once.* Ask if you're not sure. "Do you spell *Green* with an *e* on the end? Or without?" "I've

been looking forward to meeting you, Mr. Greene." "What do you think about the Chinese border situation, Mr. Greene?" And, in speaking to a third person, "Mr. Greene was just explaining to me why antique French furniture is a better hedge against inflation than gold."

5. *Don't talk too much and don't interrupt.* When people are nervous, they have a tendency to chatter on and on, not letting anyone else get a word in edgewise. If you find yourself running off at the mouth, stop. That is not the way to acquire a positive halo effect. And neither is interrupting. So don't.

Sensitive Listening

It is just as important to learn how to listen as it is to discipline yourself not to talk too much. When Governor Ella Grasso of Connecticut was asked the secret of her political success, she said that one secret was, "I've learned how to listen, to hear what is said—and what is left unsaid." Governor Grasso is obviously an expert at the technique known as sensitive listening. It is flattering—and effective. Instead of standing there silently while the other person talks, the sensitive listener becomes closely involved with the speaker, identifies and emphathizes with him. This is how it works . . .

Mr. Maloney has just told you that he made his first million by the time he was 29 years old. This is your cue to employ the sensitive-listening technique.

"You must have been pretty proud of yourself," the sensitive listener says. Or, even better, "I bet your parents were very proud of you."

The unsensitive listener smiles and says, "Did you, really? That's impressive. Truly impressive."

Now, unless Mr. Maloney has an ego as big as all outdoors (and he may very well have), there is not much for him to say to the unsensitive listener's remark. It is a bit awkward for him to agree that it was a truly impressive achievement. On the other hand, he certainly does not want to pooh-pooh it and say "Oh, it was nothing." The unsensitive listener has effectively brought the conversation to a momentary halt. And while Mr. Maloney will never quite be able to put his finger on the reason, he is never going to consider that unsensitive listener a wholly attentive person.

But the sensitive listener. Well, that is something else. Either of those two remarks tells Mr. Maloney that you have heard what he said, are impressed by his achievement—and know something of how he felt when he made that million. He can go on and agree, "Yes, I was pleased as punch." Or, "My father was so delighted that it was all I could do to stop him from calling the *New York Times* with the big news."

Let's take another case. Mrs. Samuels tells you she was the first woman appointed vice president of her company.

"That's marvelous," the unsensitive listener burbles. "The first woman vice president, hum? Very good."

What is Mrs. Samuels to respond to that? "Yes, the first woman vice president"? But she has just finished saying that. Or, "Yes, it was very good"? That is patting herself on the back. The unsensitive listener has made it difficult for Mrs. Samuels to pursue the conversation further without ignoring that fatuous remark. She will have to consider it as nothing more than agreeable background noise.

What would the sensitive listener say? Something like, "You must have felt great when you were promoted, but I'm sure that as the first woman in that position, you faced some tricky problems."

Mrs. Samuels feels that the sensitive listener fully appreciates the triumph of being the first woman vice president—and also appreciates that the lot of a pioneer is not easy

and that breaking into this "old-boy" corporate level involved more problems than not getting a key to the executive washroom.

How the Halo Effect Works

"Why work so hard to make a good impression?" Chet asked me. Chet is head of his own electronics firm, which he started from scratch nearly 25 years ago, and I have know him most of my life. "It's what you know and whom you know and what you do that count. I always judge a man on the basis of his work, not on how good or bad an impression he makes or how he looks."

I did not want to contradict him bluntly, although I could have pointed out several ways in which he uses the halo effect to good advantage. Chet has an engaging smile and a firm handshake. People meeting him for the first time always have the impression that he is absolutely delighted to meet them. That first impression predisposes them to like him—and want to do business with him.

His office suite is a showplace of contemporary design, with a Mies van der Rohe glass table and Corbusier chairs. His desk is a slab of highly polished black Italian marble on chrome legs. A sculpture of electronic components stands in one corner. And behind the desk hang three photographs. Chet with President Johnson. Chet with President Nixon. Chet with President Carter. Visitors cannot help but get some important subliminal messages to the effect that electronics is a modern growth industry and Chet is prospering—and has very good connections. The office is designed to impress just the kind of sophisticated technologists with whom Chet does business. It creates a positive halo effect.

But I decided to bide my time, not to point out his unconscious and very effective mastery of the halo effect. A couple of weeks later, I was able to show Chet that he did indeed judge people on the basis of first impressions. When I heard Roland, a young psychology instructor, mention that he planned to shave off his moplike beard, I asked him to help me.

I called Chet and said I knew two bright young men who were interested in getting into the electronics field, perhaps as salesmen. Would he, as a favor to me, be willing to spend ten minutes with each of them?

He agreed. "If they're really bright," he said, "I might have a spot for them."

Roland showed up for his interview on time. His hair was long and shaggy, just like his beard. He wore sneakers, jeans, and a blue work shirt. He was clean but rumpled. He was courteous and spoke intelligently about his interest in the field.

The next day, Roland appeared for the second interview. He introduced himself as Hobart. If Chet were to remark about his resemblance to Roland, he was prepared to explain that Roland was his cousin. But Chet saw no resemblance between the two. "Hobart's" hair had been cut and his beard was gone. He wore a grey flannel suit with a white shirt and a striped tie. The effect was pressed and crisp.

Chet telephoned me the next day and thanked me for sending Hobart to see him. "That's the kind of young man I like to hire," he said. "But that other guy. What's his name? Roland. I was surprised you asked me to see him. He's a real hippie."

I laughed. "*Hippie* is out of date, Chet," I told him, and then explained the trick I had played. And apologized.

"Good Lord!" he exclaimed. "You don't mean it!"

"Yes, I do," I told him. "I just had to show you that you do judge people on the basis of first impressions. Everybody does. It's the halo effect." If Chet had not been an old and dear friend, I would never have done this. But he was. And he thanked me. And made me explain the halo effect once more—in detail.

To begin with, clothes *do* make the man—and the woman. The first and most obvious impression is created by the way you dress.

Most people have had the experience of walking into a department store, looking and feeling less than their best. And being ignored by the salespeople. Another time, you can walk into the same department of that department store, feeling great and looking the same way. And the salespeople swarm around you.

This is the halo effect at work. It is also a very stupid reaction on the part of the sales personnel. I hope that every salesperson who reads this will resolve not to be swayed by a negative halo effect. It can only hurt your sales record. The customer who looks dowdy and depressed is usually the customer who is going to spend money to improve his appearance or his spirits, or both. He or she wants a boost. And wants it right now. The well-dressed, self-confident customer, on the other hand, may or may not be in the mood to buy. She may be "just shopping, thanks," and if she does not find exactly what she wants, she is in no mood to settle for something "just as good." You are twice as likely to make a sale to Mr. or Mrs. Dowdy as to Mr. or Mrs. Fashionable.

"We are preconditioned by our environment, and the clothing we wear is an integral part of that environment," says John Molloy, who calls himself a wardrobe engineer. "The way we dress has a remarkable impact on the people we meet professionally or socially and greatly (sometimes crucially) affects how they treat us." Harvard psychologist Zick Rubin agrees and says, "Given the power of first impressions to shape lasting opinions, it is often wise for a person who wishes to make a particular impression to present himself in that way from the outset." In other words, if you want to succeed in business, dress as if you were a success.

For women, dressing for success is a complicated matter. There are very few role models for women to pattern themselves upon. Ambitious young men can, and should, observe what the executives in their offices wear and dress accordingly. But there are not all that many women at the top, so the ambitious young woman must make her own dress rules. She should follow the masculine code in one aspect at least. And that is to dress as if she had already arrived at the top of her success pyramid. The woman on the way up should dress fashionably, although conservatively, and as expensively as she possibly can. She should look on her wardrobe as a blue-chip investment that will pay enormous dividends.

"Bankers wear suits," a young woman banker says. "And that's what I wear." A *New York Times* reporter noted, "All women on Wall Street wear three-piece suits." And a woman envirnomental engineer who spends a great deal of her time talking with mayors and city managers reports that she has a collection of expensive suits. "I deal chiefly with men and I want them to see me not only as an equal, but as an expert," she says. "So I work at projecting a tailored look, an expensive look. Even if it does not impress them, it makes me feel better about myself."

Do success-bound women have to confine themselves to tailored clothes for the rest of their working lives? Must they look like a version of the male executive? I don't think so. Women who are yearning for success will do well to take advantage of this stereotyped manner of dressing until they have established themselves. Consider it a uniform that you can discard when you make it to the top. And don't waste time and energy rebelling because you have to wear a grey flannel suit and silk blouse when you're sitting on the dais at the annual meeting.

Just as important as the way you dress is your physical appearance, the way you hold yourself, the way you walk, the way you smile.

One landmark study on the importance of physical appearance centered around a college dance. The students were told that a computer was matching each one of them with a blind date on the basis of shared interests. Actually, the young men and women were paired off any which way.

After the dance, each student filled out a questionnaire on how he or she liked his or her date. Was it on the basis of shared interests? Not at all. According to the questionnaires, the most important factor was good looks—even though the students didn't realize it. The students who had found their dates attractive wanted to see them again. Those who found them physically unattractive did not ever want to see them again. They did not believe that they were making this judgment on beauty alone. The students were convinced that their liking for the attractive dates was based on shared interests.

We tend to believe that attractive people have virtues that they may not possess. We think good-looking people are more sensitive, more intelligent, more interesting, and more exciting than those who are physically mediocre. It is the halo effect again. Other studies have shown that phyically attractive people are considered to have better jobs and more fun.

If a man holds himself confidently, has a warm smile, looks you straight in the eye when he speaks, and is well groomed, you will probably consider him attractive. And you undoubtedly attribute good qualities to him that he may not have.

Women face a more complicated set of reactions. Beauty helps women get ahead—and then it trips them up if they are not careful. Men expect more of a beautiful woman. If she does not live up to their expectations, they think worse of her than if an unattractive woman failed to live up to their expectations. That old saying, "Beauty is as beauty does," has a lot of folk truth in it. Beauty will help you get there, but it won't keep you there.

Beauties tend to be less secure than the rest of us. So much is made of their looks that they are made to feel that they are valuable only as long as they are beautiful. So if you are a raving beauty and ambitious to succeed in business, work on developing confidence in your abilities. Beauty fades, but talents and competence improve with the years.

It is harder for a woman to handle this matter of being superattractive than a man. If such a woman trips over the rug, people will whisper that she has had too much to drink. If there's a run in her pantyhose, they will criticize her for being sloppy. If people think she has an unhappy private life, that may help. Sometimes talking about minor failures will neutralize the penalties of beauty, but one has to be careful here and not overdo it. The most practical thing is to play down your beauty during working hours as much as possible. And the rest of the time? Well, if you've got it, flaunt it.

With the exception of the superbeauties, the more attractive you are, the better. Men like attractive men better than unattractive men. And they like attractive women better than unattractive women. And women feel the same way.

The halo effect is one of the most powerful psychological tools at your disposal. And like all power tools, it must be handled carefully, because it has a destructive as well as a constructive potential.

So check your halo effect.

Do you look like the kind of person you would like to know? Would like to do business with? Would like to have on your side in a negotiation?

Do you dress so that people could mistake you for the boss, not for the office boy or receptionist?

Can you recognize the make-or-break encounters early enough so that you can do the necessary homework to create a positive halo effect?

Do you act as if you were the success you want to be?

If the answer to any of these questions is no, then you had better get busy and adjust your halo.

DRESSING FOR SUCCESS

By M. G. Williams

When you catch a glimpse of yourself in a store window or mirror, do you get a little smile of satisfaction on your face over the healthy, well-groomed reflection you see? Or, do you think to yourself that you should work on your appearance a little, but not know exactly how to proceed?

Williams, who went from secretary to president of her own company with more than $1 million in revenues by the age of 27, frankly discusses the dressing problems and concerns of women in executive roles. Note the image of the "successful" executive—suits and dresses in wools, silks, and cottons, top-of-the-line shoes, and expensive leather or suede briefcase. Unfortunately, such attention to clothes and accessories can greatly influence people's impressions of you nonverbally. As a nursing administrator involved in selling ideas, programs, and your own credibility at times, you may want to use this information in order to create the most successful, competent image possible.

Don't forget that nurses in your organization are constantly forming opinions about your nursing and administrative competence from your appearance!

One of women's greatest obstacles to success at executive levels is our lack of role models—other people that we can observe to know how we should behave. Nowhere is this lack felt more than in the matter of dress. Fashion and grooming have always been important to women, but the importance of proper attire increases tenfold for the striving executive woman. Many people will argue that fine feathers don't make fine birds, but in practice a business person is greatly judged by appearance. To be considered a proper candidate for promotions and top jobs, the executive must look like an executive. This is simple enough for men, because they have a plethora of role models everywhere. Stores such as Brooks Brothers cater to the business executive striving to create an image and help him create it.

So what is the proper image for a female executive? This presents an interesting problem, compounded by the variety of garments available to choose from. Also, styles of women's clothing change more frequently than men's, so the selection of clothes can become a perplexing problem, as fashion is in a constant state of flux.

As I traveled across the country interviewing executives, I documented how each woman was dressed, her hair style, makeup, skirt length, etc., hoping that I would arrive at a composite model of dress that I could share with you. From here on in, you would presumably know exactly how to dress. But I could not establish a set pattern of dress among women business executives. The styles of dress varied considerably, and when I asked them about their wardrobes, most of them were curious about what other women were wearing. *Everyone* is confused about dress.

The styles differed according to individual personality, industry, profession, specific job, geography, and climate. Some of the taller women wore styles that would be unflattering to a shorter woman; older women tended to be less fashion-oriented than the younger ones. Women in banking dressed more conservatively than those in publishing or advertising. Geography and climate were also considerations. East Coast women, especially New Yorkers, were more formal in their appearance than were Midwesterners or West Coast ladies, yet San Francisco dwellers were more formal than those in Los Angeles. Proper attire for East Coast winters would be unsuitable for moderate climates.

So it is impossible, unfortunately, to provide absolute information on the correct way to dress. But I can discuss with authority the looks these executive women achieved with their clothing, the kind of image they conveyed, and how they went about achieving it.

CREATING AN EXECUTIVE IMAGE

How you dress communicates how you feel about yourself and who you are. Everything from your blue jeans to your evening gowns is a reflection of you. Each time you dress, you say something about yourself that indicates how you wish to be seen. This is both an advantage and a disadvantage to the executive woman. It is a disadvantage because you do not benefit from the inherent assumption of power that is enjoyed by males. You do not look like an executive, because you are a woman. It is very difficult for a woman to create a powerful image. But the proper selection of clothes can help you build an executive image, and you should do your clothes buying accordingly.

Business has long carried the banner of traditional clothing. Men learned a long time ago that they were more effective as business people if they donned traditional dress, and studies have proved this to be true. With the exception of the creative industries, such as show business or advertising, conservative clothes have become the uniform of the majority of the business community, if for no other reason than they do not detract from the business at hand. Business women should also convey a conservative image. Consequently, conservativeness is the keynote when you select clothes for business.

The degree of conservatism you adopt depends on your particular industry. Look to your male colleagues and see how they dress. If your peers are ultraconservative (dark blue or gray suit, white or blue long-sleeved shirt, subtle tie), then you should dress in outfits where the jackets and pants or skirts are of matching material. If the men wear sports coats with contrasting slacks, then you can mix and match your wardrobe, too. If the men wear leisure or denim suits, then you can be casual also. If you are unsure of the parameters permitted by your profession, dress more conservatively than you think is probably necessary. Having a conservative image in business can rarely hurt you, and, in fact it is mandatory for any notable career climb.

Perhaps the conservative image is incongruent with your personality. Nevertheless, you should adopt it if you wish to succeed. "My goal is to make money," one woman told me. "I don't like to give up any of me to do it, but I'll compromise certain things, like how I dress, during the work day in order to meet my goal. In the long run, I don't feel that I am compromising myself. It's all part of the game."

Especially if you are younger, you need to set yourself apart from the typical woman found in business, the secretary. Secretaries tend to dress alike, and you should differentiate yourself from them by adopting your own style. A little snobby perhaps, but it's all part of establishing your image as an executive type. Secretaries tend towards faddish clothes, and you can set yourself apart by avoiding fads. The fashion industry is built on the concept of constant change, and today's fresh styles are tomorrow's leftovers. Never buy fad clothing until the style has survived at least two years and only buy styles that are conservative to begin with, styles that reflect your executive image.

Although you should look toward the men in your profession to set guidelines about your dress, you should never attempt to emulate them exactly. Hoping to keep pace with the times, the fashion industry has offered suits and ties for women that were tailored identically to men's suits. On the surface, these suits would appear to be the ideal apparel for female executives assuming a typically male role. However, successful women have discovered that they are more readily accepted if they maintain a degree of femininity in their dress. Such women have learned to mask their internal toughness (generally thought a masculine trait) with a soft veneer of femininity that lets men know we are not out to usurp their masculinity. A bit of femininity in your clothes will assist you. Women who dress in clothes that are seemingly suitable for the corporate environment but are too mannish somehow make men feel uncomfortable. The quest to be accepted because you try to "fit in" backfires. Clothes that are too mannish convey an inappropriate image.

So the clothes that you wear for business should fall into the category of conservative, but mildly feminine. You do have some lati-

tude in the degree of femininity depending upon your personal preference, as long as you do not overdo it. Avoid lacy, frilly looks. You may be slightly tempted to don high fashion, especially since the stores that you shop in will carry the latest and best, but you should be cautious with it. As long as the style is not too outrageous or out of step with current fashions, go ahead and wear it. Your clothes should be pleasing but never distracting.

There are two basic looks that are suitable for female executives: the classic tailored and what I call the gently tailored look. These styles can be intermixed. You can take the same basic suit, and how you use accessories with it creates your look. If you wear a tailored blouse and perhaps a single gold necklace with a suit, you are achieving the classic tailored look. Add a silk scarf or a blouse with neckties for a soft, floppy bow and you look **gently tailored. Buy a three-piece suit and wear the vest on the days you are classic tailored, and leave it home on days you wish to appear soft and feminine. Women's clothes offer more variety than men's.**

Although you can never go wrong wearing a suit, many one- and two-piece dresses are acceptable for executive wear. Since there are so many variations of dress styles from which to choose, I cannot possibly describe those which are suitable. You must use your own discretion. For this, there is no substitute for good taste and a trustworthy sales clerk.

Dressing conservatively means being covered up. Long sleeves are preferable. In the summer, you can get away with cap sleeves, but never wear garments that are sleeveless. Mini skirts, which are now out of style anyway, are forbidden. Find a flattering skirt length below your knee, and have all your clothes hemmed to the same length. Avoid low-cut necklines or blouses unbuttoned so low as to expose your cleavage.

The color of your clothing should be conservative, too. Camel, gray, black, navy, white, or beige in a solid color are most acceptable. You can wear a subtle pattern or plaid providing you are not overweight and the pattern is repeated many times on the fabric. Randomly patterned or bright splashy fabrics are too casual for executive women. Avoid purples, lavenders, hot pinks, oranges, and reds. You can add a dash of color with a bright silk scarf, but even that should be a repeated pattern rather than a random one.

The most sophisticated look is a neutral colored outfit worn with tasteful gold or silver jewelry, very expensive, of course. Appropriate jewelry for female executives has smooth, clean lines, and is elegantly understated. Save the bangles and beads for a luau. In business, the simpler your jewelry, the better. The richest look is always understated. Your jewelry should be impeccably tasteful and not distracting in any way.

PANTSUITS VERSUS SKIRTS

A few years ago a big issue in corporate America was whether women should be allowed to wear pantsuits to work. As you might expect, the financial institutions were the last to allow it, but eventually pantsuits were acceptable garb for women, and many adopted wearing them. Of the women I interviewed, they were equally divided on the issue of pantsuits. Only about half of them wore them to the office; the rest had made a conscious decision not to.

I started wearing pantsuits when they were still controversial, and I discovered they were a great way to help position myself as an executive, for the secretaries were still wearing mini skirts. Once secretaries adopted pantsuits as their uniform, I stopped wearing them and returned to skirts and dresses.

Very tailored pantsuits are still acceptable for female executives, but they are fading. If you are considering a new purchase, buy a skirt instead of pants. You will get more wear out of it, and a suit with a skirt is now a more sophisticated look than pants.

Men have hated pantsuits from the beginning, and would much prefer to see a woman in a skirt. Wearing skirts will help you gain the power of femininity over men. I realized this some time ago when I switched back to skirts. I sensed that men were more receptive toward me if I wore skirts, and I became conscious of the effect I was having on others by what I wore. I discovered that I was more apt to gain a positive reaction from men while wearing a skirt.

I am not the only person who discovered this. A woman recently told me, "After I invested a fortune in pantsuits, I found out that men really liked dresses. I probably have 20 or 25 pantsuits, and if someone poured a bottle of bleach over them, they would look alike. So now I'm stuck with all these pantsuits when I know I am more effective wearing dresses."

This same woman had an interesting comment about the application of wearing dresses. She said, "If I am going to call on a customer, and the meeting is with a man, I'll wear a dress. If the meeting is with a woman, I'll wear pants." She learned that women prefer to see women in pants, whereas men prefer to see them in skirts. Use this knowledge to your advantage.

TO BRA OR NOT

Many of the women I interviewed confessed they went braless at home, but they all wore them to work. Even though going braless is a symbol of liberation, its symbolism is incongruous with the conservative image you wish to project. To many in our society, going braless is a suggestion of sexuality rather than independence. You have enough problems not being seen as a sex object without adding to the image. Going braless is in bad taste.

A secretary who worked for a company that I was with adopted the braless look, despite her well-endowed 38 inch bustline. She was causing quite a furor among the clients and other employees. The man she worked for was too embarrassed to speak to her about it, so he asked me to do it for him. I agreed to do it, but even I felt reluctant to speak to her about such a personal matter. Imagine how embarrassing it would be for a man to do so.

"I never used to wear a bra," an executive who started out as a secretary told me. "But when I interviewed for my present position, the man that interviewed me started hemming and hawing around, until I knew what the problem was. I said to him, 'If you are worried about me wearing a bra, I'm going to go out and buy some.' And he said, 'Oh, thank goodness. That was the only thing about you we were unsure how to handle.' " Don't place anyone in the position of having to ask you.

INVESTING IN YOUR SUCCESS

When I landed my first management job, I borrowed $2,000 from the bank to buy a new wardrobe. Up until then, my clothes had been inexpensive and casual. But I decided it was necessary I change my image, so I went for a tailored, conservative look, and only bought from the better stores. It turned out to be the best investment I could have made. I know that wearing the right clothes helped me get to where I am today, if for no other reason than the clothes helped my self-confidence. If I felt I looked good, I was more apt to confront an employee or my boss, something that was always hard for me to do. I feel that buying that expensive wardrobe was one of the keys to my success.

This corporate vice president discovered a secret of corporate success: quality clothes help make the executive. Observe top corpo-ration men, and you will never see a group of better dressers than they. Then look at the junior executives who are still climbing. The ones that already look like the affluent top executives are more apt to be promoted, because in management's eyes they better fit the image of what an executive should be. In your case, you will have a more difficult time looking like a executive under the old male rules, but you can help overcome this stigma by wearing expensive clothes. It is one of those inexplicable quirks of human nature: the more successful you look, the more successful you are apt to be. You must look affluent before you can become affluent. Wearing expensive clothes will help position you as an executive.

As part of your executive training, you should develop a discerning eye for quality in clothes. If you can't see the difference between a $20 blouse and a $50 blouse, then look again. There is a difference, and a big one, in the quality of the garment. Those who are conscious of the difference and value well-made clothes—and all executives do—will be able to look at you and immediately judge your clothes taste. Just as shop clerks favor those who dress well, so will the people making the decisions regarding your career. If you wish to be a success in business, it is mandatory that you dress well, even at lower managerial levels.

Although the cost of the garment does not always reflect its quality, often it does. Go for the most expensive clothes you can afford, and you will always feel proud of the way you look. It is better to have a few good outfits than a multitude of cheap ones that will do nothing to enhance your executive image. Do not feel badly about wearing a basic suit twice in the same week. You can change the look by a different blouse or scarf and still convey an image of financial well-being. The important thing is that it reek of quiet elegance and sophistication and reflect your good taste.

This is proper attire for the executive woman.

When all is said and done, inexpensive clothes are rarely a bargain anyway. Consider the durability of the clothing. You will get more than twice as much wear out of a garment that is twice as well made, and you will do a world of good for your image in the process. Inexpensive clothes tend to look tired after just a few cleanings, whereas quality clothes beautifully withstand the years. You can buy a lot of "cute" clothes at moderate prices, but they reflect neither class nor taste.

Styles for conservative clothes, such as the popular vested suits perfect for female executives, tend to be less faddish than inexpensive clothes, which is another reason why you can wear them longer. As I said earlier, many secretaries wear faddish and inexpensive clothes, female executives do not. If you avoid faddish clothes and buy only classic styles, the life of the item is greatly increased, and you can easily justify the expense.

Don't be a polyester princess. To achieve an upper-class look, wear clothes made from fabrics such as silk, cotton, or wool; fine wool blends are also acceptable, as long as the store or label is one that you can trust. I have a particular dislike for polyesters since so many cheaper clothes are made from it, although I agree that they are great for travelling. If you are on the road a lot, it might be wise to invest in a polyester suit or two, but other than that I would avoid them, and insist that the bulk of your wardrobe consist of pure fibers. The type of fabric you select also contributes to your classy act.

SHOPPING

Achieving a well-dressed, put-together look does not just happen. It takes hours of pavement pounding, searching through endless stores for just the right shoes or blouse, and then finally reaching a decision on the best item for your needs. Because you spend more than the average person on clothes, each decision that you make is more important, for you cannot afford to make costly mistakes.

Shopping can be fun if you have the time to devote to it, but the busy executive, especially if she has a family, has little time for leisurely browsing through shops. Finding the time to shop is one of your biggest problems. Some women, who do not have the kind of job that requires business lunches, shop on their lunch hour. This is one solution to the time dilemma, although you should use your lunch hour as a relaxing breather from the pressures of the business day.

Because of your limited time, you can alleviate a lot of wasted motion by developing a relationship with several stores that specialize in tailored clothes. Properly trained salesclerks in better stores know how to put together outfits, and once they get to know your preferences, they can be a godsend in helping you select clothes. Call them before you plan to visit the store, and give them an idea of the kind of thing for which you are looking. They can have several outfits ready for you to try on once you get there, and this alone can save you valuable time.

Salesclerks will also call you when they receive a new shipment of clothes that they think will match your tastes. And I have had them call me to give me advance notice of a big sale, and even hold items for me until I have a chance to stop by and look at them. If you are a good customer of the store, they are happy to provide these extra services for you.

Do the majority of your shopping in large cities. If you do not live near one, then plan several trips a year for the sole purpose of buying. Although most Midwest executives go to Chicago, I know a Minnesota executive who buys all her clothes in London. On the West Coast, I prefer San Francisco to Los Angeles for buying business clothes, because San Francisco caters more to the sophisticate, while Los Angeles features the chic and bizarre. But there is nowhere like New York. Fashion is the city's biggest industry, and nowhere can you find a better selection or more reasonable prices than the Big Apple. A Chicago executive said her business took her to New York several times a year, and each time she would stay another day for the sole purpose of shopping. She picked up the extra tab at the hotel herself, and said it was more than worth it because of the money she saved. She found the same items less expensive in New York than in Chicago, and always at least a year ahead in their styles.

Besides knowing where to shop, there are some other tips that will help you become an expert shopper. Wear the same undergarments and shoe height that you wear to work. When you try on clothes, sit down in them, and move about. Make sure the garment does not bind or pucker awkwardly. Check the mirror when you are sitting down, and observe how you look, for you will be spending a great deal of time seated. Make sure that the fabric does not wrinkle too badly. Crinkle a bunch of it in your hand and test how it springs back to shape. If it wrinkles too badly, it is not for you. Incidentally, a well-lined garment always hangs better and will retain its shape longer. Check the inside of the item for detailing and its interior construction. The way the seams are finished and the way that it is lined will tell you much about the quality of the garment.

If your blouse is too tight, the buttons on your bustline will continually pop open—a most embarrassing happening. Try to touch your elbows behind you back, and if the buttons burst open, it is too small. If the garment seems a little bit tight, it is better to buy a larger size and have it tailored down. The fit of the clothes is almost as important as the quality. A beautiful suit that does not hang well looks tacky, no matter how superb the quality of the garment.

Something women often overlook is the length of their sleeves. Long-sleeved blouses or shirts look best under jackets, and the blouse sleeve should be a half inch longer than the jacket sleeve. If one or the other is too long, it is a simple alteration to have it shortened.

COSMETICS

Along with the braless look and unisex clothes, the trend of the 1970s is away from makeup, a practice considered silly and frivolous by some feminists. But the completely natural look is unacceptable for life in the executive suite. The glary flourescent lighting found in most offices is unflattering, and you should wear makeup to compensate for its harsh effects.

Properly applied makeup improves your looks. Can you think of a better reason than that to wear it? Too much makeup is always tacky, but the appropriate amount of skillfully applied cosmetics gives you a sophisticated air and makes a dramatic statement that you care about yourself. Women who do not wear makeup tend to look sloppy.

There have been volumes written on the appropriate use of cosmetics, so I am not going to get into that here, but I would like to raise some observations that I have made during the years. Some women will don a $300 outfit, and then use dime store cosmetics on their faces. You can always buy a new dress, but you cannot buy a new face. Treat your skin as a valuable commodity. Pamper yourself with quality cosmetics. They will last all day, will not rub off or streak, and will make you feel better about yourself. Nothing looks worse or is more apparent than shoddy makeup.

Styles in makeup tend to be faddish, just like clothes. Every time you turn around there is a new line of cosmetics on the market. But do not get caught up in the cosmetic marketing games. You will find that even though the package and name may vary, in reality little has changed. Do not succumb to all those advertising gimmicks cosmetic manufacturers employ. Find shades and brands that suit you, and stick to them. If you feel bewildered about which shades and applications are right for you, go to a cosmetic salon and have a professional assist you. You will probably spend over $100 by the time you are through, but from there on you are set. You can simply replace the makeup as needed.

An area that seems to confuse many women is eye shadow. You should wear shades that match your outfits, not your eyes. Blue-eyed women are especially guilty of this. Many wear blue eye shadow with everything they wear, whereas they should be matching the shades in their clothes. Mascara should always be dark brown or black, no matter what color your clothes.

HAIR AND NAILS

Nothing is more attractive and sexy than long, free-swinging hair. But in the office, a flowing mane can be distracting and could be a detractor in your power over people. Hair for female executives should be no longer than shoulder length, and relatively simple to maintain.

Short, geometric styles work best with tailored clothes. If you tend towards more feminine attire, curlier styles are best. Your hair should never be so long or combed toward your face so that it is distracting when you work over a desk. If you have to keep pushing it out of your face, it will get dirtier faster and can be a source of aggravation. If you are short, hair piled on top of your head or cut to expose your neck will make you look taller. As you get older, softer hair around your face is more flattering.

Coloring your hair is acceptable (even Gloria Steinem streaks hers), but always have it done professionally by a name salon. Don't

chance those raccoon-striped tresses that are often the result of home jobs, and have your roots touched up on a regular basis.

Every time I wear a wig, I have an uncomfortable desire to take the nearest sharp object, place it under the wig, and scratch my head with it. Wigs drive me crazy. But for a busy woman, they are a salvation. For office use, wear only wigs that are close to your color and style of hair. You do not want to call too much attention to yourself. And once you develop your look, you should stick with it.

Manicured nails are a must. Have them done professionally if you can afford the time. If not, you can do an adequate job at home. The biggest problem with fingernail polish is that it chips after a day or two. When this happens to me, I become so self-conscious about it than I find myself spending the rest of the day keeping my fingers rolled up in tight little balls. I discovered that if I apply a clear topcoat every evening, it prevents the chipping. By the end of the week, you may be sporting ten coats of fingernail polish, but you can bet it will not chip off.

JEWELRY

As in the case of clothes, the jewelry that you wear should be tailored and expensive. Simple, classic designs in gold or silver are best. Save the sparkly jewels for evening wear.

Clip earrings are a pain in the lobe if you have to spend much time on the phone. Those who do usually end up spending the day with an earring dangling from only one ear. Pierced ears are a matter of personal preference, but they certainly eliminate the phone problem and are also a more secure way to keep earrings fastened.

Bracelets always bang around on the desk, and since most of the time you will be wearing long sleeves anyway, I recommend not wearing them to work. In regard to necklaces, elegant but understated gold or silver chains are always in good taste and will work well with your style of dress.

GLASSES

Avoid wearing glasses with ornate frames or ones bespeckled with rhinestones. Save the flashy specs for night. Frames that match your hair color are always flattering and will blend well with any color of garment that looks good on you.

Always wear sunglasses when it is bright outdoors, for you want to avoid squinting, which causes premature crow's-feet. Indoors, a very subtle tint to your glasses is fashionable, but if you go this route, you should invest in several pairs with hues to blend with your entire wardrobe. Never wear glasses indoors that are so dark others cannot see your eyes. This makes you appear as if you have something to hide.

SHOES, PURSES, AND BRIEFCASES

Shoes that go best with tailored clothes are clean, classic lines in black, navy, or tan leather. Boots are a fashion trend that emphasizes the covered-up look you wish to achieve, and are acceptable.

You are not going to have time to change your purse every morning, so do not worry about it exactly matching your shoes. If you use a briefcase on a regular basis, use those thin clutch bags that you can easily slip into your briefcase so you will have only one item to carry. You will look more put together that way. When you need just your purse, you can take it out of the briefcase. Too large a purse looks awkward.

On the subject of briefcases: you can get a standard style in a lighter color than a man would use. A more feminine-looking version is preferred, however. The right quality of briefcase is an executive status symbol: buy leather or suede in a chic, slim design. The size that you get really depends on your needs. You cannot go too wrong on your selection as long as you stick to a "high-class" store.

HEALTH

You are not the bionic woman. Take care of yourself. Workaholics tend to let their health suffer for the sake of the company. You are not doing anybody any favors, least of all the company, by letting yourself get run down. No job demands are so great that you have to sacrifice your health for them. Keep yourself fit.

For a more detailed discussion of this same topic, supplement this reading with Hemingway's The Well-Dressed Woman. *This book presents easy-to-read ideas for using specific styles of clothing and accessories to camouflage parts of your body that you would like to de-emphasize. Numerous sketches are used to sensitize readers visually to the effects of various necklines, styles of clothing, and types of jewelry and handbags on different figure types. In addition, lists of specific dressing "do's and don'ts" are given for individuals with problems such as heavy legs or arms, large hips or bosom, and for the different types of complexion.*

YOUR OFFICE: CREATING AND CONTROLLING YOUR TERRITORY

By M.G. Williams

Thank goodness that keys to executive washrooms are declining in popularity as executive status symbols. Women could not use them anyway (unless we demand our own executive washroom, too). The trend now is for private bathrooms complete with showers. This is just one way companies reward their executives. A plush and spacious office is another, and it is the most visible measurement of esteem a company can bestow on an executive. Many power-seekers prefer a larger office to confidential salary increases as recognition of their efforts. An impressive office is an unmistakable sign of authority.

Although the size of the office communicates territorial rights, and indeed indicates status, its relationship to the powerful corner offices is important. Corner offices are the most desirable, and offices diminish in importance the closer they get to the middle. One of the reasons corners are status symbols is that they contain more windows. Windows, then, also become a symbol of authority. In most companies, having an office with a window indicates a certain degree of status. From there, their size and number are significant.

Furnishings are also an indicator of status. The more an office looks like a living room, the greater distinction it has. Overstuffed sofas and easy chairs are popular. Other desirable trappings are muted lighting, preferably by table lamp; rosewood paneling; fireplaces and wet bars; custom wall coverings and drapes; and fine original art or signed lithographs. Desks should be solid wood and look like tables. The ultimate office does not even contain a desk. Even the quality of the carpeting has crept into the arena of executive status, thanks to a manufacturer's advertising campaign: "A name on the door rates a Bigelow on the floor." Exposed filing cabinets and typewriters are un-status symbols.

Another rule of corporate status is that the less work you have showing, the more important you must be. Overflowing in-baskets, piles of papers, and scattered books are out for status-seekers. Instead, the discriminating executive prefers to keep just a minimum of work visible. Multiple telephones are acceptable and, in fact, are encouraged, as are leather-bound books arranged in library fashion on the wall.

These trappings may seem insignificant to you, but within the value structure of business, they are very important. One of the ways a company may discriminate against you is to withhold some of these fringe benefits that a man would receive in your position. Government can regulate salary and even tangible fringe benefits such as life insurance or stock options, but it cannot provide you with an equal office. You must demand that for yourself. Status symbols are even more important for women because we do not receive the assumption of authority that a man automatically receives. If you have an equivalent office to the others on your level, it indicates the company regards you just as highly. Do not accept any form of differential treatment.

You may not control the size of your office or the number of windows in it, but, company policy withstanding, you can decorate your office to reflect your individuality. (Some firms require that you obtain permission before hanging anything; others forbid it altogether; but most are willing to let you decorate to suit your taste.) The amount of individuality you put in your office usually is in direct ratio to your position in the company. It is worthwhile, then, to invest some of your own money in your decor. As subtle as it may be, it will help position you as an executive.

Besides the status of a tastefully decorated office, you will feel more comfortable in an office that you have personalized. A touch of femininity is appropriate here. You should not be frilly, but you can reflect a certain warmth and softness to make your surroundings more soothing. Provided you have ample lighting, plants are perfect. A bouquet of freshly cut flowers every week will do if you do not have the proper conditions for plants. I spoke with one executive who kept a freshly baked batch of cookies on her desk.

Professionally framed paintings or lithographs that you have personally selected are a delightful extension of your personality. Many people hang posters, but they tend to give an office the feeling of a dorm rather than a sophisticated business atmosphere. Choose art with a discerning eye for quality, for nothing is more tacky than cheap art. You are

better off with nothing.

Photographs of your family or friends should be kept to a minimum, and you should use only photographs taken by a professional. Snapshots, especially in those plastic cubes, are unsophisticated, despite their popularity among middle management. Be snobby about what you buy for your office, for it reflects your good taste, and discerning executives will appreciate you for it.

THE USE OF SPACE

Have you ever been sitting in a chair feeling vaguely uncomfortable until you realized your uneasiness was because your back was facing the door? If you have, it is human nature, and it is something that you should remember while arranging your office. Place your desk so you sit facing the door, but not so you are backed up against the wall. Spaciousness gives a feeling of power, and you should give yourself as much room as possible. So arrange your desk so you have ample space behind you; otherwise, even if you have a big office, you are apt to feel cramped and less in control. If anybody needs to feel squeezed, it should be your visitor, and not you. The more space you dominate, the greater chance you have to achieve the upper hand in the relationship. Your desk and chair should be your throne, giving you authority over whoever comes in. Use the space in your office to help you gain power over others.

If you are fortunate enough to have a window, sit with the light beaming over your shoulder. Never sit where you have to squint, for squinting causes premature crow's feet, and we all get them soon enough. Make your visitors look into the light. This also puts you at an advantage.

When you are negotiating, always sit across from the people with whom you are bartering, and give them as little space as possible. Keep *their* backs up against the wall. When you wish to appear on more equal footing, a round conference table is perfect. In a round table, there is no position of authority as there is with a rectangular one.

The distance between you and your visitors will depend on the nature of your discussion. According to Julius Fast, author of *Body Language*, if you wish to relate at a normal business level, seat people from two and one-half to four feet from you; seat them closer for more personal interaction. If gaining power is your goal, always position yourself higher than your visitors. Dominance through height occurs throughout the animal kingdom, including man.

If you are an average-sized woman, you will have to make some conscious adjustments here. The best thing you can do to gain power is to keep your guest sitting, and you stand. Put three men on an overstuffed couch, sit across from them in a straight-backed chair, and watch them squirm. You will hold the position of power.

Because tallness contributes to dominance, taller people have an easier time gaining power. Now this presents some problems for women, but you can compensate. For example, I arrange my office so that there are two easy chairs across from my desk that are significantly lower than my desk chair. When someone comes in my office whom I want to dominate, I always ask him to sit in one of those chairs. I also have a round conference table. If I wish to deal with people on a more equal footing, I ask them to sit with me at the table.

I also use a five-foot-long desk rather that the standard six-foot version. I feel dwarfed behind the larger desk. I use a low-backed chair rather than those black leather thrones so many business executives use so I do not look quite so small. If you have the luxury of selecting your own furniture, order it scaled to your size.

A buyer in Los Angeles is notorious among salesman because of the way she uses the space in her tiny office. She keeps a bar stool next to her desk, and when a sales rep comes to see her, she sits on the stool and towers above him. She further intimidates him by asking how much time he will need (sales reps frequently fudge, saying ten minutes when they plan to take 30), and she keeps him to his work by setting an oven timer for the amount of time he says. When the time is up, the bell rings, and she sends him out the door. She is unpopular with the sales reps, but they respect her. She knows how to keep them under control.

Get in the habit of asking people to sit down when they come into your office to talk to you. Do not stay seated and let them tower over you. Either direct them to sit, or stand up yourself. Staying seated can put you at a psychological disadvantage.

People who hold meetings in their offices have authority. If you wish to control a group of people in a meeting, either hold the meeting in your office or in a neutral conference room. But do not hold it in another's office, as he will automatically play the role of host and therefore leader.

According to Michael Korda in *Power: How to Get It, How to Use It*, you can also gain dominance over another by entering his office, and, in a sense, invading his territory. But this technique of gaining power is only useful if you step beyond the accepted bounds of behavior, and infringe on the other territory. Korda suggests such ploys as using items for ashtrays that were meant for something else, giving orders to his secretary, spilling coffee, and other assorted examples of obnoxious behavior. But what he means is to "take over" the office, and in doing so, immediately gain dominance over the one whose territory you have invaded.

Such calculated behavior is inappropriate for many office situations, but you should be cognizant of dominance ploys. If you walk into a subordinate's office, you can gain dominance by merely remaining standing while you talk with him. Or you can sit down and pull your chair around the desk so you are sitting next to him. Or you can pull up a chair and lean over the desk, occupying a larger space, and therefore gaining dominance through territorial rights.

You do not always have to gain power over just subordinates. You may wish to make an impact on your supervisor. Here is what one finance executive told me about confronting her boss: "There is a point you reach once or twice a year when things aren't going your way. So you take a stand, and an absolute stand is necessary. I always do these things standing up. That's part of making an impact. Sometimes my boss will even ask me to sit down, but I always remain standing, knowing that by doing so I will be more effective."

The posture you assume, the way you hold your arms and legs, and your facial expressions, can all indicate authority. Actors and politicians know how to effect gestures and stances that suggest honesty, competency, and personal power, and you can too. According to Korda, the position of maximum power, while seated, is to have both feet firmly planted on the floor and lean forward with your hands on your knees. The person that is devoid of nervous gestures and twitches is thought to be powerful. A serene, confident facial expression can mask the turmoil and uncertainty that may be churning inside.

I was curious about the teenage hysteria over television's "Happy Days" and its cocky superstar, the Fonz. When I finally switched on the program one night, I was shocked and amazed. Somehow, I expected the Fonz to be much taller than he is. He's the shortest male actor on the program. So how does he gain all that power and authority? The answer is simple: body language. The Fonz is a master at standing with the posture of authority: legs

slightly spread with feet firmly on the floor, his arms either extended from his body in a typical "Fonz" pose, or hands on hips. He has a cool, confident look on his face; he speaks with authority, gestures with his hands to indicate sincerity, and he uses eye contact. He is an exception to the truism that tallness equals dominance.

The lesson to be learned here is particularly pertinent to executive women. Despite your probable height disadvantage, you can still gain dominance by using other ploys. Learn when to use them, and know when others are using them on you.

Now, after reading this interpretation on power and status in the office, stand back and take a look at your own office or work area (if you do not have your own office). Walk in through the hallway as if you were entering the room for the first time. What nonverbal messages does this area send to people about you? Is it full of bright, energetic colors, plenty of light, and comfortable, inviting furniture? Or, does the room almost forbid another person from entering because it is so cluttered with papers, projects, and uncomfortable furniture?

From a more personal standpoint, how does your office make you feel when you enter it in the morning? If it does not make you feel relaxed, confident, and ready to greet the world, you may want to reassess this important environment in which you spend more than one third of your life. Could you make one or two improvements on this room that would enhance your own relaxation and perhaps send messages of a similar nature to those with whom you meet in this area? Finally: don't forget to consider office space and even specific equipment or furniture when you are negotiating salary and benefits at a new job.

REFERENCES AND NOTES

1. Gardiner, J.C. A synthesis of experimental studies of speech communication feedback. *Journal of Communication* 21:17–35, 1971.
2. Ayres, H.J. A Baseline Study of Nonverbal Feedback: Observers' Judgments of Audience Members' Attitudes. Unpublished Ph.D. dissertation, University of Utah, 1970.
3. Longfellow, L.A. Bodytalk: A Game of feeling and expression. *Psychology Today* 4:45–54, 1970.
4. Some of these exercises are found in Pfeiffer, J.W., and Jones, J.E., *A Handbook of Structured Experiences for Human Relations Training.* Iowa City, Iowa: University Associates, 1969–1970, Vol. 1, pp. 109–111 and Vol. 2, pp. 102–104. Participative exercises as well as audiovisual learning aids are found in Wiemann, M., and Knapp, M.L., *Instructor's Guide to Nonverbal Communication in Human Interaction.* New York: Holt, Rinehart and Winston, 1978.
5. Jecker, J.D., Maccoby, N., and Breitrose, H.S. Improving accuracy in interpreting nonverbal cues of comprehension. *Psychology in the Schools* 2:239–244, 1965.
6. Argyle, M. *Social Interaction.* New York: Atherton, 1969, p. 415.
7. Ekman, P., and Friesen, W.V. *Unmasking Face.* Englewood Cliffs, N.J.: Prentice-Hall, 1975.

SUGGESTED READINGS

Audiovisual Aids

Brantz, M.H. Health center streamlines use of audiovisual aids. *Hospitals* 52(17):81–84, 1978.
Morra, M.E. Can you make a couple of quick slides? *Oncol. Nurs. Forum* 7(1):31–33, 1980.
Riggs, F.L., and Krug, F.T. In-house television news: Focus on employees boosts morale. *Hospitals* 52(14):91–93, 1978.

Communication Networks

Kelly, L.Y. The good new nurse network. *Nurs. Outlook* 26(1):71, 1978.
LaMonica, E., and Siegel, F.F. A professional organization that helps all of us. *J.O.N.A.* 9(5):16–18, 1979.
Nichols, B. ANA: A multipurpose representative professional organization. *J.O.N.A.* 9(5):19–21, 1979.

Nolan, M.G. Wanted: Colleagueship in nursing. *J.O.N.A.,* 6(2):41–43, 1976.
Peplau, H.E. Professional closeness . . . *Nurs. Forum* 8(4):342–360, 1969.

Consultation

Stevens, B.J. The use of consultants in nursing service. *J.O.N.A.* 8(8):7–15, 1978.

Environment

Goldstein, J.R. Nursing station design using a social theory model. *J.O.N.A.* 9(4):21–25, 1979.
Goodwin, I. A guide to planning critical care units. *J.O.N.A.* 9(6):20–25, 1979.
Hyman, R. Choosing art for your hospital: some basic do's and don'ts. *Hospitals* 53(6):95–98, 1979.
Knapp, M.L. The Effects of the Environment on Human Communication. *Nonverbal Communication in Human Interaction* (2nd ed.). New York: Holt, Rinehart and Winston, 1978, pp. 83–107.
Korda, M. *Power: How to Get It, How to Use It.* New York: Random House, 1975.
Oberlander, R. Beauty in a hospital aids the cure. *Hospitals* 53(6):89–92, 1979.

Expressing Yourself Nonverbally

Archer, D., and Akert, R.M. How well do you read body language? *Psychology Today* 11:66–69, 72, 119–120, 1977.
Beard, J.M. What is your attitude saying? *A.O.R.N.* 24(4):782–788, 1976.
Berscheid, E., and Walster, E.H. *Interpersonal Attraction.* Reading, Mass.: Addison-Wesley, 1969.
Davis, A.J. Body talk. *Supv. Nurse* 9(6):36–37, 1978.
Goldman, D. People who read people. *Psychology Today* 12(15):66, 69, 71, 73, 77–78, 1979.
Harragan, B.L. Department is the Name of the Game. *Games Mother Never Taught You.* New York: Warner Books, 1977, pp. 282–303.
Knapp, M.L. Nonverbal Communication: Basic Perspectives. *Nonverbal Communication in Human Interaction* (2nd ed.). New York: Holt, Rinehart and Winston, 1978, pp. 1–43.
Levenstein, A. Self image. *Supv. Nurse* 8(5):67–69, 1977.
Morris, K.T., and Cinnamon, K.M. *A Handbook of Nonverbal Group Exercises.* Springfield, Ill.: Thomas, 1975.

Pluckhan, M.L. Space: The silent language. *Nurs. Forum* 7(4), 386–397, 1968.

Stillman, M.J. Territoriality and personal space. *Am. J. Nurs.* 78(10):1670–1672, 1978.

Weiss, S. The language of touch. *Nurs. Res.* 28(2):76–80, 1979.

Zimbardo, P., and Ebbesen, E.B. *Influencing Attitudes and Changing Behavior.* Reading, Mass.: Addison-Weslev. 1969.

First Impressions

Beigel, A. Resistance to change: Differential effects of favourable and unfavourable initial communications. *Br. J. Soc. Clin. Psychol.* 12:153–158, 1973.

Zunin, L. Breaking the Four Minute Barrier. *Contact: The First Four Minutes.* New York: Ballantine Books, 1972, pp. 5–17.

Information Flow

Carlson, C.E., and Vernon, D.T.A.   Measurement of information of hospital staff members. *Nurs. Res.* 22(3):198–205, 1973.

Level, D.A., and Johnson, L. Accuracy of information flows within the superior/subordinate relationship. *J. Bus. Comm.* 15(2):13–22, 1978.

Somers, J. Information systems: The process of development. *J.O.N.A.* 9(1):53–58, 1979.

Mentors

Everyone who makes it has a mentor. *Harvard Business Rev.* 56(4):89–101, 1978.

Kelly, L.Y. Power guide—The mentor relationship. *Nurs. Outlook* 26(5):339, 1978.

Kramer, M. The concept of modeling as a teaching strategy. *Nurs. Forum* 11(1):48–70, 1972.

Roche, G.R. Much ado about mentors. *Harvard Business Rev.* 57(1):14–28, 1979.

Nonverbal Communication Tools

Adams, J.L. *Conceptual Blockbusting.* San Francisco: Freeman, 1974.

Goldstein, R. Photography: An effective recruitment aid. *Nurs. Forum* 2(4):46–52, 1963.

Organizational Communication and Stucture

Claus, K.F., and Bailey, J.T. Working Effectively with Others. *Power and Influence in Health Care.* St. Louis: Mosby, 1977, pp. 161–172.

Ellis, G.L. Communications and interdepartmental relationships. *Nurs. Forum* 5(4):82–89, 1966.

Fahy, E.T. A battery of techniques for dodging issues. *Image* 9(1):21–22, 1977.

Kucha, M.D. The human relations approach to nursing administration. *Nurs. Forum* 9(2):162–168, 1970.

Marriner, A. Line-staff relationships. *Supv. Nurse* 8(11):27–32, 1977.

Roberts, K.H., Cerruti, N.L., and O'Reilly, C.A. Changing perceptions of organizational communication: Can short-term intervention help? *Nurs. Res.* 25(3):197–200, 1976.

Schuldt, S. Supervision and the informal organization. *J.O.N.A.* 8(7):21–25, 1978.

Physical Appearance/Dress

Bird, C. *Enterprising Women.* New York: Norton, 1976.

Harragan, B.L. The Uniform—What to Wear as an Active Game Player. In *Games Mother Never Taught You.* New York: Warner Books, 1977, pp. 325–347.

Hemingway, P.D. *The Well-Dressed Woman.* New York: David McKay, 1977.

Hennig, M., and Jardin, A. *The Managerial Woman.* Garden City, N.Y.: Anchor Press (Doubleday), 1977.

Hoffman, L.W., and Nye, F.I. *Working Mothers.* San Francisco: Lassey-Bass, 1975.

Hughes, E., and Proulx, J. You are what you wear. *Hospitals* 53(16):113–118, 1979.

Hyatt, C. *The Woman's Selling Game.* New York: M. Evans, 1979.

Knapp, M.L. The Effects of Physical Appearance and Dress on Human Communication. *Nonverbal Communication in Human Interaction* (2nd ed.). New York: Holt, Rinehart and Winston, 1978, 152–195.

Molloy, J.T. *Dress for Success.* New York: Warner Books, 1975 (for men).

Molloy, J.T. *The Woman's Dress for Success Book.* Chicago, Ill.: Follett, 1977.

Stead, B.A. *Women in Management.* Englewood Cliffs, N.J.: Prentice-Hall, 1978.

Professional Image

Beletz, E.E. Is nursing's public image up to date? *Nurs. Outlook* 22(7):432–435, 1974.

Beletz, E.E. The public image: "A devoted heart, disciplined hand, not necessarily an inquiring mind." *Imprint* 23(2):27, 41, 1976.

Benton, D. You want to be a *what? Nurs. Outlook* 27(6):388–393, 1979

Chapman, C.M. Image of the nurse. *Int. Nurs. Rev.* 24(6):166–167, 170, 1977.

Creason, M. Registration and voting participation of four faculty groups. *Nurs. Res.* 27(5):325–327, 1978.

EPILOGUE

In our closing comments, we would like to identify several important aspects and related issues of communication that you may wish to read about on your own. First, the women's movement and related assertion techniques that impinge upon the entire spectrum of communication skills are current topics in the literature. Dysfunctional communication (discussions of frequent problems seen in individual and group interactions) is a sparsely treated, yet intriguing area. Similarly, such practical aspects of written communication as drafting a grant proposal, writing nursing care plans, and developing a nursing library, along with the nonverbal communication modes of role modeling, nursing's professional image, communication networks, recruiting with photographs, and developing interdepartmental relationships, will be essential content for some readers' needs and are covered in the Suggested Readings at the conclusion of the respective units.

Finally, as you continually improve your own understanding of and skills in communication, remember to direct funds and organizational talent to enhancing the communication skills of your colleagues and staff. These expenditures will only improve employee interactions and departmental relations and, in turn, organizational effectiveness.

Index

Index